Saltwater Game Fishing
in New Zealand

Also by E. V. Sale:

Quest for the Kauri
Historic Trails of the Far North
Four Seasons of Country Diary

Saltwater Game Fishing
in New Zealand

Fred Wilkins with E.V.Sale

REED

First published 1982

A. H. & A. W. REED LTD
68–74 Kingsford-Smith Street, Wellington 3
2 Aquatic Drive, Frenchs Forest, Sydney, NSW 2086
also
16–18 Beresford Street, Auckland
85 Thackeray Street, Christchurch 2

ISBN 0-589-01404-8

Typesetting by Quickset, Christchurch, New Zealand.
Printed by Kyodo-Shing Loong Printing Industries Pte, Ltd,
Singapore.

CONTENTS

ACKNOWLEDGEMENTS

The writing of a book on New Zealand big game fishing is possible only with the help and co-operation of many people – and so many have helped that it is not possible to record them all.

The authors are, however, especially appreciative of the assistance given at all times by the New Zealand Big Game Fishing Council, and especially its president, Ernie Wiig, its secretary, Mrs Rosemary Johnston, its records officer, Rob Dinsdale and its publicity officer, Garth Marsland; also to Arnold Baldwin and Norman Hudspith, past presidents of the council who are also New Zealand representatives on the International Game Fish Association; and to the presidents and secretaries of all the game fishing clubs, which spread from the Far North to the Far South of the country.

To look back through volumes of notes is to recall names of people who have proved particularly knowledgeable and helpful: Laurie and Judy Ross, Bingham Green, Snooks and Lola Fuller, John Chibnall, Birke Lovett, Jim Whitelaw, Mervyn Arlidge, Jack Brittain, Mrs Bev Mollard, Harvey Franks, John Going, Colin Mason, Gerry Dawson, Jack McMahon, Mrs Ailsa McLaren, Alec Stevenson, Bob Cutfield, A. C. Taylor, Don Ross, Nelson Tye, C. M. K. Peachey, Bill Clark, M. A. Cruickshank, Gary Cranston, Norm Fletcher, Miss Jill Gray, Ces Jack, Phil Lynds, John Baker, Keith Channon, Denis Hodson, Rod Bellerby, Mrs C. D. Atwood, Rick Pollock, Jeremy Wells, Pat Burstall, Rex Forrester, Mrs H. M. Wood, Bill Cooper, Dick Marquand, Don Hague, Des Benson, Douglas Reich and Brian Collins.

Special thanks are due to Dr Mike Godfrey, Don Butters and Gary Kemsley for revealing expert secrets in light tackle and saltwater fly-fishing; and to Peter Saul and David Gibson, fishery research officers, for their technical and scientific advice so freely given when sought. To the National Environmental Satellite Service of the United States Department of Commerce for permission to use their sea temperature charts.

The photographs come from many quarters, and grateful thanks are given to those who have helped in collecting them. Wherever possible, credit is given to the photographer in each case.

The authors gratefully acknowledge the maps and other art work done by Wayne Barnett of Kaeo.

Most of the fish drawings in Chapter 17 are reproduced from the official handbook *World Record Game Fishes* published by the International Game Fish Association, with special permission. While the association is not responsible for the views expressed in this book, the authors have been mindful of the principles of good fishing for which the association stands.

METRIC CONVERSION

The adoption of metrics as the standard of measure in New Zealand and subsequently by the New Zealand Big Game Fishing Council (and, as its first preference, by the International Game Fish Association) has resulted in metrics being used throughout this book for weights and distances, except for long distances at sea, which remain in (sea) miles.

For those fishermen and women accustomed to the old order, and for readers in those countries which have not adopted a change to metrics, the conversions back are as follows:

Metres (m) × 3.2808 = Feet
Metres (m) × 0.5468 = Fathoms
Kilograms (kg) × 2.2046 = Pounds

All temperatures are in degrees Celsius, for which the conversion to Fahrenheit is:

Deg. Celsius (C) × 9/5 + 32 = Deg. Fahrenheit

PROLOGUE

Big game fishing is at the top end of the recreational sea fishing in which at least half a million New Zealanders take some part. At one time the prerogative of the wealthy and the leisured (and usually of the overseas visitor who was so favoured), big game fishing is now shared, in an extended range of fish and over a wider area, by thousands of ordinary New Zealanders.

A main objective of those who have organised the sport in New Zealand, and world-wide, has been to promote ethical methods of fishing, to give the fish a sporting chance to beat the angler and to offer it the best chance of survival if it gets away. The authors of this book have endeavoured to promote practices which advance this spirit.

There is a great need to know more about the big game fish, especially the billfish, which are found in New Zealand waters. Locally they are not commercial fish but internationally they are; and the many thousands which have been taken by overseas fleets in New Zealand waters in recent years may, if such catch rates continue, represent a threat to more than just the local sport.

Through the game fish tagging programme, which has their growing support, New Zealand game fishermen have the opportunity – by tagging and recording fish and letting them go – to further fulfil the spirit of ethical fishing. In the absence of other research procedures equally as effective, they may, by catching (and wherever possible releasing) a comparatively few fish, help in the preservation of species.

To all anglers who fish in this spirit this book is dedicated.

YELLOWTAIL OR KINGFISH

One of the smaller game fish for which New Zealand is noted is *Seriola grandis*. The International Game Fish Association calls it southern yellowtail and classifies it *Seriola lalandi lalandi*, in distinction from the California yellowtail (*Seriola lalandi dorsalis*). New Zealanders generally have known it as kingfish – the Bay of Islands Swordfish Club was originally the Kingfish Club – and yellowtail means different things to different New Zealand fishermen, even being applied to koheru and trevally.

A local compromise name used for *Seriolo grandis* is yellowtail-kingfish. However, the name yellowtail has been adopted also by the New Zealand Big Game Fishing Council, and hence is the term preferred in the following pages.

Similarly the term swordfish is applied only to the broadbill (*Xiphias gladius*), and not to the marlin, which are billfish, even though to the ordinary angler they may all be "swordies".

INDEX OF MAPS

North Cape

Far North

NORTH ISLAND

1

2

3

1

2

4

5

6

7

8

9

10

SOUTH ISLAND

Tasman Sea

12

11

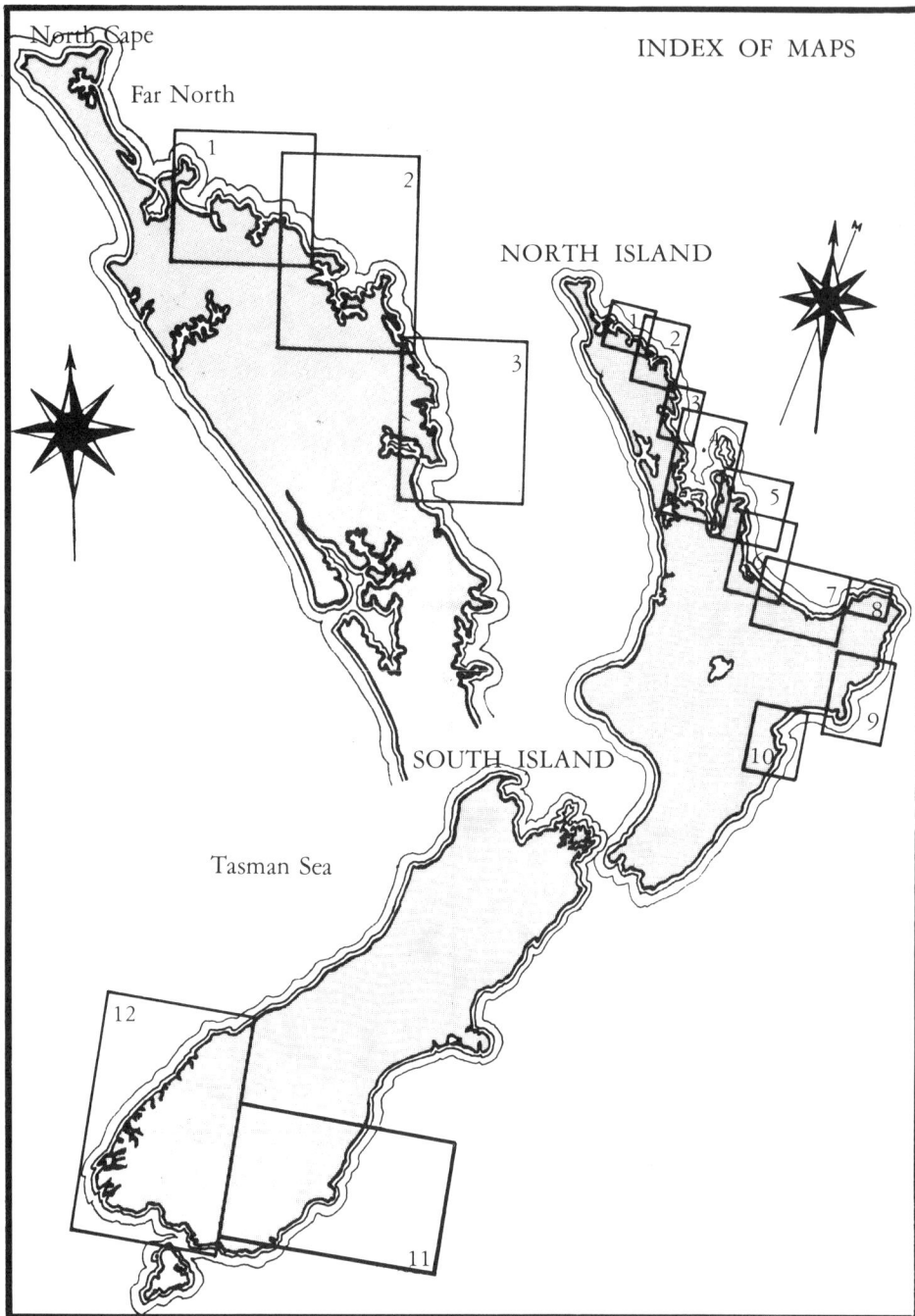

The maps of the home areas of the New Zealand game fishing clubs are printed individually through this book. The areas are: 1, Whangaroa; 2, Bay of Islands; 3, Whangarei; 4, Auckland; 5, Mercury Bay; 6, Tauranga (and Mayor Island); 7, Whakatane; 8, Waihou Bay; 9, Gisborne-Tatapouri; 10, Hawkes Bay; 11, Tautuku; 12, Fiordland.

CHAPTER ONE

Very tight lines

Fishing is a funny-serious business. Enthusiasts of all types take part.

One evening in South East Bay at the Mayor Island fishing base, when my launch *Sou'East* was beached at the gallows with a fish to weigh, a slow-motion pantomime unfolded in the bay.

Anglers were leaning out of the windows of the big game fishing base just back from the shore and others were streaming out on the beach – shouting and pointing.

In the middle of the bay, between the boats anchored thickly there, a striped marlin was tailing quietly through the moorings. Even for Mayor Island this was close to home for a game fish of this calibre.

Immediately one of the moored launches picked up its anchor, put over a bait and started to troll toward the marlin. In almost as short a time it had fouled another anchor warp, with an exchange of pointed comments between the two launch skippers. The marlin swam quietly on.

From another boat in the bay an angler jumped into a dinghy and started to row, with a freeboard of a couple of inches, furiously toward the marlin, with no rod, but gaff at hand. And on the beach a rubber-suited diver adjusted his face-mask and, spear-gun held high, splashed backwards down into the waves in his flippers.

Fortunately for them all, the marlin swam quietly away out past us – and we could see no point in joining in the joke.

If you talk to fishermen you must have time to listen. They always have a story to tell – often more than one – but are usually only half willing to tell it. Beyond a doubt that you really want to hear, lies a reluctance that you may not believe. For in big game fishing, on a last frontier where men tackle other predators larger and stronger than themselves, things happen that sound *like* fishermen's tales.

Maori tradition has, fittingly, the best New Zealand fish story of all – how Maui, from his canoe which became the South Island, fished up the North Island. Myths aside, however, the Maoris were undoubtedly superlative and daring fishermen.

Sharks were caught by the Maori not only in nets but on line, and in large numbers. Special hooks were made from hard wood, which was sometimes twisted as it grew to provide the special shapes. William Colenso, of the early Anglican missionary group, spoke of 20 canoes trolling in the Bay of Islands using rolled twine, similar no doubt to the hand-rolled line later made by a Maori from flax for Zane Grey.

This best-selling American writer, through his stories of big game fishing in New Zealand waters, first visited New Zealand in 1926 with an international reputation as a big game fisherman as well as a writer of Western novels. He brought a team of supporters, including Captain Laurie Mitchell, who fished with (and sometimes outfished) him, and an extensive array of gear of a type not seen in New Zealand before. In seven weeks off the Bay of Islands they fished up 62 striped marlin, 3 black marlin, the first broadbill swordfish caught in New Zealand waters, 23 mako sharks, 2 hammerhead sharks, 7 other sharks and 9 yellowtail.

Zane Grey came to New Zealand largely at the behest of C. Alma Baker, a New Zealander who had made his money in Malaya, and who was both a keen game fisherman himself and a great propagandist for his country. By the time Grey left he had established a world reputation for New Zealand big game fishing by his catches, had introduced radical new fishing methods (and offended some local anglers with his criticisms of their methods), and had vividly recorded fishing experiences which have been re-lived by fishermen over and over again to the present day.

During that first visit, Grey caught a world record striped marlin of 204.12 kg, the first broadbill in New Zealand waters (of 181.44 kg) and a 50.34 kg yellowtail, for which he also claimed a world record but which was somehow disallowed. But the fish he really wanted was a black marlin, especially when Laurie Mitchell landed one of 442.71 kg – a world record that stood for 26 years.

He looked likely to go home disappointed until one day off Bird Rock, near the southern entrance to the Bay of Islands, the companion launch from which Laurie Mitchell was fishing ran up a red flag. Grey went over and leapt aboard. Mitchell greeted him with a wide smile and handed over a rod from which the line ran smoothly and sweetly. There was a black marlin on it.

Grey's mumbled thanks did not conceal his great joy.

He wrote: "With chills and thrills up my spine I took a turn at the drag wheel and shut down with both gloved hands on the line. It grew tight. The rod curved. The strain lifted me. Out there a crash of water preceded a whirling splash. Then a short blunt beak, like the small end of a baseball bat, stuck up, followed by the black and silver head of an enormous black marlin. Ponderously he heaved. The water fell away in waves. His head, his stubby dorsal fin, angrily spread, his great broad deep shoulders climbed out in slow wags. Then he soused back sullenly and disappeared."

The marlin ran out to sea, taking line all the time. The launch had to run up on it to get back any line. He leaped again, "a staggering shape in black opal, scintillating in the sunlight, so wide and deep and ponderous, so huge in every way, so suggestive of immeasurable strength that I quaked within . . ."

The marlin sounded, then rose again and leaped, crashing out of the water, lifting the line tight from fish to rod, three metres above the water – ten times in two miles.

Grey felt all the mixed urges of the hunter, enraptured yet drawn by the pride of his prey. Every time he saw the fish he grew more obsessed. "I wanted him, yet I gloried in his size, his beauty, his spirit, his power. I wanted him to be free, yet I wanted more to capture him . . ."

But the marlin was a long way from capture yet. Drawn to the boat, he surged away again with tremendous power, climbed into the air again a mere 10 metres from the boat and quickened his pace out to sea. A tiring Grey was staggered to feel his reel come off the rod with a crack. Only a sudden grasp prevented it from going overboard after the fish. Grey hung on to it, allowing the line to run free, while Mitchell struggled to bind the reel seat back on to the rod. But soon it broke off again and Grey half fell into the cockpit with it. Bound on again, it broke off yet a third time.

On advice from the boatman, Peter Williams, Grey decided to go back into the familiar fishing surroundings of his own boat, the *Alma G.* which had stayed in attendance. The rod held high and the drag released, he scrambled between the two boats and soon in his own chair at last began to make an impression on the fish. But after eight times getting the double over his reel, and then having it snatched away by the strength of the fish, he made the only remaining move which seemed to be open to him — he changed lines back on to his own rod. He managed to get the leader up out of the water for the seconds needed for Williams to slip the line of Grey's heavy gear through the swivel and knot it — and then cut the line to Mitchell's rod. Seeming to accept the new challenge, the fish grew stronger and not until after the third hour did it start to weaken; and not until darkness was falling over the rocks and headlands of the Bay of Islands could Grey turn for home with his 319.33 kg,

Francis Arlidge, veteran skipper of the Bay of Islands, with a photo of himself kneeling below the great black marlin caught from his boat by Zane Grey (holding his rod, right). Peter Williams, boatman on the occasion, is standing to the left. N.Z. Herald.

three-and-a-half-metre long giant. He had bent more than a few rules, but had fished strength to strength all the way.

It says much for the fighting qualities of black marlin that it took some of the best boatmen New Zealand has known, and two sets of gear so advanced then they almost equalled the best of today, to give Grey one of his greatest fishing experiences. And more was to follow.

Don Hague, of Auckland, admits having felt a pang of regret that he was not using something lighter than a 67 kg line when, on April 23, 1978, something took his albacore bait when he was fishing off White Island with Jim and Kathleen Bayliss from their launch *Lanakai*. However, he was hoping, late in the season, to help the boat to win the award for the greatest weight of fish caught; and in those waters one needed heavy gear to be reasonably sure of

boating the big yellowtail he was hoping to hook.

"I should have been suspicious when I tried to get the rod butt into the gimbal," he says, "but I put the difficulty I was having down to the fact that I was using unfamiliar and heavy gear. By this time a 'kingi' should have long reached the kelp, judging by the way the line was disappearing off the reel.

" 'Tighten up', advised Jim – and I very nearly followed the fish over the side. It was like hitting the brakes of a car just after they have failed; you would swear it made it go faster.

"The fish had hit the bait while we were anchored and, while Jim cast off, I just hung on, rather overawed at the rate at which the reel was emptying. Within a very short time the cockpit was filled with smoke and the acrid smell of burning brake linings as the big 14/0 gave up its precious line. Jim arrived back in the cockpit in time to see a splice at 730 m disappear over the side, but – for which I am grateful – did not tell me. Buckled into a harness I tried to regain line.

"Although Jim said at the beginning that it might be a black marlin, I convinced myself that it was a big white or a tiger. As we were a long way from home and getting further away, I had nothing to lose by giving it everything I had got.

"About 20 minutes into the fight the first harness broke. I'll never know how I did not lose the gear; and I was in mental agony as I slipped out of the broken harness and got into another – a lighter one which would not stand much abuse.

"Two things I realised later had helped to determine the outcome for the fish. It had completely swallowed the bait and no doubt lost a lot of blood in the fight; and, having ripped a tremendous amount of line off, it had to tow that for miles before we could catch up. But just when I thought I was getting somewhere, the fish began to veer about. And at one time he had me out of the chair and almost over the side.

"I was almost past caring, and feeling that my strength was not up to much more, when the second harness broke.

"This time we used a kidney harness and, although my arms felt like jelly, the fish appeared to be tiring, too. I got it to about 50 m from the boat. It tried to sound but I managed to hold on and stop it. I saw its shape as it crossed about 6 m down behind the boat. A few seconds later there was a glimpse of a blue dorsal. And then out of the water came a huge head, the dark blue of it contrasting with the pink of a wide open mouth. Time stood still: and then, as quickly as it had come, the fish was gone again, leaving a huge swirl in the water.

"I worked hard and maybe two minutes later Jim had the trace. But the fish was in no way worn out and proceeded to turn the sea into foam. The slack line wound itself around the rod as I was putting it away so that I could help. My arms were shaking so much that I could hardly pick up the rod again to clear the mess, and at one stage I actually had a loop of line around my wrist.

"Fortunately Jim got a gaff in and, after a jumbled blur of minutes of spray and pain and wanting to be anywhere else, order returned. After trying to do the impossible – to pull the fish over the stern, not realising its weight – we settled for a chain around the tail. We set off on a 5½ hour tow home, from several miles out past the Volkner Rocks.

"We estimated the weight on the way in at about 300 kg but when we finally dug up a weighmaster back at Whakatane at about 11.30 pm we knew that we had a 444 kg fish, breaking Captain Laurie Mitchell's 52 year old New Zealand record." The fish was 4.09 m long and had a girth of 1.9 m.

What the anglers swore at the time was also a heavier as well as bigger black even than Laurie Mitchell's record fish of 1926 was an unofficial catch which set the Mercury Bay Club alight again in March, 1947.

Bill Clark, who still lives at Whitianga, and who was on one rod with the fish all day, recalls that there had been a get-together the night before. A striped marlin had just been caught in

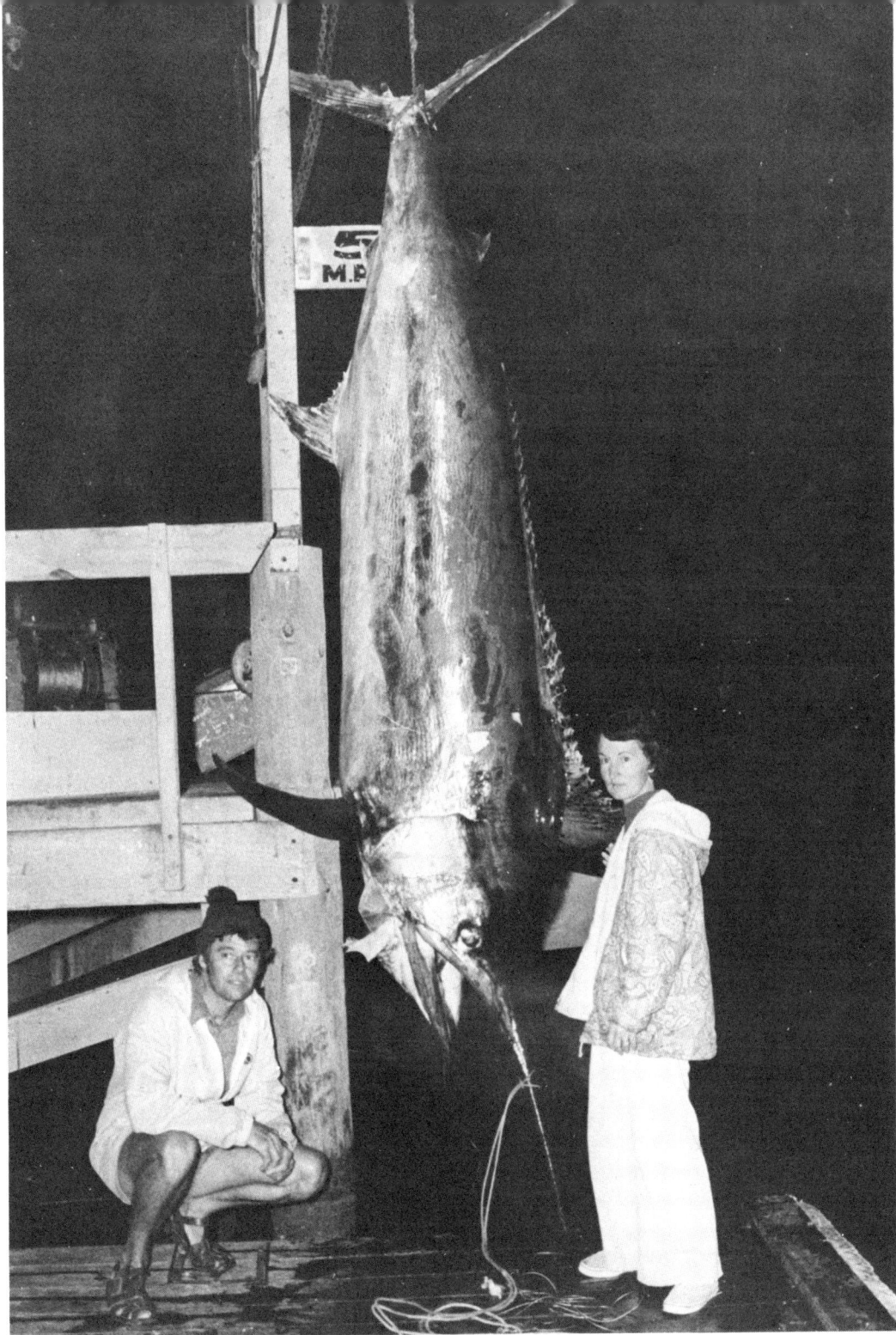

The result of the great catch described on the previous page. Don Hague and his wife Rita, with Don's New Zealand record black marlin (444.00 kg) caught on 60 kg line in April 1978. Whakatane Beacon.

13

local waters, the first for so long that it seemed a good idea to go out and see if there were any more. So nine eager fishermen, most of them pretty green, set out in the *Ronomor* (skipper Bert Chaney) at 3 am on to a dark, calm sea. There were two sets of old-style gear on board and Bill Clark recalls the one on which he did most of the action consisted of a cane rod, with a small reel and about 350 metres of line.

The expedition did not have time to lose its initial enthusiasm. Bait was picked up easily and full daylight had not long arrived before the launch was circling a likely looking school of fish on the Outer Bank, about five kilometres past the Red Mercury. Something got on the line at five minutes to seven and Bill took the rod.

"He was monstrously heavy," recalls Bill, "and we had the usual argument, when he had been on for a couple of hours without showing, that he must be a shark. I knew he wasn't because I saw him take the bait. Then he jumped three times – once so close to the boat that I thought he was going to hit us with all his weight – and took off again out to sea. This went on for about six hours. I was getting tired even if the fish was not. We could see him quite clearly about 7 metres down and we could get him up to the trace almost when we wanted to. But as soon as we tried to put on too much pressure, he would explode, dive under the boat and force us to go around in a big circle to recover. He would settle down then with no weight upon him and start swimming out to sea again.

"Fortunately it stayed flat calm all day, but all the same by now it was getting a bit alarming because we were about 30 miles out past the Red Mercury. We watched with interest a cargo ship pass inside us on its way between Wellington and Auckland.

"One of the blokes on board wanted to cut the line. Most of us by this stage were not interested in any records – we did not even think of it, there was no active fishing club anyway – all we wanted was to catch the fish and get home. So the next time we got the trace up we tied the second line to it and tried fishing it with two rods. You know, it made absolutely no difference. We had only the one chair and we could get no weight on that other line sitting on the stern. After a couple of hours we took it off.

"Finally evening started to come down, the fish was still heavy and strong, and a second cargo boat had come through between us and the land, which was now only just visible. We got the fish up to the boat again, where we had had it about a dozen times without being able to keep a hold on the trace, and this time had ready a heavy hapuku line, with the barb taken off the hook. We slipped the hook through the swivel on the trace and everyone who could catch hold, about four of us, hung on. The fish tried to shoot under the boat again as we heaved to try to get it on the back of the boat. He thrashed around and must have put a hundred gallons of water into the cockpit before Guy Dale managed to get in a gaff. That was the end of it, except that it still took all nine of us half an hour to heave the fish up alongside the cabin and back to the tuck. And then the hook, which had held the fish from five to seven in the morning until five past seven at night, just fell out."

With crew member Gordon Clark nursing a hand which had been crushed inside the marlin's bill during the final struggle, the boat turned back home, the anglers arguing over how big a fish they had caught. Back in port about midnight they found that the ball of the big steelyard had fallen off with disuse and had to be attached again with a piece of bailing wire. The weight, although later "corrected", has always been suspect. At 944 lb (428.20 kg) it was less than Mitchell's earlier record of 976 lb (442.71 kg) but the Whitianga black measured 2 ft 3 in (0.68 m) longer and was 3 in (7 cm) greater in girth.

One thousand pounds (453.6 kg) at least – that is the Whitianga tradition for its biggest fish; and the huge head, jutting out angrily above the doorway in the bar of the Whitianga Hotel, gives credence to the claim.

The huge black marlin caught by Bill Clark (right) and described on the previous page. It led to the revival of the Whitianga club after 1947. "He was monstrously heavy."

But if the big black in the Whitianga Hotel was never to hold a record, the huge bluefin tuna now mounted on the wall of the Mercury Bay Clubhouse on the Whitianga Wharf certainly did. It was the top tuna in New Zealand until beaten by an even bigger bluefin caught off Mayor Island by E. Andrews.

It happened on the *Lady Clare*, when Nelson Tye on 16 January 1967, took Gilbert Rivas and Jack Jackman out on an expedition to Richards Rock. The weather was so thick that the rock was found only by compass, but two minutes after getting there a kahawai bait was taken right alongside the rock. Gilbert gunned the boat immediately to port on a shout from the skipper, as Jack grabbed for the rod. The fish had gone straight down and for a moment there was a real risk that the line would end up around the propeller.

The fish seemed tremendously strong. It did not surface. It shot straight out under water toward the open sea, into a fog which cut visibility to a few hundred metres. Nelson followed it and called back to base by radio: "I think it must be a black."

But there was something about the strength of that first run which did not seem typical of a marlin. A good fisherman, Jack Jackman strove to get control and after a while the fish, although staying under water, was turned and started to head back toward the Red Mercury. Then suddenly it broke surface, 300 metres behind the spray and mist. The light played tricks. What could it be, the fishermen wondered? Maybe a billfish without a bill?

It was only when the fish was gradually fought to the boat that it was realised that here was a giant tuna. Nothing quite like it had been seen in these waters before. It was an hour and a half before it was brought close enough to try careful gaffing – such a prize must not be lost – and a tremendous fight still remained in the powerful streamlined body right to the end. Nelson carries a permanent scar on one hand as token of the many bits of skin lost in the final battle as the

three anglers struggled to parbuckle the fish (too heavy to haul all the way) out of the water halfway on to the tuck, and then set off home on one motor.

There were celebrations on board on the way with increasing estimates of size and weight being relayed over the air ahead to a growing crowd outside the club-house – "The biggest I've seen", "As big as a door", "Five hundred if a pound". A pair of good-sized striped marlin brought in by Don Ross at the same time were ignored as the *Lady Clare* came alongside and the club's ordinary scales weighing up to 400 lb (about 180 kg) proved not to be big enough. The tuna had to be manhandled to some heavier scales which established its weight at 519½ lb (235.64 kg) – the heaviest tuna caught on rod and line at that stage in New Zealand waters, and, it was believed, in the Southern Hemisphere.

Graham Wallace, an extremely able angler, was out drift fishing on *Sou'East* with me one morning about a mile out from the Two Fathoms Reef at Mayor Island in dead calm, mirror surfaced conditions when he hooked a tiger shark on the shallow bait. He was able to prevent it sounding and in the ideal conditions we were able to boat it in approximately 40 minutes. It weighed about 675 lb (306 kg). We then picked up a second tiger shark considerably larger, and by using the same tactics managed to boat it in about an hour.

While we were having a beer and congratulating ourselves I threw another bait over and inadvertently left the reel in free spool, with no click. Shortly afterwards I climbed up on the dodger top to see if I could sight any other boats. Another tiger shark was slowly swimming past the boat just too deep for his fin to show above the surface. He was very big indeed and by the time Graham had joined me to have a look, it dawned on me that he had taken our bait on Graham's line without our realising.

It took well over the hour to boat that fish – tigers are dour fighters, very big, bulky and heavy

The big Whitianga bluefin tuna of 16 January 1967, with successful angler Jack Jackman being congratulated by the skipper of Lady Clare, Nelson Tye.

17

like a white shark – and it was an outstanding performance by one man to cope with three such fish one immediately after the other. They were all too big to pull on board and with two tied to the anchor bollard and the third one to the aft cleat, we started to trickle very slowly home – about three miles around the island to the weigh station at South East Bay.

Graham Wallace (right) with the three tiger sharks and two striped marlin – all caught from Sou' East on 24 February, 1950. They made up a total weight of 1340 kg, then a world record for the total weight of gamefish caught by one man in a day. Author Fred Wilkins is on the left.

Chaffing Graham for being tired after catching three tiddlers I suggested that we pick up a couple of marlin to make our visit to the weigh station worthwhile. A bait dangled over the back in the wake without any serious fishing intent had not been there more than a few minutes before it was taken by a striped marlin which was soon followed by a second. These were boated without incident but they necessitated taking the third and biggest shark up forward to the anchor bollard – it sounds easy but sharks that size, still kicking, are not easy to drag around the side of a boat without hand-rails.

The first tiger shark weighed 306 kg, the second 386 kg and the big one 425 kg, just short of the New Zealand record. Inside the biggest shark was a marlin skull complete with a sword over half a metre long, and four vertebrae of what was undoubtedly a small whale of some sort. The marlin weighed 117 kg and 106.6 kg, and all in all it made up a then world record weight of game fish caught by one man in a day.

Graham Wallace and a closer view of two of the three huge tiger sharks. Inside one was a marlin skull complete with a sword over half a metre long.

About two years later I hooked the biggest fish I have ever had on a line off the Pinnacles at Mayor Island on the edge of the 200-metre depth line. We were drifting again, deep, and as usual were using 130 lb (60 kg) line on heavy gear. When a strike is made at that depth there is nothing to indicate for some time what variety of fish you have. We decided that we were most likely involved with either a thresher, or a very heavy marlin. Many of the big blacks when hooked in very deep water move quite slowly.

After about an hour and a half I was satisfied that it was too slow for a marlin or a ray and reckoned we were almost surely tied to a heavy shark other than a thresher, for it was not fast enough. Having made this decision the maximum brake possible was used from there on. The angler was Brian Armstrong of Akitia, on the Hawkes Bay coast.

Although an experienced and fit angler there were times when, even to stay in the chair he had to clamp both hands under the chair and hold himself in. I could see his knuckles white and his arms quivering with the strain while his seat was 150 cm to 200 cm out of the chair, and his rod was in a complete arc. The rod was a particularly heavy one I reserved for deep drifting; nothing less could have stood the strain. After about half an hour of gaining short lengths of line with these tactics the fish started to come quite consistently and fortunately a little more easily, and after three and a quarter hours we caught our first sight of it. It was an extremely large tiger, its stripes showing very clearly while it was still well down.

While the day was calm, there was a considerable groundswell, and as we got the thing closer to the surface I started to worry about how to handle it when my turn came. Brian got the trace to the rod tip but the shark was so darned big that my chain-snotter (a lassoo to go around a shark) began to look like a watch chain. And my gaff and gaff rope like a fly-hook on a string. It was ridiculous to think that I would hold that fish if it created any fuss at all.

Excitement was high on the boat and guesses as to weight and length were pretty extreme but the experienced anglers aboard, all station owners, decided that the fish was at least the girth of a large Polled Angus steer and in length was at the very minimum three times the 3-metre beam of the boat. I personally think it was considerably more, nearly the same length as the 11-metre boat.

I decided that I would have no show at all of boating it legitimately so, rather than risk losing it, decided to resort to any means at all to get it in, even though it would mean disqualification of the catch. More as a talisman than anything else I always carried a harpoon made for me by my father and used always on sharks before the International Game Fish Association was formed. So I disconnected the anchor warp and shackled the harpoon to the anchor chain, got all available ropes in the boat handy – and at the first available opportunity harpooned the fish. It took out the whole of our anchor warp, wrenched the bow around, and the rope went slack. The shark was still on the line and we repeated the process twice, but after the harpoon pulled out for the third time, the 14/0 hook straightened and the fish sank.

Some extraordinary tales of earlier days are told of a celebrated solo fisherman "Boy" (C. L.) Smith, of Whitianga, brother of launch skipper Roly Smith, whose boat the *Marlin* was involved in many notable catches. Boy Smith used to go out fishing on his own in a 14-foot clinker-built dinghy with an early Archimedes outboard motor. He came back with some good catches, including striped marlin, either tied to or taking up most of the room inside his boat. He fished from a steel tractor seat fastened to the centre thwart of his boat and used a sturdy tanekaha rod. Launchmen used to keep an eye open for him in case he needed any assistance, but he was of independent spirit.

One day he caught a 461 lb (209 kg) mako, a feat in itself almost unbelievable because such a fish would have the power, and usually the

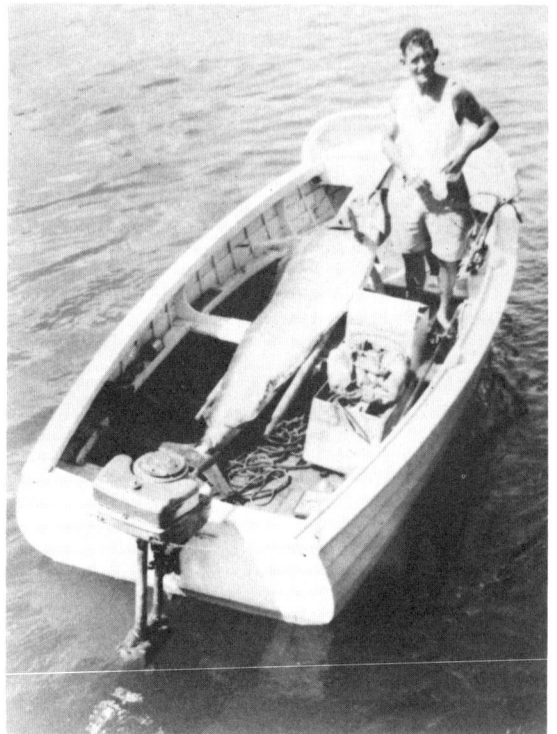

Two photographs of Boy Smith, legendary small boat fisherman of Whitianga. He shows how to bring aboard single-handed a striped marlin bigger than himself and not much shorter than his boat and stow it for the journey home. Note the tanekaha rod, the small motor and the tractor seat used as a fighting chair.

disposition, to smash the dinghy to smithereens. No-one came past when Boy Smith fastened on to the mako near Whale Rock, and the mako was too big and violent to get into the boat; when gaffed it was still very much alive. So the lone angler decided to tow it home, a distance of about 20 kilometres, behind the boat. The trouble was that every now and again the mako would get up steam and charge up and start attacking the keel of the boat with its serried teeth; and Boy Smith would have to coax an extra knot or two out of his small motor to get ahead again.

The mako was still alive when he drove his boat ashore at Whitianga, scaring the daylights out of some children who were swimming there, and got some help to haul the shark ashore. Of small additional interest was the discovery when

the shark was cut open that it had included an unusual item in its breakfast – a small mouse.

There are some dicey moments in big game fishing. No angler in New Zealand waters has yet been killed by a fish, but there have been a number of close calls, mostly with makos. Their teeth are fearsome, their strength and agility remarkable even among big fish species, and their persistence such that they are well known to bite even when dead and gutted.

Eddie Bowyer of Whangaroa, one of the old-timers of that club, was once out in a 7.8-metre launch with a friend. Eddie hooked a mako which immediately made four enormous leaps in quick succession. The fourth leap landed it perfectly in the cockpit, the sharks jaws hitting straight on to the fighting chair where Eddie had been sitting, and tearing it to pieces.

The mako proceeded to demolish everything within reach, smashing to pieces the reverse gear lever, among other things. The shark weighed in at 115 kg when the chastened fishermen ventured back into the cockpit and brought it to shore.

The only man to have been actually bitten by a mako in his boat appears to have been Dick MacKenzie, a Tutukaka skipper who was chief weighmaster of the Whangarei club for many years and a life member there. He had landed a 90 kg mako and had lashed it, apparently lifeless, on the counter, and then settled down to an hour's line fishing with his son-in-law before going home.

In the middle of this quiet episode the mako stirred to life, freed itself from its holding ropes with a tremendous whip of its body and landed in the cockpit with the fishermen, snapping wildly. Dick tried to jump for safety on to the counter but did not jump fast enough nor far enough. The shark flung itself at him and its jaws clamped on his knee. Dick's companion seized an iron bar and wielded it until the shark let go, but the knee was badly torn and streaming blood. While his son-in-law turned the launch full speed back to Tutukaka, Dick wound a rope around his thigh as a tourniquet and managed to stay just conscious until brought to shore – and hospital.

And whether or not marlin actually attack boats or ram them blindly, there are plenty of records of billfish piercing the hulls of boats. The tip of one bill, found imbedded in the hull of Roly Smith's launch at Whitianga, was within an inch of the petrol tank. There is a story of a leaping marlin putting its bill right through the coaming of a launch, and my boat *Sou' East* had six or seven swords in her, two of them right through, when I sold her. It was my practice to grind them flush and paint over them.

Not all who engage in deep-sea fishing do so with boat attached – sometimes this happens on purpose, sometimes by accident. One who was not afraid to leave his boat in pursuit of a fish was Percy Ward, of Tuakau. On one occasion, as Don Ross of Whitianga recalls, Percy hooked a yellowfin tuna during a fishing contest. He played it for half an hour, tuna being a very lively and worth-while catch – but when it was led up to the boat for gaffing it dived under the launch and through the gap between rudder and propeller.

Percy was not to be outdone. He dived off the side of the boat – in shark water – and pushed his rod and reel also through between rudder and propeller. He surfaced spluttering on the other side of the board, red anti-fouling in his hair but with the rod recovered and the fish still on.

"We backed the boat up to him," says Don Ross, "and lifted him back on board by his shoulders. He sat with his feet over the side and with water streaming out of him, and he caught that tuna. We said to him: 'Now, look. Don't ever tell anyone about this because they will not believe you.' "

One out-of-the-boat-and-in-again adventure concerned Trevor Frear of Totara North, 14 miles out to sea off Doubtless Bay in Max Spick's new boat *Waimanu* four years ago. The boat's first fish, a mako, was already tied up alongside, and then Trevor Frear got one. Bruce Harwood, the third man aboard, hooked a third. There was a scramble to get Trevor's mako tied along the side so that the third could be boated but it struggled free from the lashings and fell into the sea again, very much alive just behind the boat. While Trevor stood on the side trying to get another rope around his fish, the third one came under the boat, there was a touch on the throttle, and over he went, head first.

"I grabbed the dorsal fin of my mako" he says. "It was the only thing I could reach. There were a lot of ropes but they all seemed loose ends. Then somehow the others got hold of me and pulled me in again. There was not just my mako to worry about but the one under the boat."

It all happened so fast. "I could not have been in the water long," says Trevor. "The money in my wallet did not get wet and I could still read my driver's licence".

E. E. Chadban – the Chad of New Zealand pioneering fishing tradition – was once towed by a striped marlin while on a fishing expedition near Mayor Island. During attempts to gaff it, the marlin broke the line and the gaff rope looped around Chad's neck and under his arm, locking there under the force of the great drive of the marlin's tail as it escaped.

"I was over the side in a flick and hit the water about three metres from the boat," he said afterwards. "I had not the slightest idea of what had happened. All I knew was that I was in the water, and was going down, and was puzzled to know why I could not get up."

After a first dive the marlin jumped and started a rush across the surface of the water for about 100 metres. Chad surfaced, too, at the end of the rope and looking around saw the launch, about 30 metres away and backing toward him.

"It was then I realised that I was roped, and the swordie was again doing about 10 miles an hour with me in tow running up a wave like a respectable launch. I quickly concluded that would not do for long, so managed to get my hand under the rope around my neck and gradually worked the rope up until I slipped it over my head."

Chad then knew he was all right. But for a while he still held on to the rope with the marlin on the end and with the launch, still following him, now about 50 metres away. He then thought about what might happen when the launch, the swordfish, himself and the rope all got together – and let go. "The rest was just a matter of swimming back to the launch and getting aboard."

And there was the day I rode on a thresher. The angler who had it on his line was not a young man. He became quite distressed – I feared he might have a heart attack – by the time the fish was close enough to be positively identified. And at that stage the thresher was still too green to be boated. Rather than just cut the line and let the fish go (very much against the angler's wishes), I tried to gaff it in the region of the heart. The water flow deflected the gaff a bit and the fish ran to the end of the gaff rope and broke it, but then continued to swim steadily on the surface in a straight line with the gaff still in it.

Putting the boat close alongside again and with my wife, Fay, on the wheel keeping it there, I jumped down on to the chafing strip, a few centimetres above the water-line outside the cockpit and grabbed the rope of the gaff where it flowed beneath the water. I gave a terrific heave to get myself back inside the boat as quickly as possible but the gaff rope had looped a turn somehow around the fish's tail. He kicked, and since I had a better hold on the rope than I did on the boat, I ended up on my chest on top of the fish.

Having been around sharks for a long time I had no doubt whatever that I was much safer wrapped tightly around it than anywhere within biting distance. So I wrapped both arms and legs around it like a limpet and hung on for grim death. It was an instinctive reaction. I had a feeling that anything that stuck out was going to be bitten off.

Fortunately the fish must have been as surprised as I was and he and I managed to part company pretty smartly.

Back on board I collected my wits and gave it another go – the same drill as before but successfully this time – and got it. It was in the 220-kg-plus class – a big fish.

CHAPTER TWO

A tradition of fishing

The seas around New Zealand have always been good for fishing, and New Zealanders have always been fishermen. Nearly 2000 kilometres from Australia and with only small and distant islands of the South Pacific as other neighbours, washed by sub-tropical ocean currents and closely approached by some of the deepest waters of the sea, the country has attracted fish like a magnet, nourishing resident populations and gathering food stocks in annual migrations as the warm waters of the sub-tropics move down over its coasts each summer.

Captain James Cook, exploring New Zealand more than 200 years ago, observed Maori fishermen at work and wrote: "We were by no means such expert fishers; nor were our methods of fishing equal to theirs." Samuel Marsden, on his second missionary visit to New Zealand in 1819, was taken close inshore along the coast near North Cape all one day and recorded in his diary: "In a short time we came up with about 40 canoes full of people fishing . . . . They were fishing for none but swordfish, with short lines, and all the fish they caught of this kind were tabooed and could not be disposed of as they were to be preserved for their winter food. We saw a number of their stages on shore which were erected to dry their fish upon."

In spite of this and a great deal of other evidence of plentiful, large and interesting fish in the sea around New Zealand, European eyes were at first fixed on the whales which a convict ship *Britannia* had reported in 1791 in much the same area, and on the seals found in their thousands to the south. The idea of game fishing in the new waters hardly arose for nearly a century after Marsden's report. Les Blomfield, one of the pioneer big game launchmen of the Bay of Islands, recalled that early this century, when he was a boy, "we used to go out hunting for sharks, which were prized for their teeth. The marlin were about like flies, but we did not know what they were and we used to try to harpoon them".

And when the first marlin was fought and caught on rod and line off the Bay of Islands it was even then a secondary fishing target. The first concerted game fishing out of the bay was for neither billfish nor sharks, but for what was locally known as kingfish. Now classed as yellowtail this was a fighting fish good enough to satisfy fishing enthusiasts in the area for years, until interest gradually kindled in the obviously larger fish which so often broke lines and were sometimes seen, basking or tailing on the surface, or charging across the waves.

Credit for landing the first striped marlin on rod and line in New Zealand waters is given to Major A. D. Campbell of Scotland. He caught a 105.68 kg fish, 2.84 m long and 1.7 m in girth at the Bay of Islands. The date is variously given as 1913 or 1915 but early reports of the Bay of

The first billfish caught with rod and line in New Zealand waters, with Major A. D. Campbell who boated it at the Bay of Islands in 1915. N.Z. Herald.

Islands Kingfish Club – the continued use of the name shows where the interest still lay – suggest that another striped marlin was caught the following day, by F. P. Andreas, and a mako shark was caught on a rod by Colonel Calthorp, from India, the same season.

From there the sport grew, with the club in the Bay of Islands changing its name from "kingfish" to "swordfish and mako shark" and eventually to "swordfish" alone – the catches rising to a bumper 375 fish (including 283 billfish and 79 makos – with no yellowtail kingfish in the tally) in the 1925–26 season when Zane Grey arrived and put the place firmly on the international fishing map.

Other clubs were formed at nearby Whangaroa and down the coast at Whitianga and Tauranga – and then the gaps between were filled with clubs centred on Whangarei and Auckland, and eventually the big game centres extending to Whakatane, Waihau Bay, Gisborne and Napier and more recently to the far south, Otago and Fiordland coasts – a dozen clubs so far.

More than half a century of big game fishing and fishing research has shown that, while the Bay of Islands has maintained a special place in the local as well as the international scene, notable game fish of one sort or another are to be found all around the New Zealand coast. It is not so much fishing grounds that determine where worth-while fish are to be caught (although they do to some extent sort out the species) as the availability of good bases for boats and anglers.

Early in 1980 New Zealand held most of the world's striped marlin records, including the all-tackle record, and all but two of the line class records for 10-kg line test and above. Most of these record fish were caught in the waters down from North Cape to the Bay of Islands. The 60-kg record, however, is held in the Bay of Plenty.

The thresher records – and New Zealand holds the all-tackle record again plus half a dozen line-class records – are spread down the east coast of the North Island from the Bay of Islands to East Cape; the two world hammerhead records are at each end of this coastal strip. The two mako records are held at the Cavalli and Mayor Islands. The southern yellowtail records are again just about a New Zealand monopoly and similarly spread from off the northern tip of New Zealand all the way down into the central Bay of Plenty.

By and large, the marlin are seen more in the north and the sharks the other way round, but to this rule there are many exceptions and, until Mayor Island suffered its recent fall-off in catches, it could challenge any other fishing water in almost every category. This decline, shared to a degree by the nearby Mercury Bay Club, is probably only temporary; it is salutary to remember that the Bay of Islands, which in the 1979–80 season weighed in 605 game fish including 387 striped marlin – and which a leading boatman says could have included 600 marlin but for a fashion for light lines among inexperienced anglers – went through such a bad spell a decade ago that in one year the leading charter boat in the bay brought in only seven marlin in the whole sixth-month season. "Three of those were caught in the one day," says Snooks Fuller who was skipper of the boat, *Lady Doreen*, at the time, "so you can imagine what the rest of the season was like".

South of Hawke Bay, where the more violent seas of the Antarctic oceans begin to have their effect, big game species are still numerous, especially on the Chatham Rise, a shallow area which runs to the east coast of the South Island. The west coast of New Zealand is the less hospitable to sport fishermen, but exciting catches of bluefin tuna are now being made in its waters; a world light-tackle southern bluefin tuna has been caught in Fiordland.

Big mako have been caught, although not by game fishing, off Wellington beaches; and aerial spotting indicates that the best areas for marlin around New Zealand may be in the rough and virtually unfished offshore areas between New Plymouth and Kawhia.

The main New Zealand game fishing zone off the east coast of the North Island is about midway in an area of sub-tropical water and is fed by a warmer water flow through the area. To the north is a tropical ocean convergence – in midsummer about halfway to Fiji – where the westerly trade wind drift of tropical waters meets a sub-tropical backflow from Australia. To the south, on a line roughly through the centre of the South Island, runs a sub-tropical convergence where sub-tropical waters meet the sub-antarctic water flow moving to the east below New Zealand.

Into this area there is a flow of water mainly from the west which starts off as the East Australian Current, born of the trade wind drift from the latitudes of the South Pacific tropical islands and the warm waters of the Coral Sea. The current starts to cool as it progresses down the Australian coast and swings westward, (now the Tasman Current) to meet the west coast of New Zealand. From there it travels northward to swing around North Cape where it meets a more direct backflow from the Australian coast which has retained a greater degree of its original warmth.

Diverted (and warmed) down the east coast of New Zealand, it becomes the East Auckland Current. Further down the coast it becomes the East Cape Current, and then passes out into the open oceanic realms of the Roaring Forties.

Thus it is a warm current, with mixtures of sub-tropical and near tropical fish life, which flows down past the more northern game fishing areas, past Whangaroa, the Bay of Islands and Tutukaka, and down past the entrance to the Hauraki Gulf and across the Bay of Plenty. It creates a special environment for fish life there – an environment improved by the many off-shore islands and reefs, and varied by the way the sea bed falls away at the edge of the continental shelf – taken by geographers to be about 200 metres deep and by fishermen 100 fathoms.

If the warm current is thought of as a river in the ocean with water of different density, oxygen content, salinity, temperature, population and rate of flow, it will be seen that where it converges with other (in this case coastal) water, there will occur wide bands of eddies both horizontal and vertical, with the warm water generally overlying the cooler coastal water in a wedge. The extreme inshore edge of the warm current tends to be shallow, with the depth of warm overlying water becoming deeper the further from the confluence. The area of the wedge is potentially the best open-sea game fishing water.

The main stream of the warm current, however, directly affects only the most extreme headlands and further outlying islands down the coast. It flows fairly close to Cape Karikari, the Cavalli Islands and Cape Brett; it hits (with at least a glancing blow) the Poor Knights Islands creating there a unique marine environment and then diverts out past the Mokohinau Islands.

Its passage beyond there seems a hit and miss affair, usually well off the coast and subject to seasonal variations, but it undoubtedly contributes to the good fishing around Mayor Island and White Island and the good blue water near East Cape. Perhaps its final contribution to marine life off the New Zealand coast is made as it passes over an underwater mountain east of East Cape, where the density of phosphorescent fish life is so great that the area shows up as a patch of light on photographs taken from space.

Nothing can be taken for granted in the sea, however. There are sometimes upwellings of cold water near the coast – and there was one of these in 1970-71 which kept marlin offshore. And in from the main current the water can still be surprisingly cool; it starts that way at Tutukaka usually, warming up slowly until about three-quarters of the way out to the Poor Knights Islands, and cooling again before the warm current is really felt. A recent December reading showed a water temperature of about 18°C near the coast, 19½° at the northern end of the Poor

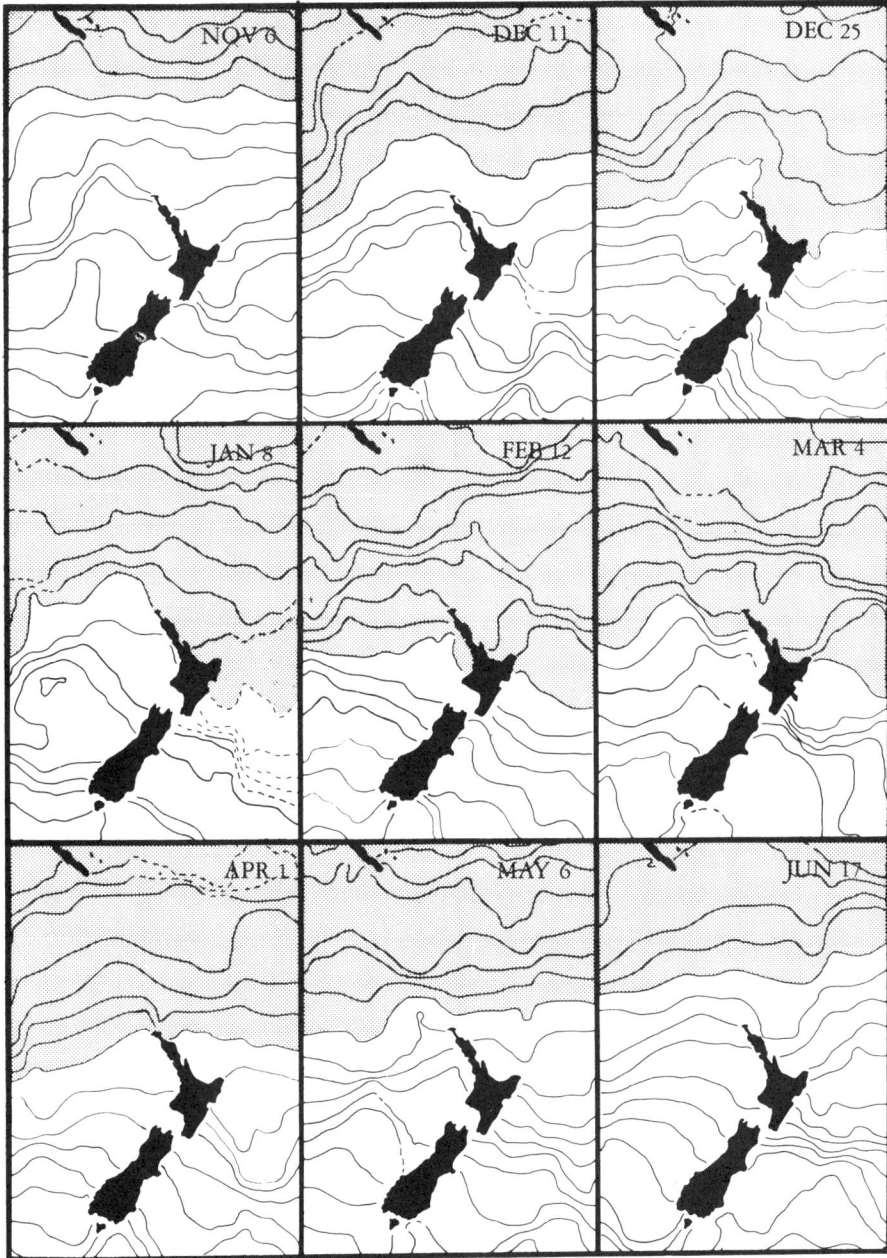

Diagram 1 STRIPED MARLIN WATER.

The charts above show the seasonal movement of warmer oceanic waters relative to New Zealand as revealed on the maps issued regularly by the National Environmental Satellite Service of the United States Department of Commerce. These charts are selected at regular intervals to show surface water temperature movements over the 1979–80 New Zealand big game fishing season. Each line indicates a variation of 1 deg C. The shading is taken down to the 20 deg C line; i.e., the surface temperature of the shaded water area is 20 deg C or above.

27

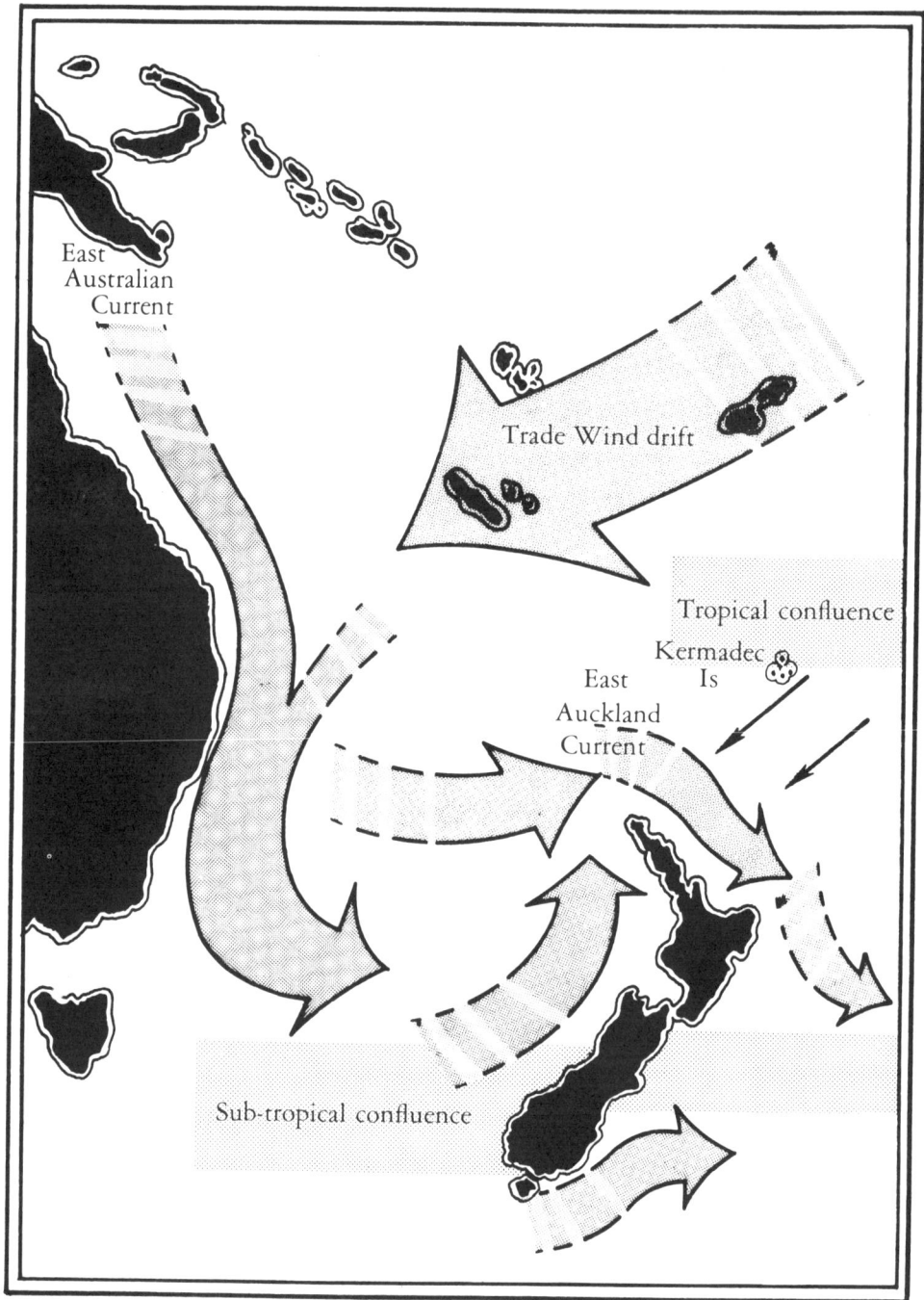

Diagram II

A stylised diagram of the main oceanic components of the East Auckland Current, with which most of the big game – and particularly marlin – fishing in New Zealand waters is associated. The thin arrows from the direction of the Kermadec Islands indicate the route that striped marlin are believed to take in their annual migrations to spend the summer off the New Zealand coast.

Knights and 22½° a couple of miles further out, in a big current line. On the edge of the current was a procession of big hammerhead sharks, half a mile apart, following what was obviously a good trail of food.

New Zealand game fishing waters are noted for the quality of the fish not their mere size. There are many records of fish that got away because they were simply too strong. Jim Whitelaw and Mervyn Arlidge agree that if the angler relaxes at the point when he seems to be gaining control, a big black marlin can turn again out to sea and from then on be stronger than the team of man, line and launch.

Real monsters of the sea, which often are not the most exciting to fish, are rarely encountered; few fish more than 453.6 kg have been caught here. They include R. Grieg's 461.31 kg blue marlin and J. Penwarden's 481.26 kg mako – New Zealand's biggest billfish and shark in the record book – B. D. H. Ross' wartime mako caught off Mayor Island which would, if it could, have taken the scales past their limit equivalent of 452.6 kg, and a couple of fish which never made it to the book. These included the great tiger shark caught off Mayor Island in 1951 by Keith Park in a six-hour fight and estimated to have weighed 680.4 kg. It took the Mayor Island scales beyond their limit of 453.6 kg so it was taken across to Tauranga the next morning, chained to the stern, and weighed in at 612.36 kg – a record which could not be claimed because the fish had become mutilated en route.

Jim Penwarden caught his big mako from Ces Jack's *Abalone* on February 17, 1970, while the boat was drifting two to three miles north of Mayor Island. It took a hard fight of three hours and a drag of about six miles before it was brought alongside.

Striped marlin here are in general bigger than anywhere else – at their minimum New Zealand weight they are about as heavy as the maximum reached off Hawaii. And for yellowtail, the maximum weight to be expected off California – about 13 kg – does not even reach the game

fishing throw-back minimum set in New Zealand. Visiting anglers have sometimes reacted angrily to the sight of the biggest yellowtail they have ever caught – or expected to see – being tossed back alive before their astonished eyes.

Few broadbill are caught around New Zealand on rod and line. The Bay of Islands Club which has caught most of them has weighed in only ten of these kings among game fish in 56 years, but Japanese long-liners have picked up – as a sideline to their tuna fishing – more than 9,000 of them in New Zealand waters in a single fishing season.

So the broadbill are about. The reason for the small number taken by anglers is probably that the broadbill is by day a deep-water fish caught usually by drifting and New Zealand game fishing is done mostly by surface trolling during daylight hours. The subsurface areas so successfully night-fished overseas are as yet quite unexplored.

The first broadbill to be caught off New Zealand was Zane Grey's great prize in 1926. Grey had already, after an hour's hot fight, lost a broadbill a few days before, one of three sighted outside Cape Brett. The one he caught took 200 metres of 39-thread (equivalent to 60-kg) line off on its first run, and showed itself enough to reveal its characteristic waving sword, before settling down to a hard fight. The 181-kg fish caused a sensation when it was sent to Russell by Grey to be viewed, and for all to share in eating.

While a record for New Zealand, this was not a world record for a broadbill, the first such record being set here, again off Cape Brett, by H. White-Wickham of London in January, 1928. The 305.27-kg fish, still a New Zealand record after more than 50 years, was caught on the drift off Piercy Island, making off with a long and powerful run before swinging in a wide circle around the launch several times. The first time the broadbill was got up to the boat it took off again without warning on a reel-screeching run, and was only finally subdued after a prolonged struggle. The fish was nearly 4.5 metres long

Tailwalking: a black marlin thrashes through calm water off Mayor Island. The two small islands to the right are Flat Top and Queen Victoria. The date: about 1933. E. V. Simpson.

with a sword of 1.2 m. The head was sent off to London in triumph.

While broadbill have a reputation for being reluctant takers of bait when they are seen coasting on the surface, Ken Collier caught another on top, on February 13, 1967, which was for a long time the New Zealand record on 36 kg line. Ken was fishing with Don Ross in the *Miss Lidgard* in green water about three miles north-east of Castle Rock off Whitianga, when the broadbill surfaced about 100 metres from the boat and was immediately recognised by its two fins. Don trolled over and dropped a trevally bait from the starboard outrigger back to the fish.

"It never hesitated, but went straight for the bait," said Don. "It thrashed furiously on the surface for a couple of minutes and then went down. Ken Collier was an expert angler and in two and a half hours we had it gaffed. The fight seemed to me to compare with that of a good hammerhead. It did not jump clear of the surface and I have never heard of one that did."

It is probably the ambition of every charter boat skipper to boat a broadbill. It was certainly Don's ambition and when he started fishing in 1950, broadbill were so rare and elusive that he made a resolution to stay fishing until he caught one. He caught a broadbill after 17 years, and 13 years later he is fishing still.

How big broadbill grow around the New Zealand coast is not known, but there should be some above White-Wickham's half-century-old local record; and there may well be the odd one above the world all-tackle record of 536.15 kg set off Chile in 1953. The Japanese catch at least 100 tonnes of broadbill a year in their long-lining in New Zealand waters and while their returns do not give the size of individual fish there must be at least a few that are big.

Perhaps one of these provided the story that Ces Jack tells. A leading skipper working out of Tauranga, Ces not only sticks to his story that the fish that Don Heatley of Taupo hooked from his boat on January 21, 1968, and lost after a marathon 32 hours was a monster broadbill about 7.3 m long weighing well toward a tonne, but he also believes that the same fish took another line from his boat a couple of weeks later, to be lost then for keeps after it had died on the bottom.

The first fish had taken the *Abalone* from the Queen Victoria rock, a few chains from Mayor Island, right up past the Aldermen Islands, a total distance including zig-zagging of about 95 kilometres. Ces Jack says the fish had a dorsal fin a metre high, like a killer whale, and when a spotlight was played on it close under the water at night, its eyes looked to be two-thirds of a metre apart.

The second hook-up from the *Abalone*, with a different party a couple of weeks later, was of a fish that behaved so much like the first that Ces

Jack told the party that "you might have cut the other fish off at the Aldermen and tied him on here".

When after approx 8½ hours the fish died and was gone forever, Ces felt it go with despair. If it was the same fish — and he felt it was — not only was it a fisherman's dream, but he had spent altogether 40½ hours in trying to catch it, more than a working week.

Another broadbill estimated at between 360 to 450 kg got away from Fred Bogun of Mt Maunganui in the Bay of Plenty, in 1980. The broadbill came up like a rocket at 2 pm and took a kahawai bait first strike. In the fight that followed the broadbill was brought to the boat no fewer than eight times but fought away each time. The last time, after 9 pm at night after a seven hour fight which did not appear to have tired it, the swordfish ran out with over 300 metres of line, felt to the angler as if it was turning over in the water and then the line went

Greyhounding: its colour fired up, a striped marlin leaps across Bay of Islands waters, grace and strength in every line. Tudor Collins.

slack. Hauled in, the line was found to have gone at the point where it was tied to the trace.

As I write, the most recent boating of a broadbill was by William Hall of Auckland in February 1980. It was the first swordfish to be taken in the Bay of Islands in 12 years, and weighed 241.77 kg. It was sighted on the surface but trolled skip baits and lures did not interest it. However, two minutes after the fish disappeared beneath the surface, a live kahawai bait that it had previously ignored took off and within minutes the fish was hooked.

"There was no screaming of the reel as I would have expected," said Bill, "but the line went out slowly in fits and starts taking three to six metres with each small run. At the end of approximately five minutes we must have had a total of about 180 metres out when we decided we had nothing to lose by striking the fish and, gently winding in all the slack, we struck with the boat." Bill fought the fish on a hard line for 3 hours 10 minutes before bringing it to gaff.

While broadbill are noted in New Zealand both for their reputation and their rarity as catches on rod and line, and mako for their

Flying: striped marlin demonstrate their capacity for fast, low skipping across the waves before the camera of Tudor Collins — famous photographer of big fish and big trees.

An unusual shot from the air of marlin working a school of fish. The photograph was taken from a tuna-spotting plane working in conjunction with the skipjack purse seine fleet, near the Mokohinau Islands. Ministry of Agriculture and Fisheries.

Volkner Rocks, with White Island in the background. One of the Bay of Plenty hot spots. R. Hague.

Bill Hall's Leilani II, *from which several recent record catches have been made. His is one of the few tuna towers so far installed on New Zealand launches.*

Mrs C. Pedersen of the Whangarei Deep Sea Anglers Club with the 260.40 kg blue marlin she caught on 22 February 1979. It set club and New Zealand records which still stand. The record was originally claimed on a 24 kg line but the line overtested by 3 kg. However, the fish took the 37 kg line record and is the heaviest blue marlin caught by a woman in New Zealand waters.

ferocity, it is the marlin for which big game fishing in these waters is noted; and particularly the striped marlin, which for size are matched only by those off the Australian and South American coasts.

The striped marlin are beautiful fish with their iridescent bodies which sometimes seem to light up as they tackle a bait, their long bills, and their tremendous, leaping, fighting qualities. The fishing season really begins when the first marlin is caught, not usually these days until well into December, and some of the sparkle of it ends when the last striped marlin is caught, usually around June. But during the six-month season the striped marlin are caught in their hundreds.

The total catch for all clubs for the 1978–79 season was 565, but the catch was up to 692 in 1979–80, with the Bay of Islands club alone weighing in 387. The Bay of Islands records also show the typical rise and fall of the marlin season – with monthly catches of: December, 4; January, 38; February, 95; March, 172; April, 36; May, 40; June, 2.

The marlin catches have been on the rise in the northern grounds over recent seasons, but there is no sign of falling weights that might suggest overfishing. The average sizes have, in fact, been increasing and the numbers have gone up without increased fishing effort.

The more commonly suggested reason for the poor seasons which occurred for striped marlin off the northern New Zealand coast (and the subsequent recovery) has been that on their annual migration to New Zealand down a line believed to centre on the Kermadec rise, many were for a period taken by overseas fishing fleets on their long lines. The Japanese showed increased fishing activity in the offshore areas out from the Far North fishing grounds at about the time the local catches declined, and the catches have certainly improved since the fishing fleet changed its strategy and its area of interest by pursuing bluefin tuna off the far south of the country for most of the season. They still fill up with their former main catch, yellowfin tuna, on

their way home at the end of the season however, and it may be more than coincidence that they end their north-bound fishing about opposite Mayor Island and Whitianga. Striped marlin were still scarce there until the 1980–81 season, when Mayor Island waters staged a remarkable recovery, producing a tally of 214 game fish, including 58 marlin (striped, blue and black).

No link has been established between our striped marlin population and that in any other waters, although tagging has established such a link between the black marlin stock in New Zealand waters and those off Queensland where, in this instance, the fish tend to run bigger than ours. Black marlin are, however, tremendously prized in New Zealand waters for their fighting qualities, and a number weighing more than 350 kg and one of 444 kg have been caught here. It was long felt that Captain Laurie Mitchell's big black which held the world record for a while at 442.71 kg might have gone above the 1000-lb mark (453.6 kg) if it had been weighed soon enough.

The black marlin do not seem as sensitive as striped marlin to water temperatures, although they undoubtedly like it warm to judge from their numbers and size off the Cairns fishing grounds. They tend to be caught off reefs and other foul ground even close inshore in New Zealand waters. Blue marlin, however, which are perhaps the most aggressive of the marlins caught off New Zealand, are clearly oceanic fish, liking the warm blue water off the coast in full summer. They rarely stay longer than does the blue water, and rarely come close inshore out of it. It is perhaps significant that recorded catches of this splendid fish have increased greatly since the fishing launches started to patrol further out to sea as the old-established inshore grounds started to become less productive in the 1950s and 1960s.

A fish which has been caught only recently, and in small numbers so far, has been the shortbilled spear fish, the first of which was taken on rod and line from the *Ngarangi II*, skippered by Noel James of Te Puke. At the time it caused much speculation that it might be the smallest marlin ever caught here when it weighed in at only 20.41 kg, but it was identified by John Moreland, the National Museum's ichthyologist as the first short-billed swordfish ever recorded in New Zealand waters. Closely related to the striped marlin, the fish was indigo blue in colour, small in girth, without stripes and had a dorsal fin running the length of its body. Even in its home tropical waters this fish is something of a rarity.

When the New Zealand record bluefin tuna was caught by E. Andrews, of Pio Pio, fishing from the *Luana* on February 3, 1970, the boating took only an hour, but in other ways the huge sleek fish was a handful. It was decided to keep the huge fish in the beer room at the Mayor Island Lodge overnight so that it could be taken away and cast the following day. Fishing club beer rooms are not usually small but the only way the giant tuna could be fitted in was with its tail up in one corner and its nose down in the opposite one. It would not lie down. And the next day it took a dozen men to manhandle it down the beach and over the rail of a launch for transport to the mainland. The cast now hangs in the Mayor Island clubhouse, along with black and blue marlin, and a couple of broadbill, all of handsome size.

A separate population of bluefin tuna provides the new Fiordland Club with good sport and has given Miss S. Vincent the world record for this fish, one of 22.22 kg caught on 10-kg test line. The New Zealand men's record on 10-kg line is also held by Fiordland, jointly by B. Vincent and R. G. Marquand. New areas discovered off the West Coast of the South Island offer further good catches for this fish, which is, however, also the prime target for the Japanese fishing fleets. A good tuna properly processed is worth $2000 in Japan, so commercial competition for the species in the south, where the tuna boats now congregate early in the season, will continue to be fierce.

The yellowfin tuna, however, which comes lighter while still being a splendid fighting fish, has been in recent years down-rated by the Japanese fishing fleet. Good fish keep coming up, and half the New Zealand records have been set in the last ten years, these records shared between the Bay of Islands, Tutukaka and Whakatane.

There are two more big game fish for which New Zealand has established a reputation. One is the hammerhead shark, for which Mrs H. M. Wood of Lottin Point holds the world women's 60-kg line class record of 184.16 kg and Robyn Hall of Auckland the 15-kg line world record for women of 86.18 kg.

Perhaps a more exciting fish still is the thresher shark for which a New Zealand angler, Brian Galvin, fishing out of Tutukaka held the world all-tackle record of 335.20 kg. This was broken, again from Tutukaka, by Mrs Dianne North's 363 kg fish.

CHAPTER THREE

The open challenge

Game fishing off the New Zealand coast ranges from the highest professionalism to the sheerest amateurism; and fishing being what it is, success will not always go to those who most deserve it. Skilled deep sea anglers have sometimes fished, and not just here, for years before they have caught the fish of their hopes, while others can get records at their first hold of a game rod.

It is well worthwhile for any top-line fisherman who wants the best sort of fishing to come to New Zealand, for it is all here. The world's best striped marlin and some of its best game sharks and smaller game fish like yellowtail are to be caught here. The facilities ashore and afloat are good, and they will find fellow anglers and boatmen worthy of their own skill and experience. Coastal waters are a sheer joy just to be upon and have made New Zealand a place apart.

It is also a place where the average New Zealander can enjoy himself, for fishing is a sport for everyone. The sleek, extensively equipped launch which trolls over the Taheke Reef by the Cavalli Islands – a famous ground for famous fish – may find itself in the company of a sheep barge fitted with a fighting chair which may well out-fish it. A party cruising north to the Cape should not be staggered to pass a fishing trawler on which a crewman sits on a crayfish pot, trolling for marlin from an improvised outrigger. The Old Man and the Sea Trophy, awarded by

the New Zealand Big Game Fishing Council for the most meritorious catch each season, has reflected this broad spectrum of anglers. It has been won by women as well as men, of course; by some of the world's top anglers, such as Sir William Stevenson, the first man to catch three game fish each weighing over 453.6 kg; by an angler with one arm; by another with no legs; by one who was blind; and by a 14-year-old boy, William Bannister.

Fishing with the family can turn into something of an epic struggle, as Fred Cotterill of the Whangarei Club found. On Saturday, February 29, 1964, Fred was fishing from his launch *Jeanette* near the Pinnacles off the Poor Knights Islands. His crew were his sister, his wife and his 14-year-old nephew. Late in the afternoon a black marlin struck, the reel screamed and almost immediately the launch's engine stalled. While the two women tried to restart the engine, Fred held on while the marlin continued to take line, which was crossed at this stage by two other launches unaware of the strike.

By the time the engine could be restarted, the fish had taken out 700 metres of line and the *Jeanette* had drifted perilously close to the jagged rocks of the Pinnacles. Then, as Fred began to recover some line, the steering chain broke. The two women, fresh from their struggles with the motor, now had to lie on the floor of the cockpit and work the rudder with an improvised tiller made from a stub of wood about 10 cm long. Throughout the four-hour fight that followed, Fred's nephew controlled the throttle and yelled orders to the women at the improvised tiller.

Darkness came down on a lumpy sea as the fight went on and the marlin, still full of fight, attacked the *Jeanette* and pierced the hull with its bill. Eventually gaffed, the marlin weighed 169.19 kg from a 37-kg breaking-strain line, one for the record book.

The usual game fishing boat has at least someone to steer and someone to help in boating as well as its quota of actual anglers. But one-man catches, sometimes of mako, and sometimes from very small boats, are part of the local fishing tradition.

One of the first of these recorded occurred off Whangaroa when Alan Sanderson, one of the pioneers of the local club, was left in his 3.5-metre punt *Humdinger* on the fishing grounds while the launch which towed him there went off for some serious fishing. It returned to find Alan patiently waiting in the punt with a 108-kg mako tied alongside.

Big fish are not to be taken lightly, however, and the more amateur the fisherman the more he or she needs to be warned to take care if fishing alone.

A debate that is continually revived with every large billfish caught with its bill broken, is to what extent, if at all, billfish use their bills as fighting spears. Considered expert opinion is that billfish do not customarily use their swords for fighting, although there are times when it seems they may. A 136-kg mako shark was caught on a hapuku line out from Whangaroa Harbour recently which had a broadbill sword right through its body.

Makos, of course, seem prepared to attack anything. A 325.68-kg mako caught from Ray Dinsdale's *Caramia* had already had a chunk bitten from its side by another shark when it was hooked but did not seem to have lost any of its vigour or ferocity – it bit a large section out of the launch's stern ladder when brought

Memories of Grey – a mako caught at Mercury Bay by Roma Grey, Zane Grey's brother. Tudor Collins.

alongside. And John Going, on investigating a threshing in the water off the Poor Knights one day, found a large broadbill, of about 200 kg, being attacked by a large mako which was gouging at its sides with open jaws. The broadbill was almost dead when they reached the scene. They managed to gaff the broadbill but were unable to get the tail up because the fish was so heavy. They then set about trying to catch the mako – a huge specimen they estimated at between 350 kg and 450 kg.

It was at first disinterested but eventually,

A worthy broadbill prize: Bill Hall with his 241.77 kg fish caught off the Bay of Islands in 1980 on 36 kg breaking strain line. Monty Miller.

when tried with kingfish bait, showed signs of returning appetite. However, efforts to keep the bait in front of the mako only succeeded in the loss of both fish for the gaff was dislodged from the broadbill and it sank into the depths with the huge mako circling around.

This book deals in detail with the technicalities of fishing gear, baiting and best ways to fish as I see them for New Zealand waters, but it would be a pity if the oddities and improvisations to which fishermen are prone should go right out of the game, or if it should be assumed that nothing but the very best and most modern gear will catch a fish.

Before the influence of Zane Grey in particular came to be felt — he introduced split cane rods to the scene — and before the modern fibreglass rods were even invented the New Zealand game fisherman used tanekaha rods which he usually made himself.

Tanekaha is a New Zealand tree, sometimes known as the celery pine. It grows to about 20 m high but when young it has a tall slender form,

The magnificent head of a broadbill caught at Whitianga on a 37 kg line.

straight in grain and with heavy white wood of good strength. Walking sticks made from these saplings found a ready market as far away as London, but their true worth, as every fisherman of the day knew, was in bending to a good fish. Anglers used to sort out their preferred size in the bush, cut it themselves and put it in a creek for about six weeks to flush out the sap, and then into a drain pipe filled with linseed oil for a two- to three-week soak. The rod would then be ready for final dressing, the fixing of rings down its length and a roller tip at the end. They were indeed very good rods.

Some mighty deeds were done with rods cut from the bush, as when Mrs Rita Beaver in April, 1951, caught a 389.18-kg mako, then a world record and still the New Zealand women's record on 60-kg line. A 54-year-old grandmother, Mrs

Beaver was fishing out of Whangaroa Harbour with her husband, a commercial fisherman, and Bert Louden, one of the most notable of the Whangaroa anglers. Mrs Beaver had never caught a game fish before and the menfolk decided that it was time this was put right. When a very small mako swam past the stern of the boat Bert said: "That's the fish for you." He hauled in a line which was on the drift, whipped off the large kahawai bait, and attached a strip of bait more suited in size to the small shark. He tossed the bait over, and up from under the boat surged a huge mako which snatched it. For the four-and-a-half hour fight which followed, the rod she used was one of Bert Louden's, and made of tea tree.

Bert Louden caught 150 game fish with his wooden rods. Not all the old rods were equal to the task imposed on them of course, and when Stan Ellis, an early Whangaroa angler caught his first world-record thresher of 316.16 kg, it was on the second rod to be used on the fish, substituted "by skilful handling" the account says, when his first rod broke.

Big game fishing is not usually the physical strain that one might imagine. There are skills that can be easily learned, such as in the correct method of pumping and winding, to lessen the strain. Harvey Franks of Tutukaka remembers a woman he judged to be in her late thirties and weighing about 57 kg, who brought to the boat a 243-kg blue marlin in two hours – something he did not think she would have the strength to do had she not settled down to methodical fishing.

The idea of teasers – brightly coloured pieces of board or metal – to arouse the interest of fish before putting out baited hooks, was introduced by Zane Grey to New Zealand and the idea still lingers, although most fishermen around New Zealand agree that it is better to "fish for keeps" right from the beginning. Most teasers show tooth marks after a little use, backing up the idea that if they had carried a hook they would have caught a fish instead of just teasing it, but, as fish have become more and more difficult to catch,

BAY OF ISLANDS SWORDFISH
CLUB

28-2-80		
ANGLER	ROBYN	HALL
FISH	3k/MARLIN	
WEIGHT	98 kg 217	110½ kg 243
TACKLE	24 KG. B/S	
LAUNCH	LEILANI II	
15 kg	S/MARLIN	

Mrs Robyn Hall, holder of several records on lighter tackle, with a striped marlin and a black marlin. Graeme Townsend.

fishermen have looked at every possible idea to capture their interest. Thus bottles are sometimes towed along (empty, of course) to clank together and flash in the sun; or rattles of coconuts are dragged underwater, and idea born and still used in the Pacific Islands.

Lure fishing has two problems of cost that tend to make it less practised than it might be. The first is the cost of the lures themselves — unless you are prepared to make them yourself out of some frayed rope or strips of plastic. You stand to lose more of them than you would off ordinary hooks set with bait. The more important cost, however, is that involved in trolling them — for to drive a boat at a lure speed of 10 to 12 knots uses three to four times as much fuel as ordinary bait trolling at three to four knots.

So although lure fishing has exciting possibilities, fishing with baits is still the more popular method here, and is, perhaps in terms of actual catches, the more effective. Advice on the best baits to use is given later but in times of desperation almost anything may catch a fish. There are records of game fish being caught on an old sandshoe and a length of radiator hose. Then there were the two anglers (who shall remain anonymous) whose background was in the country rather than on the sea. Not only did they pour wine on the water before casting their bait, but they formed the notion that, because fish must eat the rubbish that is thrown overboard from ships, big fish should have got a taste for vegetables. So they tried fishing for billfish and sharks with cabbages as bait — enclosed in little net bags to keep them on the hook. Their skipper was so ashamed that he implored them not to bring their lines out of the water when there was any other boat around.

Stories abound about a fish taking a second bait after having got off the first hook, then usually finding that they have bitten once too often. Off Whakatane, when Graham Bourk, Peter Willetts and Lee Stewart were fishing near the Raurima Rocks, the same fish was hooked in turn by each of the three anglers. A medium-sized shark, it first took Peter Willetts' line and whipped the rod from his grasp while the boat was being manoeuvred into position. The next time it was brought to the boat but tore itself away while being gaffed. When it was caught at the third biting, it showed the gaff marks of the second encounter and trailing from its mouth a second line at the end of which was Peter Willetts' missing rod.

Deep trolling is a new idea to Don Ross, a

A black marlin broaches, alone on the sea with a bird.

World record: Klaus Rober and the 183 kg striped marlin caught on 24 kg breaking strain line in the 1980 Bay of Islands International Bill Fish Tournament. Graeme Townsend.

Mrs Dianne North and here world all-tackle record thresher shark. It was caught from the launch Mastro *owned by Garth Marsland (background) in February 1981.* Northern Advocate.

charter skipper working out of Whitianga, and there is nothing like learning with someone who is learning himself. He got the idea from watching marlin swim up near a school and then disappear, presumably fairly deep under, and wondered what success he might have if he could get a bait down where they were. The first time, he tried the idea for about three days but had no luck at all, so put it aside and began again about a year later, this time giving it a longer trial. He started to catch fish. Over a fortnight it was apparent that he was catching more fish than by surface trolling.

His first attempts were with big Japanese paravanes used by commercial fishermen, but these were unsuccessful. Then he tried window sash weights to assess what sort of weight he needed to get his bait down and found that something even a bit heavier was needed, up to about 18 kg. The lead had another advantage, it seemed to go very quietly through the water. So he has evolved a system of very slow trolling, still with baits out on outriggers (the speed is not enough for lures) and a deep trolling line off the stern of the boat (sometimes in combination with a shallow heavy troll) as well.

The heavy trolling line runs almost vertically down from the back of the boat. The weight, still in about the same cylindrical shape as a window sash weight, is let down on a thin line to minimise "fuss" in the water and the risk of having the weight forced up back toward the surface. The weight itself is connected to the top of the trace on the main line with a very light tie which breaks when there is a strike. The weight must then be hauled up at speed to get it out of the way – it is no easy task to get 18 kg of lead up 30 metres in a hurry, and a winch is handy for this – to allow the fish to be played in the ordinary way.

One thing that was quickly learned was that the lead weight had to be on a steel trace as well as the main line, because sharks have a tendency to attack the weight before the bait. So far, Don has tended to use 37-kg line but, because the fish

down deeper tend to be smaller if more numerous than those near the surface, he is changing over to 24 kg, with always the fear that if a big fish takes the deep bait the gear may not prove heavy enough.

Deep trolling, however, is not a Don Ross invention, nor a Whitianga monopoly. It is done on an increasing scale abroad with increasingly elaborate gear which has not yet been widely adopted in this country, and may well be adapted to suit local conditions and experience.

There are strict rules to big game fishing to be observed, at least in spirit, by all sportsmen, and if an angler has in mind the possibility of a record fish, the utmost care must be taken to keep to the letter of the rules at all times. Every year sees record claims disallowed because the double is not the right length, perhaps, or most commonly, when the line overtests above its rated strain. One can be lucky, of course, as in the case of the 260.40-kg blue marlin caught by Mrs C. Pedersen of the Tutukaka Club which was claimed as a record on 24-kg line. The line failed the test by 3 kg but the fish was still heavy enough to take the New Zealand record for 36-kg line.

Records are, of course, often as much a matter of luck as of skill – sometimes bigger fish give in easier than smaller, younger ones – and often the margin is not very great. Under the rules of the I.G.F.A. a new record fish of over 45.36 kg must exceed the existing record by at least one half of one per cent of the existing record, and, if it is heavier by less than this margin, will jointly hold the record. The striped marlin caught by Johnnie Boyle from Goldie Hitching's *Luana* on December 30, 1974 on 60-kg gear was only 1.82 kg heavier than the existing world 60-kg line record of 178.71 kg, but it needed to be only 0.89 kg heavier to set a new world figure.

While marlin are caught commercially well off the coast, moves to embark in a local commercial fishing of game fish have so far not eventuated, for two main reasons.

The first arose from the action of the Tauranga

Club in having a restriction placed on commercial fishing for marlin when it began off Tauranga in the late 1940s with what was known as the drum system. The commercial fishermen, supplying a canning factory in Tauranga, would roll about 50 metres of heavy baited hapuku line, with the usual steel trace and hook, around a drum and toss it over in marlin water. The line would be tied back on itself at the chosen drifting depth, so that when a strike occurred, the tie would break and the drum revolve allowing enough slack line for the fish to swallow the bait and hook on.

Passing game fishermen were angry to see the drums bobbing about with the tugging of big fish, and hooked marlin leaping around them. When fish were exhausted, they would be collected, and the drums and lines rebaited and reset. Bob Gray remembered seeing a commercial boat coming in past the Bait Pond at the Mayor with ten or a dozen "swordies" on as the game fishing boats were going out after breakfast.

With the argument that the commercial fishing was a threat to a sport which was a tourist drawcard, Cyril Dentice and Stan Deans convinced the Government of the need to place a limit of four marlin a day per boat and to restrict fishing for them to rod and line.

Even with the new 200 mile limit, commercial fishing of marlin has not surfaced again in inshore waters, for marlin has a mercury content higher than the minimum legal level allowed in foodstuffs sold in New Zealand. The local limit is a mean level of 0.5 parts per million; and some overseas markets also require a mercury clearance to accompany shipments of fish products. The permissible safe levels vary from country to country, with Japan, for instance, having a level of 0.4 ppm for locally caught fish although it will accept "open ocean" fish with higher levels.

Mercury is accumulated by most fish in the sea and marlin, being at the top of the food chain, thereby accumulates more than others. A survey done last year gave New Zealand striped marlin a mercury content ranging from 0.14 ppm, to 1.44 ppm, with a mean of 0.99. This level of mercury, while it makes the sale of striped marlin illegal in New Zealand, does not deter those who catch marlin from eating it themselves or passing it on to friends. It is commonly accepted that they would need to eat a lot of marlin to assimilate much mercury from it and marlin flesh is so rich that few people could eat enough to be in danger.

As it is, the days have gone when most game fish caught were dumped after being weighed ashore – with perhaps only the jaws of makos and the spears of billfish being kept, as souvenirs. It was a practice that did the sport's image no good, and which has dwindled as it has been realised that the fish is generally much too good to eat for it to be wasted. Smoked marlin – striped or black – probably take the gourmet prize and most big game clubs have a local expert to deal with the catch for members. The fish is usually smoked in slices, the process taking five to six hours. Blue marlin and broadbill (if you can catch one) grill and bake beautifully.

In some areas where marlin is plentiful enough to satisfy all appetites, sharks are still dumped but in most places all but a few of the sharks are also regarded as good eating. Thresher shark is good cooked almost any way. Small mako also cook well and in some places overseas are regarded as epicure fare. Big mako are less in favour and most people reject hammerhead. The tunas and albacores, of course, make good eating, as does kingfish. Game fishing is no longer just for sport.

44

CHAPTER FOUR

Gear for the sport

Every sport has its proper equipment, and the gear for game fishing is perhaps more specialised than most. However, as the fish are much stronger and larger than the angler, making the catching of them a test of applied skill rather than of brute strength, and as the angler may be man or woman, young or old, fit or handicapped in strength or health, choice of the right gear is doubly important.

With the ending of the era of the tanekaha rod went the wooden reels designed on the pattern of the salmon and trout reels of England, without gearing, free wheel or brakes. They were hard work to wind; if the fish had to be allowed to run, the handles whizzed around as the line went out, at great risk to the angler's knuckles; and the only way of slowing the reel, apart from nudging with the thumb to prevent an overrun, was to push a leather strap against the whizzing spool until friction slowed it down, or it started to smoke.

The main credit for introducing new gear and new ways of using it is given to Zane Grey. He introduced not only whippier or faster action rods, but geared reels with mechanical brakes, and persuaded the local anglers not without reluctance to change to reels set over the rod and not under it. He contended that this positioning of the line enabled greater work to be done with the rod (and – his critics used to say – he liked demonstrating just how much work whenever he

could be sure that he was being watched).

His claim is still accepted by rod makers, although a few purists wonder why. I find the mechanics of the fact more interesting because they have a wider application. In my opinion the wider reel with its two harness points, combined with the slot in the butt cap or nock, eliminates rod twist. When the angler uses both hands to manipulate his reel, he is held in a proper stance with shoulder, hip and leg muscles all taking an even strain. This gives him far greater pulling power, plus far greater and faster control of both reel mechanics and line spooling.

It costs about the same to equip oneself for big game fishing as it does to play golf with good gear or go skindiving with top equipment – which means that it does not come cheap. The price goes up each year, so comparison with other sports is more relevant than a figure, but it goes to confirm that time spent in making the outlay wisely is well spent. Those who fish from New Zealand charter launches will find that their skippers will provide gear that usually suits them, however anyone who gets hooked to the top end of a big game fishing line is likely to think about some of his own. If ever he has the luck to fight a big fish to near mutual exhaustion and hankers for another he will surely then want his rod custom-built.

A set of game fishing gear consists of a rod, reel with line, trace and hook or lure, a fishing

Les Blomfield, one of the best known of the early Bay of Islands launch skippers, handles a "knuckle duster" reel. N.Z. Herald.

harness and a few accessories such as a glove. The rod is a composite – no longer a single pole – consisting of tip, line guides and a butt, joined by a winch-fitting incorporating a pin to fit a slot in the tip ferrule which holds the guides in alignment with the middle of the reel spool. Personally, however, I prefer the guides to lead to one side, so that the line has only to be flicked one way to achieve level wind on retrieve.

Apart from the tips (which are mostly, but not all made here), most of the components of modern game rods available in New Zealand are imported. Some tip blanks are imported, and the local manufacturer is also in turn an exporter. Rods can be assembled tailor-made to suit the individual angler, but most are bought off the rack in a range intended to suit varied but standardised requirements.

Tips for lighter rods are often made of solid fibreglass but those for game fishing are usually hollow, of various constructions and combinations of materials. Under international game fish regulations, the tip must be a minimum length of 101.6 cm. Tips are cut from one section or other of the tapered blanks (which are made in slow and fast tapers) according to the stiffness required.

Buy to your need and not for price. You will get some idea of what a rod is meant for by a weight capacity marked on it, but the prime requirement for the most effective and enjoyable angling goes beyond that into a question of balance.

Balance requires that the line, reel and rod are all of matching strength, and that they also match the angler. The sort of fish being sought will determine the strength of line to be preferred and also the lengths. These factors will also determine the choice of reel, and the line weight (or strength expressed as breaking strain) will determine, along with the strength of the angler, the sort of rod to be used. The general preference is that the line should be strong enough to bend the rod tip to an angle of 90 degrees.

Consequently, the person who is going to use

the fishing gear is of prime importance in the balancing of that gear. If a big and strong man, gear that is matched with his physique will allow him to enjoy angling techniques to match his temperament and strength. The fit and pugnacious sort of angler is happiest with a rod tip stiff enough to test him pretty severely in deflecting the rod tip by 90 degrees in playing a fish. That choice dictates far more direct transmission of shock both ways, but punishes the angler more than the fish because the tip is the fish's lever against the man. So the longer and more inflexible a rod tip we have, the more we handicap ourselves. A very stiff stick makes for a really hard slugging gutwrenching sort of a fight, and when used on a hard fish is more prone to line failure and torn-out hooks.

On the other hand those who choose angling of a more relaxed nature (because of their physique or maybe their health and temperament) will look for a greater degree of flexibility of rod tip to suit their choice, and in doing so will reduce their handicap.

This question of backbone or flexibility of rod tip has a direct relationship with the type of butt. Since the tip is the fish's lever against the angler, the butt is the angler's lever against the fish. Therefore, if considered alone, the longer the butt the less handicapped the angler. There are practical limitations and the International Game Fish Association rules a maximum allowable butt length of 68.58 cm. It allows enough latitude to permit personal or individual balance by lowering the chair gimbal or shortening the rod butt, as the case may be, to adjust the reel height to the angler's arm, and backlength and strength. When combined with the tip length minimum of 101.6 cm – the I.G.F.A. ruling – it makes a pretty sensible sort of standard.

Most straight butts fitted in New Zealand are about 43-cm long, and curved ones a few centimetres longer. The choice whether to have a butt straight or curved governs the maximum pull the individual angler can put on a fish. A curved butt is of very great assistance when lifting heavy, slow-moving or dead fish, because it allows the seated angler to keep the rod tip down and his back vertical. But what we gain on the swings we seem to lose on the roundabouts, mainly because the curved butt severely limits elevation of the rod tip and thus curtails the pumping arc. The straight butt remains my favourite for all but deep and ultra-heavy fishing.

Any butt, of course, needs to be strong because all the strain that the tip of the rod is taking is transferred straight through to it, and a butt will quite frequently break where it has been turned down to permit its entry into the winch fitting. The ease of handling a rod, particularly for convenience in winding the reel, may well depend on the length of the butt. It is not really practical for the tackle dealer to keep a range of butt lengths available without having details of the chair gimbal heights. Anyone wanting a shorter or longer than standard butt would need to have the existing butt cut down or, where possible, extended. This is easier for wood and aluminium, which are the most common materials, than for fibreglass which is both expensive and heavy. Incidentally, the grain of a wooden butt (which is usually turned from hickory) should, for strength, be edge-on, or vertical, when looking down on the rod in its fishing position.

Another point: The rod butt fitting (or gimbal nock) sits either in a pouch in a waistbelt worn by a standing angler (when a shorter than usual butt aids angling convenience), or more commonly fits in a gimbal, or slot with a pin through it, in the front of a fishing chair. Because nocks are made to various designs by different manufacturers and especially in different countries, there is a possibility that the rod butt will not fit on every boat. As a precaution against this, the gimbal fitting on a boat should be roomy enough to allow say 50 mm of play for the average butt fitting. If this does not cope with a particular problem then alternative butt fittings are usually available.

Next comes the hardware, guides and reel seats. I prefer good strong roller guides and tip fittings which can be dismantled for servicing to all others I have used. A new breed of ring guides with a near friction-free synthetic material is becoming well favoured, especially when using lines of fine diameter, but when fighting a really good fish there is apprehension and heartbreak enough without having to contend with prematurely fraying line.

Light backbone (flexible) rods need more guides than their stiffer counterparts to keep the line clear of the rod when it is heavily arced, and to reduce the friction area on the line at the guide. The number can, however, be overdone. The bindings for the guides stiffen or add backbone to the rod where it is bound and therefore leave the areas in-between subject to greater stress than would be the case if the taper was the only distributing factor. Guide designers are trying to overcome this problem but, as the strength of the lugs by which the guide is bound to the rod is always a plus point, the problem will remain.

A big standard game fishing reel will take nearly 800 metres of the all-tackle (60 kg) line, and the fast bill fishes may run out all of that. Fish taken near the bottom in very deep water may take nearly all (and sometimes all) of this length on their very first run. Bigger reels than necessary to take this much line are, however, not often used these days because not so much fishing is now done in the all-tackle class in New Zealand waters. If a reel of this capacity is used for lighter line test, the difference in capacity is best used not so much for extra length but for a backing of thicker line, giving the effect of increased gearing and a faster retrieve without infringing game fishing rules.

(The components of fishing gear are rated, by the way, by different systems. Rods rate in kilograms, from 1 kg to 36 kg, about the heaviest used in New Zealand waters; reels for bigger game by a rating which ranges upward from about 9/0 to 14/0 for local conditions; line by kg-breaking strain up to 60 kg, the international

These two photographs show the spectacular agility of striped marlin on the line. They were taken off the Bay of Islands by Frank Cunningham.

A broadbill broaches off the Poor Knights Islands. The fish dropped the bait after sounding and returning to the surface. The photograph was taken by G. E. Angus of Dargaville from the launch Arrana.

A 132 kg striped marlin which was landed by Colin Lee off Leilani on 31 December 1978. The fish, which was hooked through the top of its broken bill on a lure, took five hours to boat. Carol Atwood.

The smile on the face of a mako. R. Mac-Donnell.

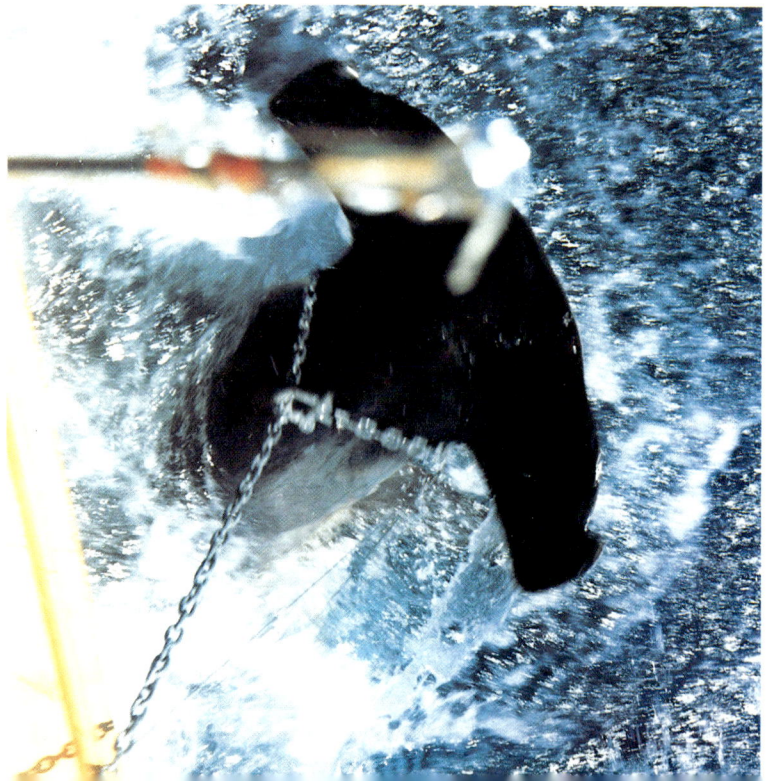

Angler John Baker, from Whakatane, can relax now with this very lively hammerhead well secured to his boat Mado. R. Hague.

When Lord and Lady Mountbatten fished in the Bay of Islands in 1956 with Dr Harold Pettit, they alternated, with success, from Alma G. *with Francis Arlidge (above) and* Pirate *with Jim Whitelaw (below).*

all-tackle limit, and hooks by a system seemingly similar, but unrelated, to that for reels, with 12/0s and 14/0s the standard sizes for bigger fish.)

Few anglers will live out a career without seeing at some time the last turns of their line pulled off their reel by an unusually determined fish, but the reels will usually take enough line for the skilful angler to avert this. The move to lighter line is encouraging a choice of smaller reels but it is unwise for the average angler to game fish around New Zealand with less than about 600 metres of line. This allows for eventualities such as a second run by a fish before adequate retrieve from the first run, the need to take the boat clear of obstacles while fighting a fish, and to give a margin for less than average evenness in spooling. Remember, too, that a manufacturer will occasionally be over-optimistic about the amount of line his reel will hold. Choose a sturdy reel with a reputation for reliability and availability of parts.

Line comes in three main types – braided synthetic, with or without a core of fine synthetic monofilaments, layed up synthetic, and solid monofilament nylon. Lead-core multifilament line is normally used only in fly fishing. Monofilament tends to stretch more, lasts better but is weight for weight a little greater in diameter than the better braided lines. It has an advantage in lighter tackle fishing (3 kg, 6 kg, 10 kg) because its in-built stretch eases the shock on gear from a strike or sudden drag.

Under international game fish standards – for competitions and for record qualification – lines are graded in their breaking-strain in kilograms – 1 kg, 2 kg, 4 kg, 6 kg, 8 kg, 10 kg, 15 kg, 24 kg, 37 kg and 60 kg with 37 kg the heaviest now recognised in events conducted by the New Zealand Big Game Fishing Council. This metric grading is in place of the former rating in pounds of breaking strain and the even earlier classification of lines by their number of linen threads.

For tournament fishing or record attempts, therefore, the angler should use only recognised

tournament pre-tested line, and the really keen angler will pre-test to breaking point himself. I test my lines by using them to suspend a drum or bucket a few centimetres above the deck. After wetting the line, quickly fill the drum with water until the line breaks, and then weigh the drum and contents. For light lines, a spring balance between the line and bucket is more convenient. (For tournament fishing something more sophisticated would be appropriate.) Gaff handles, a shark waddy or rod butts make good suspension bars. Remember that in this case you want to know how weak the line is – the point above which it will certainly break. Some manufacturers, seeking to show how strong they make their lines, give a figure that it will not break below. If ever in doubt, use a line that is rated lower (2 kg or 3 kg at least) than what you want.

Strength, on the other hand, is the main requirement of a big game fishing hook, and that means that it has to be made from a good grade of tempered steel. Hooks of hand-forged and tempered carbon steel, made mainly in Japan, are available in New Zealand but are rarely seen on game fish shelves because of their price, about $4 each at the time of writing. There are also stainless steel hooks of various grades and sizes. I have had little experience of these because I do not approve of non-degradable hardware on the line in big game fishing. The most commonly used and most readily available hooks are of galvanised steel. They are perfectly satisfactory and will last several seasons with reasonable care.

I use 12/0 to 14/0 hooks, usually in kahawai bait. Otherwise, the size of hook depends on the bait and rig to be used – small baits, small hooks; big baits, big hooks; and appropriate sizes in-between. The rule holds good even for most of the exotic baiting methods found so effective in some localities.

It is not generally appreciated (hooks are not always marked this way and store assistants may therefore look blank when asked) that hooks come kirbed both ways. The kirb is the twist of

A party of fishermen with a black marlin caught off Cape Brett in 1945. The successful angler, Mr W. W. Patterson, stands at the tail of the fish.

On a short line from the rod tip, a striped marlin leaps in Mayor Island waters. Eddie Simpson.

the point of the hook away from the line of the shaft, virtually all hooks being kirbed except those used in lures. When I find hooks with opposite kirbs, I keep them in pairs to use when trolling because they help to keep the baits apart. When using any of the many versions of my reversed hook rig, if the kirb is used to set the point out from the side rather than over the back, the ratio of hook-ups to strikes shows considerable improvement.

Straight (plane) hooks are used on lures because kirbing tends to make the lures spin. And a last word on hooks – if you are fishing to tag and release your fish, the hook and trace used should be as light and as corrosion-prone as procurable.

In big game fishing especially, hooks are linked with lines by traces. The strength of the hook and the strength of the trace are inter-related because a fish fouling its tail in the trace may otherwise straighten a hook out. When using a light hook, it is advisable to shorten the trace to the minimum length necessary to protect against biting or chafing against the teeth and, as far as possible, relate the hook chosen to the strength of the double line.

Traces were originally made of cable-laid galvanised steel. A later development, still much used, is the use of cable-laid stainless steel. And there has been a more recent move in favour of heavy monofilament nylon – one major argument against which is that it will stand up neither to the biting of heavily-toothed sharks, the fraying action of lighter-toothed sharks, nor even the roughness of marlin jaws if these fish are deep-hooked.

As I do not like stainless traces for the same reason as stainless hooks (and even heavy all-nylon traces would seem ever-lasting) I am left with the old-fashioned trace of galvanised steel, when I can procure it. I prefer a short trace of about a metre of galvanised steel wire attached to a long leader of monofilament. The galvanised hook and trace will rust out completely in a few weeks in an escaped fish.

Leaders are joined to hooks and swivels with crimped sleeve loops nowadays, and attached to the line with snaps or a variety of suitable knots and plaits. Of the various types of swivel-ball-bearing, barrel and box swivels, my preference is for the ball-bearing type for big game fishing. Its main advantages are that it turns so freely, is small in size and makes very little fuss in the water. Big game lines are usually of such small

The results of a bumper day's fishing are laid out for weighing in South East Bay, Mayor Island, in the days before the limit of four billfish a day per boat was introduced. Sou' East, the boat nosed up to the beach, has just unloaded the first of seven gamefish aboard. The total catch for the day brought into South East Bay was 23 fish.

diameter that they offer little resistance to spin and will twist up very badly if used with poor swivels. Most swivels are manufactured and marketed by breaking strain — their own safe load — which should exceed the weaker part of the rig by a considerable margin to allow for wear and flaws.

It is not absolutely necessary to use fishing harness with big fish; however, it is always prudent, and on hard fish absolutely necessary if the gear is to be used properly. The harness comes in three main types, the first designed for the standing angler — a very light affair that slips over the shoulders and is worn with a waist bucket. It allows the angler to drop a hand off the rod when, for instance, he has to move

around the boat and needs to hang on to something. This type of harness is usually made from webbing.

The other two types of harness, usually made of padded leather or form-fitting canvas, are designed for use in the fishing chair, permitting the rod to be supported and worked by the angler's body, while freeing his hands to control reel and line. Shoulder harness, a waistcoat-type of light leather jacket, is the choice of most anglers for light to medium fish.

For heavier anglers and heavier fish the kidney harness is often preferred, sometimes with a section on which the angler sits when in the chair. It has the double function of holding the back part low down, giving more leverage, and, when the angler lifts from the chair with legs rigid to the footrest, allows him to utilise his body weight in addition to his back muscles. The rod is clipped to the harness and the angler may feel initially that there is a danger he will be pulled over the back of the boat. It *can* be a danger, but it does not affect the average angler with his average fish, tucked into his chair with his feet firmly on the footrest, floor or against the transom.

Many anglers like to wear a cotton glove on the left hand (opposite for left-handers, of course, who will already have been struck by the fact that very few reel designers have considered them, leaving them to use right-handed reels cranked the wrong way, or to cultivate a degree of ambidexterity).

The glove assists in thumbing the reel cheek, without burns, for instant additional brake, or when spooling the line on retrieve. Some anglers, applying temporary additional brake on the line without re-adjusting the reel, use their gloved hand to pull the line at the beginning of a pump as they reel in.

Lures, which are dealt with more fully separately, simulate fast-moving fish, preferably a food fish of the species sought. A jig is a slow-moving food fish simulator, some with shaped and painted bodies and an action designed to simulate slowly moving or darting fish, and is the slow speed counterpart of the small feathers, squid and dummies. Spinners are lures for smaller fish and used in surface trolling. Strangely enough the latter type are often miscalled jigs and, to add to the confusion, are called spinners even though they do not spin. Anything that does is near useless for catching saltwater fish.

Many of them are just very pretty merchandise and perhaps catch more fishermen than fish, but, with the coming acceptance of downrigger fishing, which I am confident is just around the corner, some may be found very effective.

It is one thing to hook a game fish and get it after a hard fight to the side of the boat, apparently beaten, and another to get it aboard or lashed to a deck-cleat for a definite catch. For this final stage, every boat should carry several gaffs of sizes to suit the fish being caught. For big fish, such as marlin and sharks, I prefer a gaff made of stainless steel about 11 mm in diameter, heavily barbed and shackled to a gaff rope. The gaff is slotted into a shaft, a wooden pole similar in size to a hayfork handle, not permitted to be more than 2.43 m in length. There is also a restriction on the length of the gaff rope which, measured to the end of the rope from the shackle onto the gaff, may not exceed 9.14 metres. These gaffs with detachable heads are called flying gaffs.

It is prudent to carry two of these gaffs, with a bite of about 150 mm, and two smaller flying gaffs of slightly lighter section but same length of shaft and rope and a bite of about 100 mm, for bringing aboard kingfish and medium-sized tuna. One of the lighter ones, at least, is a necessity, and it is also advisable to carry a fixed gaff (with hook permanently attached to the shaft) with a smaller, non-barbed hook, for smaller game fish and bait fish such as kahawai. This needs to be sturdy, of about 8 mm stainless steel and a bite of about 80 mm.

A small hand-gaff similar to a bale hook can also be handy in lifting heavy fish, always difficult to handle because of their protective slime and rounded shape.

CHAPTER FIVE

Big game boats

Boats for big game fishing, like the gear and general techniques of the sport, are seldom ideally suited to all localities, even where similar fish are found. Hence, although New Zealand's most heavily fished game-fishing grounds cover only the comparatively small stretch of inshore waters from North Cape to just around East Cape, there are considerable differences in boats and boating practices from centre to centre.

New Zealand game-fishing boats have evolved as modest in both size and power compared with many types overseas. Perhaps a shortage of indigenous millionaires could have had a bearing on the size of the boats, but, encouraged to try, local game fishermen have found that game fish large and small can be caught from all sorts of boats.

The fundamental requirements for a well-equipped boat are plenty of cockpit space, at least one swivelling and gimballed chair, a built-in bait tank, freezer space for frozen bait, and adequate storage for rods, harnesses, tail ropes, gaffs, tagging gear, wire cutters, baiting gear and so on. In addition to room for all this highly desirable if not absolutely essential cockpit equipment, there should be storage for an assortment of leaders and lures, snaps, hooks and swivels.

The boat itself should within broad limits be chosen with characteristics suitable for local conditions. For instance, fishing grounds which are well out, in an area where rapid changes bring winds predominantly offshore, dictate boats of good stem height and a fine entry rather than full sections forward, for those are the predominant characteristics of a good head-sea boat.

In addition where the prevailing winds are predominantly onshore, I would prefer features which promote directional stability to ensure an easy trolling run back to port, and the best possible control on bars or in otherwise difficult harbour entrances, so often associated with onshore weather patterns.

Speed, if available without undue sacrifice of those other characteristics, can by judicious use give more fishing time in a chosen area and bring more good areas within daily reach, and also make it easier, when weather signs warn, to beat the making sea back to home.

In areas where drift fishing is a significant factor, stability of a boat combined with an easy motion is of prime importance if those on board are to enjoy their fishing. This harmony of movement is seldom adequately achieved other than in boats that drift with the quarter to the sea. If the freeboard forward offers more resistance to the wind than the complementary underwater sections do to the water or – to put it another way – the freeboard aft offers less wind resistance than the underbody offers to water resistance, the boat will drift diagonally down wind, quartering the oncoming chop or swell. When combined with a low centre of gravity, light draft and moderate deadrise, this gives the easiest and most comfortable drifting motion possible, with the fishing gear held well clear of the boat and in full view all the time.

I started big game fishing as Captain Arthur Fletcher's deckhand-cum-cook in 1929 in *Naomi*, a double ended ketch-rigged motor sailer built for the German Ambassador to New Zealand in Wellington just before the First World War. *Naomi* was bought by John Mowlem of Tauranga some time after the war and was Mayor Island's first properly surveyed charter boat. She was better suited to the job than her motor sailer designation would seem to indicate, because she was designed to motor rather than sail. When adapted to big game fishing, her broad beam,

cruiser stern, big dead-wood and curiously full sections forward gave her excellent drifting comfort.

Later on I skippered a boat called *Kingfish* owned by Major Mirrielees of Tauranga and fished by Ernie Chadban of Tauranga and Whitianga. As it happened she too was an ex-motor sailer but by some quirk of design had almost exactly opposite bottom features. She had steep dead-rise, high stem, deep fore-foot and very fine entry. Consequently she was an outstanding very wet head-sea boat, but drifted broadside and rolled very heavily. As one angler put it, she was a very fine and safe ship but could "roll the water out of your whisky" and "ran like a hen". In other words, she just would not run straight in a following sea.

Curly Steedman's *Dauntless*, from which Herbie Burch's broadbill was caught, another

Naomi, *the ketch-rigged motor sailer which was Mayor Island's first fully surveyed charter game fishing boat.*

outstanding boat in her day, was a beamy, straightforward power boat. Like the other two, she was round-bottomed, but had a much harder turn to her bilge, and a tuck stern sloped out to about half a metre overhang. She was an outstanding drifter and the slope on her tuck turned the water down very effectively both when drifting and when backing up to play a fish.

Later still I was in charge of the Air Department fleet of fast flying boat tenders at Mechanics Bay, Auckland, and so gained a lot of experience with fast load-carrying planing hulls. During that time I started on the design of a faster than usual game fishing boat, subsequently built and called *Sou'East*. She is a deliberate and successful compromise, with the closely-studied

Another famous early boat: Bert Chaney's launch Ronomor *of Whitianga trolling along the northern coast of Mayor Island.*

desirable characteristics of the boats mentioned plus very good handling and sea-keeping ability. The knowledge gained from the 20 years during which I owned and operated her has since been used in *Sea Runner*, a new boat designed in conjunction with my son. Although she is not yet fully operational she is showing remarkable characteristics and figures. I feel that cost of fuel and its availability will force the adoption of a new approach to our sport.

All the four boats I mentioned earlier – *Naomi, Kingfish, Dauntless* and *Sou'East* – were round-bottomed, a shape in my opinion more comfortable to live aboard at sea than that of hard-chined boats, which tend to have a quicker motion at anchor or drifting. Where it is necessary for someone to sleep aboard because of exposed anchorages, on already uncomfortable nights, the quick action and the noisy slapping of

Virginia, which when skippered by Charlie Miller was the second of the pioneer Mayor Island charter gamefishing boats. The skipper aboard in this later photograph is Ray Chadban.

chines is not an endearing feature, compared with the relatively easy motion and quietness of round-bilged craft. So, in spite of the modern predominance of hard chines, based mainly on fashion, availability and speed, the round chine boat has, in my view, more to recommend it in such localities than the chine boat has. If drifting again becomes a significant fishing technique, this type may well regain widespread popularity.

In the Bay of Islands hard chine boats have been well to the fore since the very early days of our gamefishing history and in the hands of the early great professionals such as Francis and Mervyn Arlidge, Jim·Whitelaw, Les Blomfield,

Peter Williams and others must have caught a total of gamefish that could be eclipsed only by Japanese longlines; and they are still looking good and going strong.

New Zealand's major established game fish grounds are mainly in the very benign waters of our north-east coast, which is unique in that it is richly endowed with good small boat harbours seldom more than 30 miles apart. Most of them have good road access and trailer boat launching possibilities, even where there are no actual ramps. We are a boat-minded people and trailer-boats are everywhere, so it is hardly surprising that big game fishing, once the sport of the privileged few, is now a widely enjoyed pastime.

Much to my amazement, and that of other "old timers" like me, these small trailered newcomers operate at distances offshore and in

Alma G II originally and now again in the Zane Grey, *at the Hole in the Rock, Piercy Island, with Mervyn Arlidge at the wheel.* Tudor Collins.

weather that at times horrifies me. It says much for the reliability of modern outboards and the skill, stamina and faith of the skippers. As pleasure boats, defined as such because they are not "plying for hire or reward", they are not subject to the Ministry of Transport's paternalistic, expensive, and often incomprehensible requirements, which add so much to the commercial boat charter rate; even so, their safety record is impressive.

Between these extremes, there are day charter boats and cruisers. The day-boats leave port after breakfast ashore, run out clear of tidal waters, usually in 30 to 40 minutes, stopping only to catch bait when required. When favourable water is reached, bait and/or lures are put over and the day's fishing begun. Late in the day, at about the same point, the baits are picked up and the run home made in time for dinner.

The cruising boats are generally bigger and are designed and equipped to accommodate the charter party of one to five or six aboard for the full period of the charter. By day their fishing activities are the same as those of the day boats, but it is usually planned to bring them at day's end to overnight shelter in some neighbouring port or anchorage.

The three northern game fish clubs – Whangaroa, Bay of Islands and Whangarei – have a wide choice of grounds at a variety of distances from base, offering a range from short

Fred Wilkins' Sou' East flying the vice-regal flag with Lord and Lady Norrie and their daughter Rosemary aboard in the mid 1950s.

day trips to long cruises, and hence encouraging the use of a wide selection of boat sizes and types. Auckland has its best game fishing around and beyond Great and Little Barrier Islands and needs some big boats for this area as well as the great many smaller craft which come out all along its populous and well-favoured coastline.

Whitianga and Tauranga tend to need bigger boats again – Tauranga, in particular, because Mayor Island, the centre of its fishing, lies nearly 20 miles out to sea. Such a distance requires too much travelling time, there and back, and allowing for fishing in between for other than a very long day. This situation led a good many years ago to the establishment of a motel type of fishing camp on Mayor Island, with more than a dozen Tauranga-based charter boats picking up their charter parties on the mainland and fishing with them out to the island. The anglers sleep and live ashore and go out daily on the launches, finishing the final day back at Tauranga.

This situation has led to the development of a slightly different sort of charter launch from the rest of the coast, pretty big, rugged and very good sea-keeping boats. They have to be all these things because they spend all their summer, apart from their trips into and out of Tauranga to change parties, out at sea, or subject to sea conditions because Mayor Island has no all-weather anchorage.

Whakatane needs the same big charter boats – White Island lies even further from shore base than Mayor Island and shares the disadvantage of lack of all-weather anchorages. However, excellent charter boats are available tailored to the American light-tackle anglers specially interested in the giant yellowtail for which the area is justly famous.

The use of what are known as tuna towers – high platforms from which lookouts can see deeper into the water and further afield – have not taken on much in New Zealand yet. One of the country's most experienced and knowledgeable skippers, Snooks Fuller of the Bay of Islands, has used one for some seasons but primarily for photography: he can see a long way further and better from 6 metres above the water. Another is in use on Bill Hall's new *Leilani II*. To New Zealand eyes the towers make boats

A fine new boat. Carey Fuller with a hammerhead shark and striped marlin he caught from Lucky Strike, *the new boat of Snooks Fuller (on the flying bridge with his wife, Lola Fuller).* Monty Miller.

look top-heavy and unstable, but those who have used them say they act like a mast on a yacht, giving it a heavier heel but slower and kinder movement. It is, therefore, more comfortable in boisterous conditions but reduces the boat's overall safety margin in extreme conditions.

Coaching is a very important part of a professional skipper's obligation – when it is expected or requested. There are skippers who lack the knowledge or ability to coach, and anglers who know too much to accept it, but there is just nothing in fishing to equal the intense satisfaction shared by a good angler and a good skipper working a hard fish in complete understanding. Such people can make their boats and their gear an extension of themselves to such a degree that the use of them is completely automatic and near faultless. If even one of them, usually the professional, knows his fish as he should, he will quickly determine what sort of fish they are fighting even when it is unseen, approximately where it is hooked and, on an assessment of location, weather, time and angler, decide what strategy to adopt in fighting it.

When all this is checked out with the angler we have a team and, if the angler knows the necessary techniques, we are down to the nitty gritty of judgments, tactics and luck. By judgment I mean decisions based on a mental movie of the fish, what it is doing, what to do about it; by tactics – the choice and application of techniques to apply to achieve that; and by luck, the grace to get away with our mistakes and misadventures. As in any team, each must be prepared to advise and be advised, on the basis of acknowledged strengths and weaknesses, so in a long fight the lead will be picked up and relinquished quite frequently.

Mental fatigue after the first hour becomes a perhaps greater hazard than its physical and more obvious counterpart. The mind tends to wander and, when guided back to the job in hand, there is difficulty in picking up the threads. If rapport

is what it should be, a "what page are we up to?" query should be all that is necessary to get the picture rolling and to slip back into full communication again – if not dissension is inevitable.

Physical fatigue becomes evident in short temper and slowed-down reactions, impaired co-ordination, discomfort and actual pain that divert the mind. The skipper has the least physical duress but, if he is good enough, carries the extra burden of spreading his attention to include the total environment.

It is he who remains aware of weather patterns, neighbouring traffic, the time factor, the angler's condition and efficiency. He who operates a pre-determined programme of spreading line wear and influences the direction and distance the fight takes them, shields the angler from the restlessness, concern, helpfulness and other intrusions of party members at inopportune times, and above all keeps his cool.

There are anglers who are so good that they neither need nor appreciate more than the minimal co-operation and, some who would rather lose a fish than be helped, but I cannot recall an occasion on which I have seen either concept survive a really tough fight by a really big fish. Usually when the going gets tough enough the angler finds himself so emotionally involved that there is just no way he is going to let that fish beat him, and he accepts what support is available.

Fortunately there are a whole lot of fish that simply cannot be fairly beaten – team or no team – and there is no feeling like that of watching a very hard fought, and very big, fish swim victoriously away while we sit not only tired, unbelieving, disappointed and frustrated, but admiring, reluctantly glad and with the darndest fellow feeling and liking. At such times the "good luck to you mate, you earned it, let's have a drink" covers a welter of conflicting emotions.

CHAPTER SIX

The craft of baiting

The first fishing done on most trips – in spite of the deep-frozen reserve in the freezer or chilly bin and maybe a couple of live ones caught last thing the night before and kept alive in the floating bait tank, tethered over the side – is to stock up with a fresh supply for inboard live-bait tanks. Some of these fish may be already baited up on short snapper traces to be used for a quick switch for a cagey fish following our troll but not biting. In such cases, it is often worthwhile to snap the live bait to a standby set of gear, drop it overboard, stop the boat and revert to drifting. It very often does the trick, and even when it misses, there is at least the satisfaction of having tried.

When fishing for kahawai, it is good practice to use a sub-surface trolling board or other such gadget on a hand line that will run a lure about a metre or two down, plus a couple of very light rods with appropriate surface lures. Kahawai are first-rate light tackle game fish. As in all lure fishing, it is wise to use a variety to attract them and, if necessary, to keep making changes until the most productive for the time and place is established.

I do not believe that kahawai are the best of marlin bait, but on most of our marlin grounds they are more readily available than anything else and, as fresh bait is more productive than stale, they are invaluable. Because I have often seen marlin herding and feeding on koheru, I have a very strong preference for them as bait. However, it would seem that the marlin are not very selective feeders, so it is reasonable to assume that all their fellow travellers of appropriate size are grist for the marlin mill. Since kahawai are not oceanic travellers, mackerel, tunas, pipers and so on must be more familiar, even if not preferred food. (Incidentally, I believe finning marlin to be full-fed fish in some comatose state approximating sleep; and the cagey follower of trolled baits to be a similarly full-fed but more active character prepared to keep an eye on the meal until he has the larder space to gather it in. If this simplistic logic has any merit at all, it follows that the smaller the bait, the less cagey the fish and the more strikes.)

Trevally, another once prolific indigenous fish, also makes very good bait, especially when small, and it trolls much better than kahawai. Trevally seldom take lures but when located in schools, which are usually over offshore reefs, can be jagged on a "Taranaki" on a hand-thrown line or heavy bait-caster. Why it is called a "Taranaki" I do not know. It is a cluster of three or four big (12/0 – 14/0) hapuku hooks welded together to form a large triple or quadruple hook which, when pulled quickly through the densely packed schools, makes a very productive jag. I prefer plane hooks but kirbed are also used.

Mackerel are quite often encountered offshore in large, fast-moving schools and can be caught in the same way as kahawai with selections from the same assortment of lures, but much faster trolling speeds are required, if only to keep up with them. Sometimes the schools will be seen to be "dusting" very densely and at others to be identifiable only by a characteristic heavy ripple on the surface. They are good bait but have to be very carefully rigged and set because of their very soft flesh and round shape, which makes them inclined to spin.

Bonito, or skipjack tuna as they are now known, also fall to our selection of kahawai lures. Although good drifting baits, they do not last long when trolled. They have the typical very round tuna shape, delicate skin and extremely soft flesh and tender mouths, so spin badly and break up very rapidly in any other than the

This close-up of the jaws of a mako shark, taken in the 1920s, shows the teeth that anglers are still anxious to avoid today.

calmest trolling conditions. Like kahawai, they are good sport on sufficiently light tackle. They are very fast and dive deep but are not aerobatic. Careful handling is required to prevent the hook from tearing out.

Squid are bait which as yet have found little favour here, although used extensively elsewhere. They have not been readily available here in areas where drift methods were commonly used, and it is hard to see how they could be effectively used when trolling. It seems likely, though, that with the advent of night fishing, they will be both caught and used frequently and found to be very productive in drifting.

Shiny mackerel and piper are the only fish I have identified that I have seen marlin actually chasing, so I have always gone out of my way to get them. I have done very well with mackerel – when occasionally obtaining them from trawlers. They troll quite well when used on appropriate

hooks and traces. The piper have been successful when drifting, but so has nearly everything else I have tried, and I have not had enough experience with them to evaluate them properly.

Shiny mackerel are very like the koheru so prolific in many of our more northern harbours but less well known further south, so for a very long time I thought they were the same fish. They are beautiful fish, brilliant bronze green, gold and silver in colour, with tiny little scales that make their skin look like highly reflective shot silk. No doubt it is the reflective characteristic that causes the water over their schools to appear slightly gold or brassy in colour, for those I have seen seem to remain about a metre under the surface.

It was curiosity about the colour that diverted my troll thirty odd years ago to give everyone aboard our first-ever close look at something which must be quite common but which I had never imagined, let alone heard of at that time.

Fortunately the day was very calm and I had cut the motor to drift past while looking for an explanation of the colour. I spotted two slow-moving striped marlin about three metres down, and a little to one side of what looked like a very large brown-gold ball. Almost unbelieving, I realised that this was a tight school of yellow fish huddled tightly together in a huge ball of about two metres diameter. It was being slowly circled by several marlin, which were obviously herding the fish and, as we watched, occasionally picked some off the outside without breaking up the formation.

There seemed to be always three to four marlin close-herding the school and quite a lot of others, showing as only shadowy forms, very much deeper down. They were all striped marlin, easily identifiable because at what may be called "shadowy" depths, the stripes show up almost like skeletal ribs.

A school of trevally— less frequently seen these days — foams off Mayor Island.

Days of carefree fishing: Tudor Collins took this photo of the unloading of a catch at Whitianga when the Mercury Bay club was young.

After watching for some time and getting over our excitement, I tripped the outrigger baits well clear of the school, let them down to where I judged the deep fish to be, carefully moved around to the side of the colour patch and gently pulled the baits past the side of it. When close and still deep, both were taken quietly and slowly. Still paying out line, we moved quickly away and were well clear before applying drag.

We boated both marlin, found the school again and in the same way hooked another pair, but one of them hit the air immediately we tightened up. When we returned to the area after boating them we were unable to find any sign of what one of the chaps called the "marlin kerbside

restaurant". Needless to say, from then on no patch of colour has ever been passed by, and I have several times found precisely similar deals, and a few that were different.

One was a patch which was milky white instead of brassy-coloured and was found to be a balled up school of what appeared to be anchovies, with the striped marlin again going about their same performance. We took two fish in the same way, but we had seen only three marlin, which may be why the school then broke up and we saw the anchovies scattering on the surface with a pursuing marlin in the middle. We saw it take one little fish in mid-air. Trying to watch all that and attend to a double-header and all its attendant excitement at the same time was difficult.

The other such occasion with a difference

66

Stan Ellis, one of the best known of the early Whangaroa game fishermen, with an impressive catch at the Whangaroa Harbour weighing station. Tudor Collins.

occurred on a family holiday trip after the season was supposedly over and all the fish had "gone back to South America" (a sort of fishing equivalent of "where do the flies go in the winter").

After a very boisterous morning which we spent in a bay, the sea dropped to a flat calm and the day changed to provide a perfect autumn afternoon. So I took Fay and Chris, my wife and two-year-old son, and John and Ada, his godfather and godmother, for a short troll around for no reason at all but to enjoy the perfect conditions. Of all the lucky things to happen we found marlin, more than I had seen before, perhaps 30 or 40 of them, around a very large ball of shiny mackerel, perhaps three to four

metres in diameter, in perfect viewing conditions.

We floated on a cobalt blue mirror and watched the whole show, highlighted by the late autumn, warm and extra-bright sun. The water was so clear and unrippled that its depth seemed only a backdrop. The colours and lights of the most colourful of mackerels and of the marlin shone against it. The excitement and conflict of emotions aboard was all that our incorrigible two-year-old needed to supercharge his natural ebullience and unpredictability, so in almost automatic response I grabbed him off the coaming, stuffed him down the cockpit/cabin companion way and shut the door to keep him safe.

After everyone had recovered a little from the wonder of it, I dropped the hurriedly retrieved baits to see what else was in store for us. As usual we hooked two marlin, but dropped one of

67

them. On our return I found the situation intact, but as I prepared to pick off another two fish, a school of very large kingfish – I guess about 20 kg each – tore right in past the marlin and broke up the ball. The mackerel immediately huddled under the boat, pressed hard against it, and the boat really echoed to the thud of the kingfish taking them from it. It must have been the kingfish making all the noise, because later inspection showed no scars or broken bills which would have been inevitable if we had been hit so hard by marlin.

In the middle of all this, the marlin joined the fray outside the boat and the next thing we were surrounded by near-flying mackerel being nobbled on and over the surface by half air-borne marlin, and kingfish literally cannoning off each other in their frenzy.

Baiting methods are extremely variable, even within the broad requirements of trolling and drifting and the bait fish available, for we then encounter the wonderful world of fishermen's fancy and invention. Everything feasible has surely been tried, even down to a lock of mother-in-law's hair to scare away sharks. On the other hand appeasement, too, is a frequent practice. A drop of the "best aboard" often goes over with the bait, as a tribute to the local sea god, or monster.

Some baits and some rigs cannot be used for trolling although most trolling rigs can be used for drifting. For instance the popular live baiting method of shallow-hooking the bait fish just in front of the dorsal fin would be quite impossible to troll, just as would my drift-fishing version of the reversed hook rig I dreamed up at Mayor Island in 1936.

In the drifting version the hook is set firmly in the bait, high in the back and a little behind the front spine of the dorsal. This places it much further forward than the setting for trolling. In both cases the point faces backward toward the tail, the kirb is out from the dorsal, and the eye of the hook is firmly sewn high on the back, where it lies when the hook is set. In the drifting

version the trace is left free, attached only to the eye of the hook, but in the trolling rig it is taken forward along the shank of the hook, tucked under the gill flap and tied lightly to the firmly-sewn mouth and nose. Further ties may be sewn along the flank if needed to keep the trace flat and neat.

With all trolling baits, I either break or strain the backbone to render the bait as flexible as possible, I think this desirable even if for no other reason than that it makes for a better troll with less tripping and more natural action.

For drifting, I prefer live baits if possible, even though dead ones seem to be taken just as readily – once they are found. I think that it is probably true that live baits attract predators from greater distances. When using live baits, however, there is a grave danger that the trace will sink below the bait fish, which can, and frequently does, become entangled in the line, making cutoffs inevitable when the baits are taken. If the drift is to be a shallow one, this danger is best guarded against by attaching a float to the top of the trace and taking care to keep the line direct.

Other trolling methods traditional to New Zealand and which are permitted by the International Game Fish Association are those with the hook set through the nose of the bait fish, or a few centimetres away from the nose on a bridle of strong twine. In the days when marlin were more plentiful and the number of strikes missed or fish lost was of less concern, these methods had much to commend them, for the fish struck were mostly foul-hooked and consequently much more lively than those caught by my system, which is designed to hook deep, and usually does. However, many hooked in the jaw and horny throat perform every bit as well as those hooked outside and these can be released with much less injury. Those hooked inside can also be released if galvanised steel hooks and traces are used and cut short on release.

My method is based on the fact that marlin are gulping fish. Lacking the dental equipment to do otherwise, they have to swallow their prey whole,

Diagram III

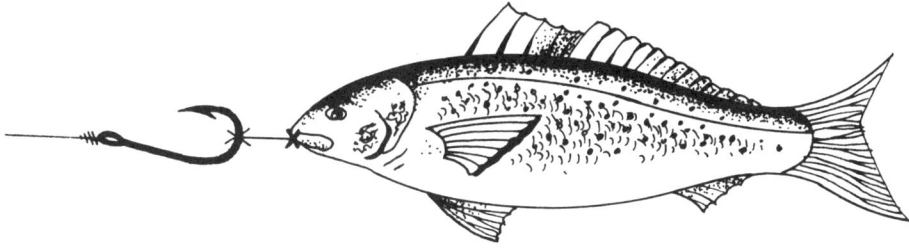

The old-style method of bridle-rigging bait for trolling.

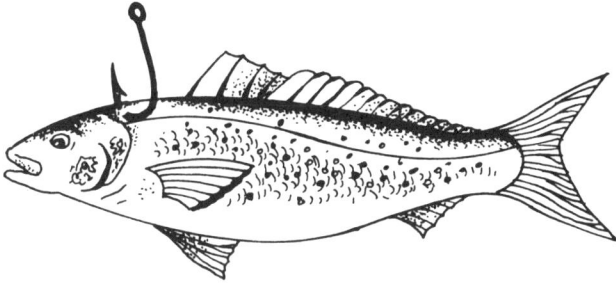

The former method of hooking bait for drift fishing (live or dead bait).

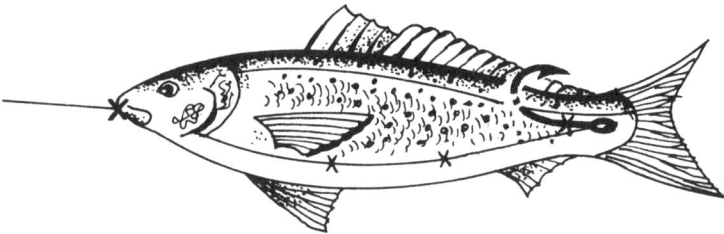

The basic baiting method I introduced for trolling.

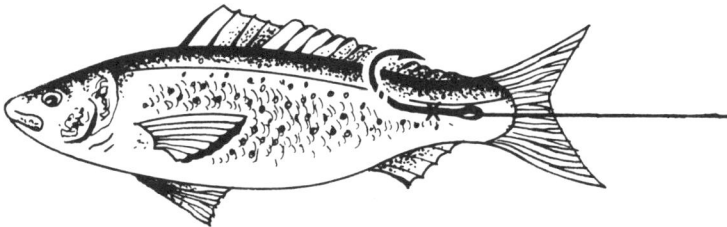

My baiting method adapted (one alternative) for drift fishing.

and this is best done head first. Hence the hook setting with the point facing the tail, which allows for easy swallowing and an almost certain hookup if the fish attempts to disgorge or when the angler retrieves or strikes, unless the rig is broken or the point is imbedded in the bait. The business end of the hook is pointing the right way. Kahawai, kingfish, tuna and mackerel are all suitable baits for this rig.

For the system to work well, it is essential that the nose tie should be as light as possible to keep the bait trolling, so that it will break clear at the strike and not impede the swallow. It is therefore a bonus that on a slow drift, even with a dead bait, the nose tie can be dispensed with. A live bait will swim with the drift and handle even a fast drift quite well. Setting the point further toward the head in the drifting rig is also more productive when biting fish such as sharks come along. Unlike the gulpers, biting fish usually bite the bait in half and, when the hook is located at one end of the bait or the other, show plenty of sense in leaving us the bit with the hardware. Therefore, having the hook in the centre is the better bet. For trolling, it is located further back simply because it lets the bait troll better.

The other two rigs are also used for both gulpers and biters but are less productive for two reasons. First, in their very productive years, they were generally used in conjunction with "swingers", which were later outlawed by the International Game Fish Association. In my experience, as many or more fish were caught on the unbaited swingers as on the baited hooks. Secondly, if the theory behind my method is correct, gulpers were badly impeded by having to swallow a lot of heavy and in those days very stiff trace wire with their meal. When and if they got it all down, and disgorged it as they usually did – mostly above the surface in full view – the hook that had been turned around to be taken harmlessly down, once again turned around to follow the bait harmlessly out. This would happen unless the angler was fortunate enough to strike just after the bait was swallowed and before

it was disgorged. If,.on the other hand, he muffed the dropback technique, he often unwittingly buttoned on in accordance with modern lure fishing techniques, in which the hook always faces forward and relies entirely on the impact of the strike to effect a hookup.

Broadly stated, therefore, rigs are divided into reversed hooks and forward-pointing hooks. Only those with reversed hooks are specifically intended for the deep-hooking of gulping fish. They are almost 100 per cent effective when swallowed, if properly rigged. They are less effective than the forward-pointing rigs for impact-hooking, but at least equally effective for biting fish.

It is in the bracket covering forward-pointing hooks that the full spate of individual fancy and inventiveness is encountered, but most of those which differ from our rigs already described have been evolved under very different conditions from those pertaining in New Zealand.

Ultra-slow trolling allows extremely limp baits to be trolled upright rather than on their sides, as in the other bait trolling. The baits have the backbones removed or carefully broken to allow a swimming motion and may be rigged with hooks either reversed or forward pointing. The essential requirement in rigging, however, is that the hook must be rigged under the bait fish to form a keel which ensures the natural upright position usually desired.

Slow trolling is then essential, for the bait is so limp – to allow the swimming action and to prevent spinning – that if it is allowed to flap it will quickly dislodge the hook and then break up. Unfortunately the big diesel engines in most modern game boats react badly to the light loading of such slow running. However, it seems likely that the cost and shortage of fuel may foster a new interest in the old drifting methods, even sail-assisted. If so, this fishing method may gain wider usage, especially if considered in relation to downriggers for which it would seem ideally suited.

Our present wide ranging, fast trolling, lure

Diagram IV

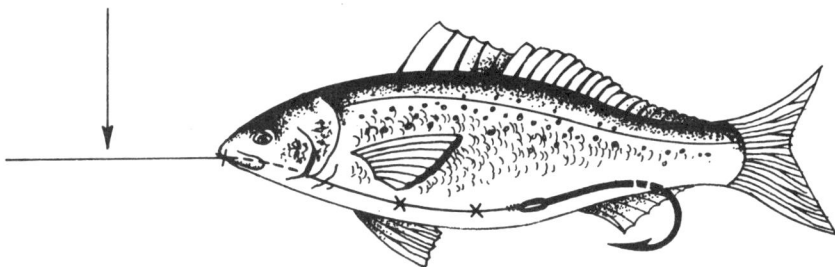

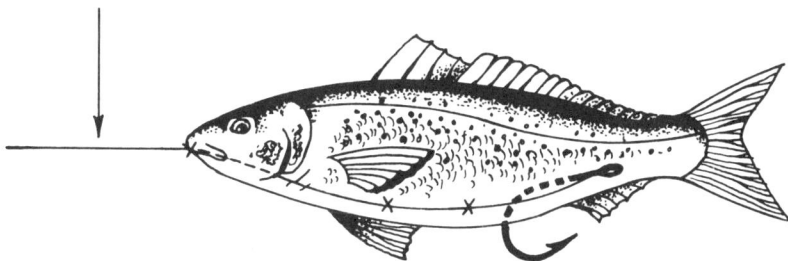

Baiting of drifters or swimmers (when backbone is removed). The hook is set below to keep the bait in a natural position.

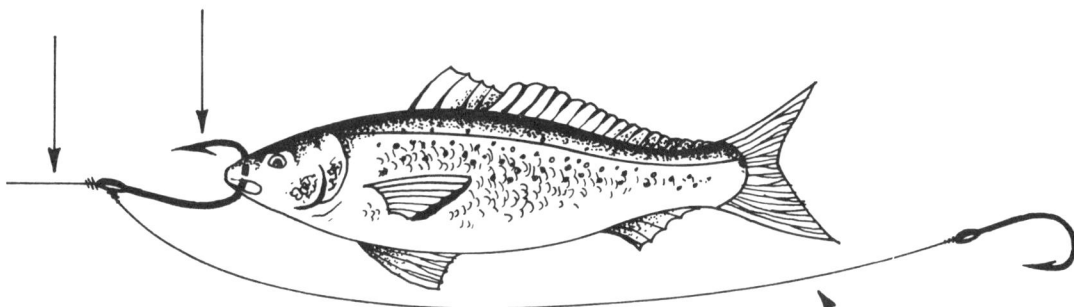

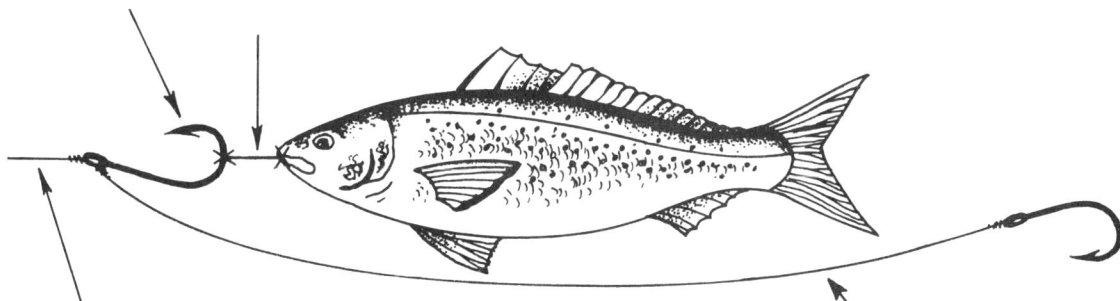

Old style (and now illegal) swinging hook rigs.

71

and bait-fishing methods are remarkably successful in the light of our near ignorance of our quarry. However, they are becoming frighteningly expensive.

We must therefore learn more about the factors governing the distribution of marlin in the various areas. However obvious, it is a task beyond the resources and knowledge of most anglers, but it is what they really need to know. The Ministry of Agriculture and Fisheries has an officer doing part-time general research on marlin, and his efforts are greatly appreciated: perhaps the time allocated could be increased.

For the launch owner there is now a range of very sophisticated electronic equipment available that can be used to supplement and extend his existing skills in finding fish. Power-hungry, large and expensive, this equipment was not feasible until recently, even in our largest game fishing boats. Fortunately size and power needs are no longer beyond the average game boat of nine metres or more, although price is still a factor in its adoption.

I personally would like (for a start) satellite navigation, a chromograph sounder and a controlled depth salinometer and temperature recorder: the satellite navigation for a near-constant position record; the sounder to tell us when sub-surface fish are below, plus their depth and heading; and the temperature recorder and salinometer to tell us the warmth and kind of water at their level. The daily records of even one such boat over a season would be very revealing and, when added to surface observations, such as satellite surface temperatures at the times recorded, would give us a better evaluation and understanding of surface clues such as so-called tide lines, upwellings, eddies, water colour, the behaviour of birds, schools and finning fish, and the influence of tides and weather. *Sea Runner*, my son's boat, was designed and built with special emphasis on the characteristics we thought necessary for privately conducted research along these lines; and when fully equipped will, I am sure, be the tool we need to

answer a lot of the questions I have puzzled over for so long. It will probably also open up further puzzles and, sad to say, prick a lot of pretty theoretical balloons.

We are right on the verge of a very great change in the sport and the prospect is exciting. For one thing we, in this country, mainly for convenience and partly because it did not seem necessary, have completely neglected night fishing. Other than the little-heard-about Japanese operations, most New Zealand anglers know little if anything about the availability and behaviour of game fish at night. It seems the time is right to find out. Dwindling catches in some areas, whatever the reason, make the newly developed overseas sport of fishing at night for broadbill an opportunity for the venturesome here.

It should be possible to establish whether we have an adequate population of these fish in accessible waters, and then if so, it will be all on. The little I know about broadbill does not excite me very much, but I badly want to know about the night behaviour of the marlin.

Darkness means nothing to electronics, little to man and probably little to deep-ranging fish. Equipped with modern electronics, we may be better off at night than we are in daylight without them, and with the attraction of sufficient lighting and lighted baits, fish should come. If successful, it may lead to launches remaining offshore through reasonable weather instead of returning to base every evening, with significant savings in fuel and related costs. A sail-assisted drift-cum-slow troll would be just as comfortable at night as during the day, and a small drogue is easy to live with.

Again, greater efficiency in fishing could be achieved through the use of a simple grid type chart of the areas fished from its base or bases. With the aid of radio reports from each boat, a daily plot of fish sighted and caught could be kept by each club and could be a valuable research tool, especially if used in conjunction with the other procedures which will be in use on *Sea Runner* and hopefully other boats. A daily analysis of the charts, updated by early morning reports of boats which have stayed out, and by daily satellite temperature charts, would greatly assist morning decisions by launch skippers on where to head for. The area decided on before departure might well have to be a "one shot" deal for the day – and we need a better procedure than following blind hunches or following the leader.

Diagram V HOOK RIGS: LEGAL AND ILLEGAL

1

1. Double lines are measured from the start of the knot, braid, roll or splice making the double to the farthermost end of the knot, snap, swivel or other device used for securing the trace, leader, lure or hook to the double line. The length of double line on line classed 1 kg through and including 10 kg is limited to 4.57 m. The double line on all classes of tackle above 10 kg is limited to 9.14 m.

2

2. Leader measurements on classes 1 kg through 10 kg are limited to 4.57 m and on all classes of tackle above 10 kg the leader is limited to 9.14.

3

3. The length of the leader is the overall length including any lure, hook arrangement or any other device. NOTE: The *combined* length of double line and leader is limited. On tackle classes 1 kg through and including 10 kg the combined length must not exceed 6.1 m and on all classes above 10 kg the combined length must not exceed 12.19 m.

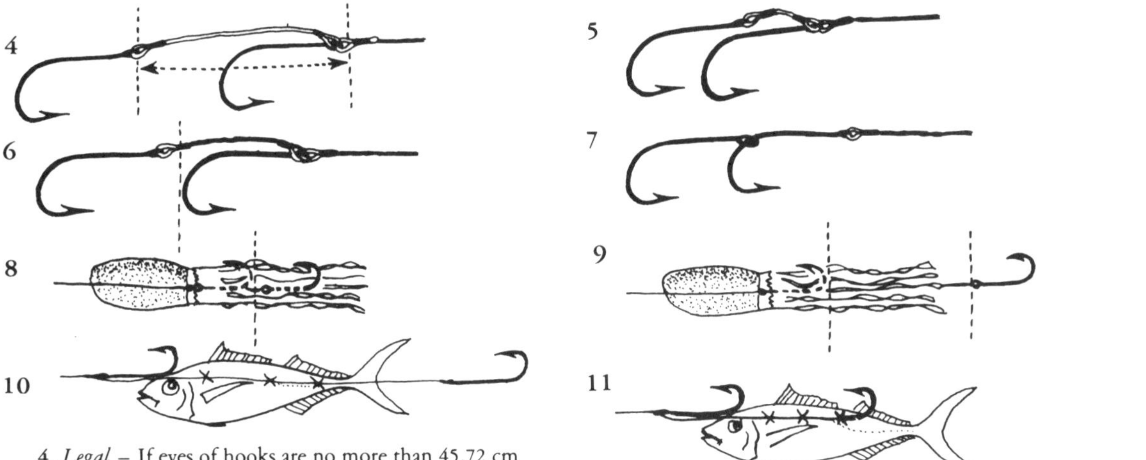

4

5

6

7

8

9

10

11

4. *Legal* – If eyes of hooks are no more than 45.72 cm apart in baits and no more than 30.48 cm apart in lures. *Illegal* – If eyes are further apart than these distances.

6. *Legal* – Eyes of hooks are no less than a hook's length apart (and no more than 45.72 cm in baits and 30.48 cm in lures).

8. *Legal* – Eyes of hooks are no less than a hook's length apart and no more than 30.48 cm apart, and the trailing hook does not extend more than a hook's length beyond skirt.

10. *Not legal* – Back hook is not firmly imbedded in or securely attached to bait and is a dangling or swinging hook.

5. *Not legal* – Baits or lures, as eyes of hooks are less than hook's length (the length of the largest hook) apart.

7. *Legal* – In baits and lures. The point of one hook is passed through the eye of the other hook.

9. *Not legal* – The second or trailing hook extends more than hook's length beyond skirt.

11. *Legal* – Both hooks are firmly imbedded in or securely attached to bait. Would not be legal if eyes of hooks were more than 45.72 cm apart.

CHAPTER SEVEN

The art of angling

The art of angling is the very simple practice of stopping a fish from doing what it wants to do and making it do what the fisherman wants, under rules and with equipment that handicap the fisherman, who by virtue of the handicap becomes an angler.

Broadly speaking, when we hook up the advantage lies with the fish, but in the course of a successful fight it gradually passes to the angler. The lighter the gear the greater the fish's advantage and therefore the longer the fight before the initial advantage is whittled away. However, the broad pattern remains, provided the tackle is not out of all reason and fairness. This means gear not only suited to the angler but also to the size and weight of the fish he seeks. The contest is only fair when kept as personal as possible, and when, despite the best efforts on both sides, the issue remains in doubt right until the bitter end.

In such a contest, the speed and hysteria of the first run of practically all fish caught on or near the surface, coupled with the tail-walking and leaping of marlin, the aerobatics of makos, and the occasional leaps and tail thrashings of threshers, leave us helpless to do anything but avoid over-run in most cases. In the case of the average marlin, however, if the aim is to subdue the fish with the utmost despatch, throwing sudden weight on them while they are mostly airborne will pull them off balance and cause

them to crash back in again on their sides. One or two such crashes is about all it takes to spoil a good fight, but it can be a handy technique if tagging is the principal aim.

From then on, follow the rule as best the circumstances will allow. Try to stop the fish doing what it wants to do, give it slack line if it rears its head and shoulders out with mouth wide, especially facing you, and never let it run with line over the shoulder. Not only does this almost nullify your best efforts but it also creates a very grave risk of break-offs due to fouling the tail. They are all very powerful fish and if the line snubs the tail when the body is bent, even heavy all-tackle traces will frequently snap like string when they straighten.

Probably the hardest and potentially most dangerous move to counter is the steep and fast straight run downward. Not only does it promote the "line over the shoulder" situation, but it is usually done at considerable speed and if not checked early more often than not results in a dead fish on the bottom – sometimes even stuck in the bottom like a dart. I have been told of a number of incidents in which fish have been retrieved with the sticky green mud of deep bottoms still clearly evident on the heads, sometimes right back to the eyes, and have seen others.

It is almost impossible to raise a dead fish from the bottom without breaking rules; and this backbreaking job can be avoided only by prompt action early in the descent. I know of only one technique that will definitely do the job. It is hard to master when applied to fast-moving fish but will work when expertly applied, even in the line-over-the-shoulder situation.

Everyone tends to resort to jerking when the going gets tough, and this is a simple reversal. When considered as a "flying object" the fish obviously trims against overpull. So the idea is suddenly and regularly to drop-back to it and thereby throw it off balance. If the timing and tension is right, we subject it to a sustained series of re-adjustments which by correct timing all become over-adjustments, at least as distressing to it as they would be to a running man. If continued, they will reduce it to a state of compliance. Anyway, it works.

If you are lucky you will have got over the first hurdle. You will have stopped it from doing what it wanted to do and from there on it is mainly a matter of outlook. If it is just the fish that is wanted, when and if control is gained keep it on a short line, slap it down when it jumps, put it into a circle and "psych" it with half rolls and rotation reversals. Have two gaffs, an umbrella and plenty of help.

On the other hand, for a fight, assist the fish to jump by easing brake on fast runs (when not sounding) keep the line short to minimise drag, ease the brake and thumb the reel to avoid overruns, retrieve any slack that may occur, watch closely for underwater changes of direction after jumps, and enjoy the greatest show on earth – or water.

When and if it settles down to steady swimming, reduce the immersed bight of line to safe proportions to guard against any sudden acceleration and consequent break-off, put the pressure on, move to a position broad off the shoulder on the side it is hooked, if you know it, and work it into a circle pivoting in the centre. Everything else being equal, once the pattern is established pressure may be eased a little. This

allows it to use the circling against the line pull to recharge its batteries a bit after the jumps and break out again if it wants. With luck it'll jump again or if not will settle down to steady swimming again or try to sound. Either way, the techniques already described are the best I know and can be applied to produce a "psyched-out" or played-out fish.

I have tried to describe only the basic moves in the game as an illustration of my methods. Fortunately fish, fishermen and the sea are individually pretty unpredictable and when they are taken in combination ensure that no one fishing trip will ever be the same as another, and no fight will ever be a stereotype. The apparently simple business of beating a fish with the best of expensive gear and a high-powered, highly specialised game boat can be, and often does become, a mighty precarious business with all the ingredients of high adventure. The fish themselves and the things they do often outshine our best lies. Pity the poor fisherman then, star in a drama beyond embellishment, who gets only disbelief when he tries to recount it.

On a trolling strike it is always difficult to tell the inexperienced what to look for. Some strikes are unbelievably fast, both mako and marlin. A mako taking a trolled bait will often shoot up out of the water to a height twice its own length and dive head-first on to the bait. In spite of all those stories about a mako having to turn over to bite, it seldom misses. This is a marvellous sight and if on a close or rod-tip bait, pretty scary. The moment the shark disappears from sight one has that queasy feeling that at any moment it will jump again and land right in the cockpit.

Makos in the air go high, spin, somersault, kick and snap their jaws all at once, and at the top of the jump, of course, are in slow motion. They can keep it up for a time-stopping age. When they hit the water between jumps they seem to literally bounce back up again, and very frequently loop and twist so much line around themselves that no tension can be applied, so that they become uncatchable.

If Bill Higgins ever reads this, he will surely re-live such an occasion out off the Two Fathom Reef at Mayor Island on a mirror-calm day when we were beaten just that way by a really big mako. The incident is still vivid to me. It was one of the biggest makos I ever saw perform so aerobatically and by the time it settled down it was just festooned in streaming loops of line. Throughout the show Bill avoided a break-off and, when the mako swam quietly off, we carefully followed gently retrieving line until we were so close behind that we tried to lift some of the trailing line with the gaff, and had plenty of time to admire the fish and discuss tactics before it broke away.

It was years later that I realised that what we should have done was to tie a balloon to the line, cut the fish adrift and with the balloon to keep it located while close to the surface, rebait and hopefully hook him again. That way we might just have promoted and won a second round. For sheer lethal beauty of form and motion, you cannot beat a mako.

Marlin on a very fast take usually lunge rather than dive at the bait and just keep on going – fast. They then usually disappear, pause and hit the air. If the pause is brief and the fish hits the air fast, it is odds on that it is foul-hooked or has tangled in the trace so the best drill is to move in behind it and work close on a taut line, if there is time. Otherwise it is liable to shake loose or swim out of the entanglement. By such tactics a lot have been caught that were fouled in an unbelievably tenuous fashion.

On the other hand, if the pause is protracted and followed by the appearance of the head and shoulders above the surface, thrashing deliberately from side to side, it is almost a certainty that it is gill- or throat-hooked, very firmly buttoned on and unlikely to provide very much in the way of fireworks.

Much the same thing can be said of the other occasions when the pause is long and the speed deliberate, whether the fish breaks surface or not for a start – very likely gut-hooked and probably

pretty securely. In both cases care should be taken – where possible and appropriate – not to pull on a short line to an open mouth.

A green thresher in northern waters will often announce itself on the troll by cruising up alongside a bait and hitting it with its tail, the blow by the flat of the tail on the water sounding like the crack of a stockwhip. The blow may even knock the bait from one side of the wake to the other and this will usually trip the outrigger clip. The boat should immediately be stopped and the bait allowed to sink in simulation of a dead or stunned fish, and to minimise the chance of tail hooking from further clouts. Threshers are tough enough even when jaw-hooked.

One is acutely aware of the power of a thresher's tail even when the fish is apparently subdued beside the boat, for the boatman is then clearly within stunning range himself. I had a demonstration of the reach of the tail one morning on Mayor Island when we were called from breakfast by a report that there was a live thresher on the beach. We all emptied out of the dining room and ran down to the shore. There was only a small sea running, but the thresher must have been caught on the top of a breaker and was on the beach two metres from the water.

I had always thought that one was safely away from the lashing tail when in front of the fish, but this thresher was curling its tail right over its head and digging out a hole in the sand about a metre in front of its nose. Its power, reach and speed were just incredible, beautiful and frightening. It reared, twisted, bucked and spun, sending wet sand flying, and lashing its tail like a flail. When it lashed the sand ahead of its nose it lay chin and pectorals flat on the sand, while the rest of its body twisted and lifted high up completing the arc of its tail.

Keeping well clear, we threw loops of rope over its pectoral fins and dragged it down to the water, where it swam off apparently none the worse for its stranding.

I am not sure whether it is officially agreed that there are two separate varieties of thresher

Sly customer: a thresher shark of about 200 kg moves up on a bait, with an eye just showing and long tail showing above the water.

sharks in New Zealand waters but I recognise at least two different-looking fish. One is green-grey coloured and the other quite rust-coloured on the back. Those I have seen up here in the north have been predominantly of the green variety, but since I have not seen any over 130 kg to 180 kg I suspect that the larger ones were of the red variety – or maybe they gain the reddish tinge when they become big. At Mayor Island, where most of our larger specimens are caught, they are predominantly reds and are generally from 130 kg to 260 kg. They are usually hooked while deep drifting and are moderately fast, extremely tough dogged fighters and can be counted on to stretch both angler and gear to the utmost even in ideal conditions.

Before the advent of modern tackle, so few were boated when hooked on the deep drift that for many years we could only indulge in fantasies on the monsters we could not stop. Our tanekaha rods and 270 m cutty hunk linen lines just could not cope, mainly because the combination of short line length and heavy diameter demanded such heavy brake on a fresh fish that, if the rod was thick enough to take the strain, it was too stiff to cushion the speed-friction strain on the thick line. Breakoffs immediately above the double were the usual outcome. Tanekaha rods, while effective on surface fighting fish such as the bulk of marlins and makos, put the angler in the position where he had to lower his tip to save his rod and thereby almost surely break his line, or ease his brake and almost surely have his line run right off.

Most of us chose to protect our gear and fishing time by keeping our baits on or near the surface. Probably because we occasionally picked up threshers as well as the usual run of marlins, makos, tigers, blue sharks and whalers, we did not realise that our "monsters", instead of being Moby Dicks, or Zane Grey's Great White Sharks, were mostly threshers and deep-feeding loners. By the time we had found out, we had learned so much, and had had so much fun in the process, that there was no room for disappointment.

Here on these northern grounds the small green threshers commonly taken on the troll provide a fishing spectacle I had seen only once before and, when it occurred, was to me so strange a concept that I could hardly believe my eyes. It happened at Mayor Island. The fish was a typical big red and why it behaved like a small green is anybody's guess. I was fishing with Bill Higgins, Harold Oliver and party at Mayor Island on one of those memorable perfect days. We were trolling through one of the island's less productive areas on our way round to the Maori Chief when someone shouted that there was an eel behind his bait, on its tail. Every shout on a trolling boat punches a near-panic button and concentrates all eyes and attention on the baits. I have often wondered if this might explain why fish so often, when about to take, suddenly abort their approach and disappear (like the hunter and shepherd who always looks past rather than at the shy animal?) Anyway, by the time I had figured it for what it was – a thresher's tail about a metre exposed, upright and from our angle like an eel, the fish lashed at the bait and hooked itself in the tail. Seeing a hookup is always a great advantage, and in this instance we were in only 40 metres or so of water and not far from an open bay with clear shelving sand bottom. We had a good angler on with 60 kg line and perfect weather. A big fish tail-hooked – it was just over 220 kg – is very difficult to fight and, if it can get into or is hooked in very deep water, it is an exhausting test of an angler's skill, stamina, gear and (let's face it) luck. This particular fight has remained

one of my vivid memories because it was a copy book exercise and we won it only by the slimmest of margins. It is not often that the angler, the gear, the fish, the weather and the location all add up to a clear-cut pattern of balanced odds and furthermore provide a perfect coaching opportunity.

The obvious strategy was to keep the fish from heading into the deep and work it into shallow water in case it should quit on the bottom and face the angler with the sometimes impossible job of lifting it to the surface in accordance with the rules. And with gear often stretched and worn by the fight to a state well below par, breakoffs at that stage are very common. In order to do that with our tail-hooked fish we had to hold station behind it and actually steer it. It sounds simple, although it is anything but, and resolves itself into a series of bouts in which boat and fish waltz around each other, with the angler maintaining as steady pressure as possible and leaving the initiative to the fish until a repetitive tight circular pattern is established with the boat in the centre.

Immediately the pattern was completely predictable and the fish approached the quadrant that found it heading in the direction we wished, we allowed the boat to sag toward it, while still maintaining constant pressure and angle and thereby set him on our course. By keeping our pressure, engine and propeller revs constant and guarding against thumps and bangs in the boat, we kept our catch at it for as long as possible, and then repeated the process until we were ready to slug it out and bring the fish to the gaff.

In this case we gaffed a bit too soon; the fish was more "psyched" than exhausted and as soon as the gaff went in it went berserk. The gaff was on a 6 m rope, cleated down before use; but the rope broke at the cleat and that big fish actually planed on its pectorals with its tail lashing the water, in a big semi-circle around the boat while we collected our wits and wiped the spray out of our eyes. The angler was still in the chair, with the reel on the light brake setting adopted when the trace was taken, and such was our luck that neither the tail nor the gaff had fouled the line. So after the last great flurry we had little trouble in boating it. It happened 20 odd years ago but I still have a very clear mental picture of it — in colour, both visually and verbally.

Before the introduction of outriggers here, trolling for game fish was done entirely from the rod tip, and was an extremely efficient method when practised with the complete concentration and quick reactions which successful "drop back" required. Fishing was done from the chair with the angler "sitting in" and harnessed to the reel. The reel was set with little or no brake, and the weight of the trolled bait was countered by

Curly Steedman at the wheel of Dauntless, *one of the early Whitianga charter boats and fourth on the Mayor Island scene. In those days, before the adoption of outrigger fishing, the angler sat always in the chair, alert for a fish and ready to release line to it immediately.*

holding the spool or the actual line with the gloved hands. For the occasional brief spell, or to give time to light a pipe, a wooden match wrapped once in the line and then twisted twice would sometimes be used as a fragile line stop across the bottom guide to take the weight and free the hands. "Drop back" was done immediately the fish came up and hit. The line was released and the fish helped to take the bait away with the least possible drag.

Because there was a lot of jerkiness in the performance, the spool tended to out-run the line and cause what every fisherman knows as an over-run. It is pretty fatal, because it usually tangles the line and automatically cuts it when the weight comes back on again. The only way to check is to manipulate the brake or apply the gloved fingers to the cheek of the reel as delicately as required to damp down the speed of the drum to the run of the line.

When the angler is very excited it is not an easy thing to bear in mind and watch very carefully. Anyone who has not experienced a fast and hard strike – marlin, tuna or mako – direct from the hand-held rod, simply cannot imagine the shock that it is. It is an absolute shock, physical as well as emotional. The immediate impression, (or mine always was) is of almost actual contact with the fish, I suppose because of the short length of line between the reel and the fish compared with the distance when fishing from an outrigger. The close up view of the head, mouth and eyes of the fish scattered my wits.

It was all so quick too. The reaction to it all was that I had not caught the fish, but the fish had caught me. It seemed to take an awful long time to get things into focus again and drop back and check the over-run but, if that awful long time took more than a moment, only good luck could save the day. Consequently a lot of fish

The Ngaroma *with a big black marlin on the counter and The Aldermen Islands in the background.*

were lost that would now fall to the automatic drop back of wide-spread outriggers.

Game fishing started off the American coast with drift fishing, followed by fast trolling – a method by which good results were being obtained here too when Zane Grey came to New Zealand in 1925–26. Still not completely satisfied, the Americans started kite fishing – flying a large kite behind a boat which was on the drift or trolling into the wind. The fishing line was clipped to the kite line, and the kite was allowed to take it as far from the boat as practical. The thought behind it all was that the boat was probably scaring away fish, but it must have been a frustrating business. The next step was the trial of outrigger poles which, while they did not get the baits quite as far away from the boat, were more controllable and adaptable to weather and sea conditions.

When outriggers proved practical it was realised that they also defined a larger working area behind the boat – laterally between the outrigger lines and as far back from the boat as

practical to set baits or lures. The first outriggers were ambitiously long, to the extent that they were dangerous to the stability of some boats, but it was soon realised that, by pruning their length down to a compromise, a fishing area as big as required was still provided. And as had already been established in the days of fast rod-tip trolling, good catches could be made right in the wake of the boat.

A charter skipper called Bill Hatch (a famous "name" in American game fishing) was employed as fishing guide by Michael Lerner who brought outriggers here just before the Second World War. Bill Hatch's job was to co-ordinate and direct the expedition's fishing and, if necessary, to teach and advise the New Zealand professionals, or guides as they called us. He was a particularly nice chap and what I learned about outriggers proved invaluable. The expedition brought the hardware necessary to fit bamboo poles or such-like to local boats as improvised outriggers.

I was skipper of a boat at Mayor Island called *Tui*, which was fished by Mrs Lerner for the six weeks of their stay in the Bay of Plenty. My boat was accordingly equipped with outriggers under the direction of Bill Hatch, who coached me in the use of them. The same thing was also done in the Bay of Islands with launches and skippers there.

I was intrigued with the increased scope – that is, greater fishing area – provided, and the consequent ability to fish with more gear from the one craft. When I later built *Sou'East*, I fitted her with outriggers and used them in accordance with what I had learned from Bill Hatch.

The year 1938 produced a good fishing season in the Bay of Plenty. The weather was good and fish were plentiful. Once the expedition realised how plentiful the fish were, the outriggers were not used all the time, and it became the habit to use them only when the anglers felt like seeking shelter from the sun, rain or wind or needed to vacate the chair for other reasons, for the outriggers would keep their baits fishing safely

for them in their absence. This was the other predominant feature which made me consider outriggers worthwhile. Up to then, as described in the rod-tip troll, anglers had to sit in their chairs holding their rods all the time.

Today outriggers are considered a "must" in all big game fishing – perhaps an overstatement of need but not of practice. While being aesthetically pleasant, they make it possible for a boat to use a greater number of baits or lures at the one time, and to keep it set up and fishing without the angler being tied to constant attendance. Outriggers not only permit a great increase in comfort for anglers during a long day at sea, but they perform a useful role in eliminating the "finger trouble" so frequently encountered when a sudden strike occurs on the rod-tip, and is even more in evidence during the panic of a double strike. This is possible while outrigger trolling if the reel is set with the minimum drag needed to prevent over-run, while the weight of the trolled lure or bait is taken by the clip on the outrigger halyard.

There are as many opinions on length, stiffness and appearance of outriggers as there are on practically any other part of the gear, fishermen being fishermen. However, as with all equipment, usage is largely dependent on the fisherman. I personally prefer an outrigger of what might be called short to medium length (between 3 and 4 m long) and – at the risk of being called biased – one which is somewhat stiffer then the dominant fibreglass poles in use on the northern grounds. The outriggers I developed in the Bay of Plenty, and were first built and fitted by Bill Higgins on his *Nor'West*, were designed to overcome the inherent whipping tendency of the then commonly-used heavy bamboo poles. These, if used beyond 3.5 m in length, required fore and aft stays to stablilise them, and this resulted in a clutter around the boat.

My outriggers, designed on a girder principle, required no stays of any sort, only telescopic spreading arms. The design allowed an in-built

Quo Vadis, with its Mayor Island-style outriggers folded up, cruises quietly home with a couple of tuna at the stern. Tudor Collins.

non-varying stiffness to the choice of the individual. I still consider them extremely efficient and good-looking even though I shall not be using them on *"Sea Runner"*, our new boat. The reason is mainly a question of speed. My original outriggers would offer too much resistance over 20 knots. I shall, however, stay with my preference for a stiffer outrigger than in common northern use.

The usual practice in New Zealand is to tow baits, one off each outrigger, at approximately 5 knots – a speed which will vary in relation to the size of baits and surface conditions. Rough water tends to break baits free of the clips and this

means loss of fishing time in retrieving and resetting them. The aim being to keep baits trolling at all times in all working conditions, with as light a clip as possible, the skipper has to vary clip weights and boat speed to suit conditions.

In-between the outrigger baits at least two smaller baits and/or lures are usually trolled, one close in the wake and the other back to a point just inside the outrigger baits. Such an arrangement, and where the baits and lures are set, is a matter of personal fancy but is a good working minimum. Some people like to run a lure well back beyond the trolled baits, but this practice has the disadvantage of being prone to foul-ups by fish taking either of the side baits and

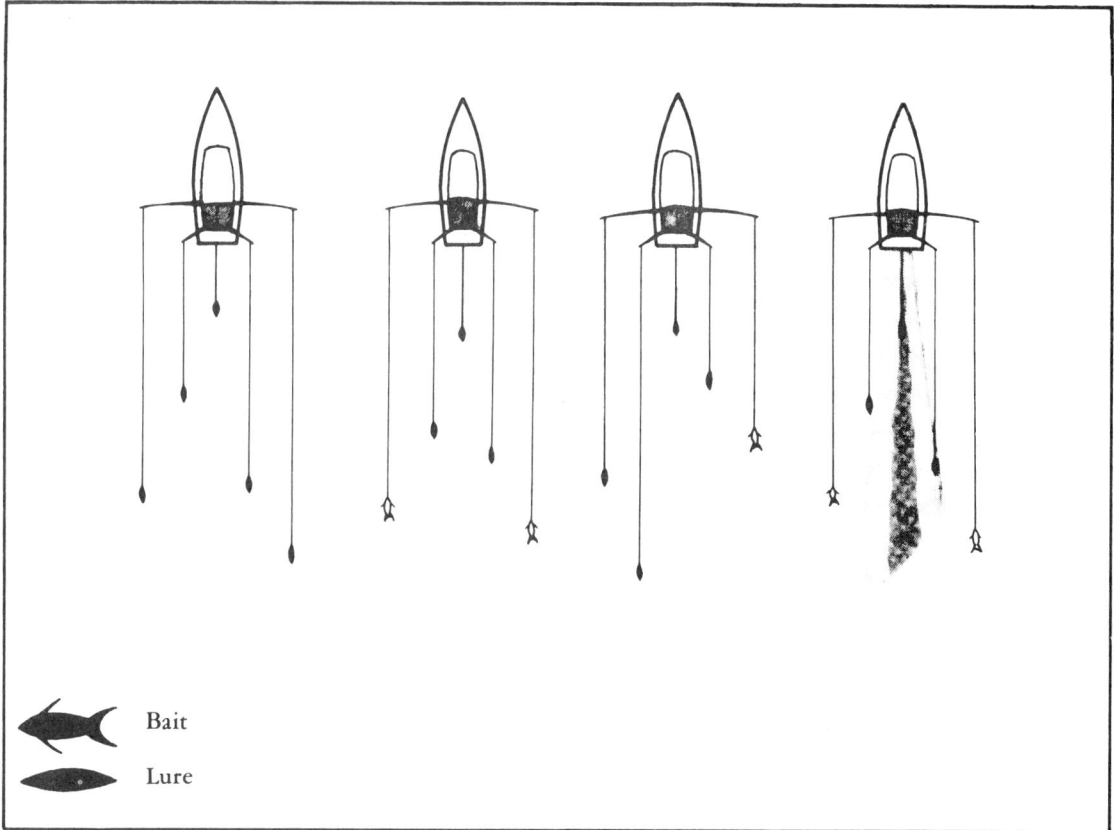

Diagram VI

Patterns of trolling: these patterns (with baits and lures indicated) are maximum settings from a boat. The outer baits, on outriggers, determine the fishing area in and beside the wake (indicated on the right hand diagram). Fewer lines are often preferable and the disposition of baits and lures is a matter of personal preference.

cutting across the wake. For this reason it is usually considered preferable to keep all lighter gear (the heavier lines are usually trolled on the outriggers) between the boat and the outrigger baits.

If lures are used in conjunction with trolled baits, they must be chosen for their effect at the speed which suits the baits – about 5 knots. If lures only are used, including off the outriggers, they should all be chosen for the speed to be used, for there are lures designed for both high and low speeds, and most are very ineffective outside their designed range. The system learned by Laurie Ross, skipper of the charter boat *Maraqueta* and president of the Whangaroa

Club, from a Hawaiian expert and since applied successfully on his home grounds, has only one drawback – it requires fast trolling at a time when speed equates with high fuel use and thus high operating costs.

But as Laurie puts it, zooming around at 11 knots with big fish coming in to take a lure in the boil of the wake right off the rod tip is exciting fishing. All hell breaks loose with almost no warning and an angler has to be standing by, to grab the rod as soon as the lure is taken and to point the rod like a gun at the fish so that the line screams straight out on the first take. Simultaneously the launch skipper must gun the boat up in a short burst of extra speed to strike the hook; and then must throttle down to follow the fish, putting in a loop of line which will keep the pressure on the fish until some of the line lost in the initial burst by the fish can be regained.

There is nothing in fishing to approach the excitement of this strike on the rod tip, and all the exhortations to an angler to keep calm and think, apply even more when a lure is being used. With marlin the hook does not sink deep into the horny area of the mouth and of the many marlin lost on lures about half go straight after the strike. The fish, as soon as it realises that what it has taken is not a food fish, will stop, and shake its head to try to throw the hook clear. Hence the initial burst on the throttle in the key second or two when the line must be kept tight. The brake, incidentally, is set fairly tight for the take and the strike – perhaps as much as 10 kg on a 24 kg line, which explains why the angler has to be quick to his rod and to point it at the fish if something is not going to break.

And because the hook is unlikely to be more than lightly bedded, every precaution must be taken during the playing of the fish not to pull it out. The greatest danger, apart from relaxing tension on the line, is to allow the fish to change sides, so that the line instead of pulling the hook into the mouth, pulls it out. It may be necessary to circle the fish to achieve this object. But the second point of major risk in losing a fish comes right at the end when the fish is being brought up to the boat. Then if the angler relaxes for a moment, and the fish chooses to give its head a final shake, it is away. Laurie Ross says he tries to solve this – and with good success – by taking the trace in one hand and holding the bill of the fish against the boat with the other until a gaff and a rope can be got home.

Marlin can be caught this way not only efficiently but humanely, because the hook is not deep and does the fish little harm – a big plus point if it is the intention, to tag it and release it. With the trace cut off short the hook will soon fall out. In fact, in most cases when a marlin is

boated on a lure, the lure falls out into the boat as the fish comes aboard.

A method of lure fishing that Laurie Ross has come to appreciate involves setting two big jet-head lures – the ones with holes in the head – on outriggers and set – there is an art in this – so that they "smoke", sending off trails of little bubbles, and then setting two other lures in close to the boat in-between. One of these can be a large lure that ducks about all over the place, causing a lot of fuss in the water and drawing a lot of attention. The other should be a small, steady lure set just beside and fractionally in front of the fussy lure. If a marlin scorns the smoking lures and comes in close to inspect the big lure it is often tempted to strike at it, usually several times without success, and will then settle for the small lure coasting so quiet and vulnerable alongside. The angler then has a big fish on his line, almost eyeball to eyeball.

Once I got into deep drifting and started to hook into quite a few threshers and other big fish, and after breaking quite a bit of gear, I realised that fishing deep required some significant departures from surface angling, and eventually developed a different approach. As a charter boat operator I was anything but a free agent, and could depart from standard fishing practices only when the interest of my charterers would permit, but I was fortunate in having several who were very experienced, and like me, very curious. One of our earliest setbacks was our first complete stripping of a 550 m line.

The angler was Mick Groome, in company with Brian Armstrong, Ray Christophers and Eric Duncan, all well known anglers from Dannevirke. It was a beautifully calm day and our bait was on or near the bottom in about 150 m of water, just in from the 200 m line. As usual, we had nearly twice as much line out as depth of water under us, leaving us with approximately 250 m on the spool. The take was deliberate and started a run-off at about 5 knots, which neither hesitated nor varied in the ages it seemed to take to strip us clean. The angler was

A striped marlin which has been hooked not in the mouth but around one of its pectoral fins.

young and strong, the heavy split cane rod really powerful and the line a near-new 60 kg test. With that combination I had no doubt at all that in 250 m we could at least turn nearly anything.

With motors running, rod bent to the limit, harness creaking and daylight between the angler and seat, we waited. And waited, and tugged, and pulled, and jerked, and the line just ran steadily off straight down into the water. There was nowhere for us to go, we could not follow the line down and nothing at all that we could do but keep the pressure on and hope. By the time we were down to the last few turns on the spool, the hope had become a kind of scalp-prickling acceptance and, as the end loop left the pin and, it seemed, simultaneously hit the water and disappeared straight down, someone said "skunked".

That was the first time. There have been two others since and each of those occasions cost us 725 m, for I never again worked deep drifting with less, even though it seems that the only gain on such occasions is time – for the fish to stop. Unlike surface fishing, a change of direction by the catch is of no immediate help, unless it is a rising turn back toward the boat, but even this can still take line because at that stage line/water friction is the major problem. It takes time and a lot of slow, even pumping to overcome the combined effects of belly in the line plus the line's inherent elasticity, which in terms of rod tip travel becomes a big factor when most of the line is out. Even if the fish does the decent thing and apparently stops, it is quite a while before we achieve a sufficiently direct line to be able to make our presence felt.

If then we manage to transmit a variation of strain past the cushioning effects of line belly and stretch, the fish will move a short distance and apparently stop again, and after a while will start making more definite responses.

If we have managed to stay at an effective distance, the very fact of our constant pull from above starts it upward and we are in business. Usually the fish will come up quite a long way before baulking. In the process, quite a bit of line will be retrieved and consequently our effectiveness greatly improved. Then when the fish jibs it goes into, or is put into, a circle at the reduced depth by our constant pressure on it, and from then on is best thought of as a fixed-wing flying, rather than swimming, creature. Threshers use the area of their pectorals against our pull just as an aeroplane banks in a turn, while fish with smaller pectorals use body depth in the same way.

In the early stages, at the reduced depth, the circling fish will usually regain quite a bit of depth, but the pattern of the fight is established, and will be repeated over and over again unless accidentally or deliberately broken by applied angling techniques. Since the circle is the fish's best defence because of the pectoral area or body-shape, we should not allow it to persist and, since it comes about because of our steady pull against it, the obvious thing to do is to make a quick shift of position to outside the circle.

The sudden relaxation and then resumption of tension from the opposite side causes the fish to half roll and puts it into another circle of opposite rotation. The time factor is important so in preparation for the manoeuvre the boat should be sagged into the fish while circling inside it and when as close as possible gunned along the line until outside the circle. Then the reel should be braked hard until the new circle is established. It is a simple and extremely effective technique and, when properly done four or five times at regular short intervals to a fish that has settled down to dogged never-give-in resistance, can be counted on to "psych" it into quitting.

Sometimes the opportunity occurs early in the piece but, if taken then can cause an awful commotion when the gaff goes in. In the case of threshers and makos the boating of green fish is especially dangerous, because unlike the others they can reach right into the boat. The mako's tendency to leap into cockpits is well known. I recall one of my very early such encounters with a really big thresher. After we had gaffed and roped it and untied the trace from the double, it started a demolition act on the boat and could not have done better if he had been on contract. There were only two of us on board, and by instant agreement we skipped to the foredeck and watched that darned fish remove our open-sided dodger, smash our windscreen, chair and rod, tangle the double line round his tail, break his ropes and take off really fast with our gear. I for one had the feeling that we were lucky the rod was broken or he would have been back to catch us.

It was an expensive lesson and, taken young, was one I never forgot. The things old Bill, ex-deep sea diver and ship's fireman, said to me when I got his boat back home again will never be forgotten.

CHAPTER EIGHT

With lighter tackle

One of New Zealand's most experienced light-line fishermen is Don Butters, a Wellington dentist who has been fishing with tackle of 10-kg breaking strain and under for 20 years. With this light tackle some 200 mako have been caught as well as a good many yellowfin tuna before they became scarce off Whitianga about 1970.

Enduring "a lot of raspberries about trying to catch sharks on cotton", he has not only been top boat in Mercury Bay Club on a number of occasions but holds the New Zealand records for mako and yellowfin tuna on a 10-kg line – the mako, of 157.4 kg, was for three years a world record. His son John with a 32 kg mako is the New Zealand record holder in the under 3-kg line class, and John's wife Judy holds the New Zealand record for the heaviest mako caught on a 6-kg line. So Don speaks with some experience.

He started off at Whitianga in 1960 using an ordinary snapper rod and an 8.1-kg line, hooked a yellowfin tuna between Whitianga and The Aldermen Islands and brought it aboard after a three-quarter hour fight.

Impressed with the speed of the fish and the excitement of fighting them, he kept on seeking tuna on lines which hardly seemed adequate to the task and in 1967 caught a 50.35-kg yellowfin tuna on a 10-kg rated line, to break his own record for the fourth consecutive time and give him a New Zealand record which still stands.

And when the prime run of yellowfin tuna

eased in the fishing waters of the Mercury Bay Club of which he is a member, he switched to mako which he felt sure, given the patience, could also be caught on light line. Since then he and his friends have caught not only 200 mako but a few hammerhead, and some 250 blue pointer sharks, though never a marlin to the time of writing. He has had a couple on the line but they tend to roll up a light line and break it with fin or tail.

Most of this fishing is done on 10-kg rated line (the heaviest used), but a number of the fish have been taken on 6-kg and half a dozen on 4-lb monofilament (rated as 3-kg). His son John Butters was using a 4-lb monofilament line when he caught his 30.84-kg mako for a record in January 1979 – and when tested by the Department of Scientific and Industrial Research the line broke at 2 lb. This fish, hooked 2 km off Goat Island, near Whitianga, worked steadily out to sea, jumping as only a mako can, leaping more than twelve times.

Don Butters himself still has a New Zealand record in the 157.4-kg mako he boated in 1973 on a 10-kg line after a fight of 6½ hours. It was the heaviest mako on any tackle caught by the Mercury Bay Club that season.

Part of the secret of such light tackle fishing lies in the patience of the angler, and a willingness to lose a few, although Don says he has caught more than he has lost – 75 to 80 per cent of those that have been on the line.

Most of those that have got away have not broken clear but have regurgitated their bait (and hook) right beside the boat, and have recovered and swum off.

One of the fundamentals of light tackle fishing is to try to play the fish fairly close to the boat as excessive line in the water produces enough friction for the speed of the fish to break the line, especially if the angler has inadvertently left a little too much drag on the reel. The greatest danger of a line break is when a fish is being brought in to the boat, almost played out. The angler, in his excitement and anxiety automatically tends to drop the rod tip, thus losing the cushioning effect of the flexing tip. The fish must always be played with the rod tip high if it is not to shake its head and snap the line.

Normal wear and the effect of the sun soon weaken the line anyway so the first 20 metres or so must regularly be thrown away.

Essential also to the technique is the use of small, very sharp hooks (about twice the size of snapper hooks) because with the light line a heavy blunt hook cannot be sunk home.

The trace used needs to be strong – about 400 lb breaking strain is common – but everything else is light, so light that in trolling most fishermen prefer to work without outriggers for fear of chafing the line. They therefore revert to the older style of fishing off the rod tip with its techniques of manual control of line release and over-run, and the attendant excitement of direct contact from the outset with the fish. In drift fishing, usually three baits are put out, one hanging over the side to a depth of 10 metres or so, and the other two on floats, one about 30 metres and the other 50 metres from the boat and both 6 to 8 metres down. The floats are attached to the doubles by cotton, so that the weight of the bait is taken by the cotton rather than the line, and when the fish strikes the cotton breaks and float drifts clear.

A favoured trolling bait is flying fish, but

kahawai, English and horse mackerel, squid, or a tuna lure with a strip of kahawai tied to it will do on the troll, and even snapper, golden snapper and tarakihi on the drift. Successful light line methods of rigging the bait include a single hook through the lips of the bait fish, or two hooks, one near the tail and one in the belly with the line trailed from the nose of the fish, where it is tied.

The art, when the bait is taken, is not to make a swift strike, but to wait patiently, easing out the line to allow the fish to move away with it, sometimes for four or five minutes, taking maybe 400 to 500 metres of line before allowing it to feel anything. A mako will then usually take off like a rocket, leaping far more on light tackle than on heavy, because the thinness of the line produces almost no restraint and there is only a small irritation from the bait. Makos on a light line will jump as much as three times their own length out of the water and frequently leap 10 or 12 times.

As soon as they settle, it is time to start regaining line; Don Butters turns the boat and follows the fish, playing it off the starboard bow of the boat if at all possible, keeping it about 50 metres from the boat because with too much line out the fish will break if anything but a minimal drag is used and at no time should the angler apply drag equivalent to more than one third of the breaking strain of the line. For much of the time the fish may cruise about 20 metres down under the boat occasionally diving deeper or coming to the surface to jump again. The chase can go on for a long way – the record 157.40 kg mako caught on 10-kg line was hooked just outside Red Mercury Island and boated about 8 km outside Cuvier Island, travelling about 20 km in 6½ hours.

Occasionally a mako will sulk and refuse to play, possibly through being deeply hooked, and Don has boated a 99.78-kg fish in under half an hour on a 10-kg line.

After fishing with light tackle for 20 years Don Butters prefers to fish on tackle which gets lighter all the time, although in some ways he finds less satisfying the fishing on the lightest monofilament line because of its stretch. This is really light fishing, using a little game rod, with rings because the line tends to slip down beside rollers. It comes close to another even lighter style of game fishing which is gaining in stature and popularity – saltwater fly fishing.

Don expresses his philosophy of light-tackle fishing as follows: "Over the last 10 to 20 years the number of large fish being caught is getting fewer each year but it is still possible by using progressively lighter gear to obtain great satisfaction in playing and catching smaller fish which on heavy gear would put up virtually no fight and have almost no chance of escape.

"One mistake by the light tackle angler allows the fish to escape, in most cases unharmed, and it is this emphasis on skill and patience which restores fishing to a sport. What greater satisfaction than to boat a mako of perhaps only about 40 kg knowing that it has been a battle of wits and skill which may have lasted for as long as 3 hours over a distance of 5 or 6 km with the possibility at any stage of victory to the fish. Whenever a fish such as this gains his freedom, the angler's best wishes should go with him because he has fought gamely and successfully for his life and has provided the angler with something far more important than just another fish tale, he has provided an irreplaceable memory to be treasured forever."

Prominent among the new generation of saltwater fly fishermen in New Zealand has been Dr Mike Godfrey, of Mt Maunganui, the only New Zealander with a world record in this branch of saltwater fishing. The fish which set this record, a 14.51 kg yellowtail caught with a 10-lb tippet on May 12, 1979, and another yellowtail weighing 9.52 kg, gave him first and second places in the fourth annual International Game Fish Association contest in this fish and line category.

Dr Godfrey is a member of the Mount Pleasant Boat Club. Most club members do ordinary fishing but they include some keen saltwater fly fishermen, which led to the club being granted observer status with the New Zealand Big Game Fishing Council.

The basic requirements of such gear include a standard fibreglass or graphite rod with plenty of butt strength, capable of throwing a No. 10 line and preferably with an extra grip up the butt section.

A couple of good saltwater reels are needed, preferably one for 6-lb and one for 10-lb class. A large freshwater fly reel with at least 250 metres of backing can be used but a corrosion-proof reel avoids the tedious task of unwinding the backing each time the rod is used, for washing and then rewinding again.

The line can be a fast-sinking shooting head or a floater for very shallow waters. Dr Godfrey's preference for kingfish is a shooting head attached to 30 metres of braided monofilament and then 250 metres of braided dacron backing of 9-kg breaking strain. The braided monofilament gives a useful guide to how much line is out and how deep the fish is, as his line changes colour every 10 metres.

The leader or trace is made up of less than 30 cm of heavy monofilament of 15 kg to 24 kg attached to the fly, then a minimum of 30 cm but usually 45 cm of the test line – 6-lb, 10-lb, 12-lb, or 15-lb class, and then about a metre of 15-kg breaking strain monofilament attached to the fly-line with a loop. The advantage of a loop is that a quick change can be made of traces and flies, if they are kept ready attached to each other, as Dr Godfrey does, with all knots pre-tested at three quarters of the breaking strain of the line. He uses a uniknot, which is excellent for matching unequal lines and for attaching flies to heavy monofilament. If wire is used, either fine piano wire or the new "Twistweld" would be suitable, says Dr Godfrey, who adds: "What may not be realised is that the maximum load put on the line via a fly rod would only be 1.8 kg to 2.7 kg, and that is with a far greater bend in the rod than would be normally used playing a fish.

Test it yourself with a spring balance.

"One of the more interesting aspects of saltwater fly fishing is in the flies used. The local yellowtail feed well on piper and my flies are 10 cm to 15 cm long with white feathers and bucktail overlaid by a blue-green dyed synthetic fibre for the back. The head is made from two oval pieces of old squid lure, tied on either side, and sealed in with five-minute glue after painting on the eyes. The head takes up most of the 3/0 or 4/0 hook, and all the feathers, and so on, project beyond the bend to prevent them from hooking around the shank during casting. For very shallow water a floating fly can be made with a large muddler pattern."

The boat must be stationary during fly fishing and a rewarding technique is to anchor in a suitable spot and burley from the stern. One angler may do some "stray lining" with piper bait while the other is fly fishing. If a kingfish is caught on a bait, the fly fisherman waits until the fish is seen and then casts, because there are often other kingfish following behind. Dr Godfrey once put a fly straight into the mouth of a 11.79-kg kingfish following another to the stern of the boat. It was caught on a 6-lb line which unfortunately overtested and his record claim failed.

The biggest problem with yellowtail is their habit of diving for deep rocks. Tauranga is a deep harbour with a sandy bottom and it is possible to follow a fish there. In winter the yellowtail gather at the harbour entrance where up to eight fish have been seen at a time swimming in the burley trail. "Casting into the 'pack' is then fantastic," says Dr Godfrey, "as the fish average nearly 9 kg. The heaviest caught in the 1978–80 season was over 27.21 kg, hooked in three metres of water and played for nearly an hour on a standard 9-kg game rod. My heaviest on the fly was the 14.51-kg fish on a 10-lb line and we travelled about four miles in the two hours it took to land it."

Yellowtail is probably the prime New Zealand target of the saltwater fly fisherman, but skipjack,

barracouta, kahawai, trevally and snapper may also make for good fishing. At one stage Dr Godfrey asked the I.G.F.A. if it was permissible to run the nylon test tippet through a thin plastic sleeve to protect it from the skin, in catching a mako, but the I.G.F.A. turned it down.

Gary Kemsley, of Taupo, another expert in the field of saltwater fly fishing, sets out the basics as follows:

Tackle

Two outfits are recommended for saltwater fly work. A light No.7 or 8 outfit will suit for estuary fishing and for calm-water fishing for smaller species. A heavier No.10 to No.12 outfit will be required when fishing for larger species or when fishing in heavy conditions.

Rods

Rods should be stiff enough to punch a line into strong winds and to lift the fly and line from surf and turbulent currents. The rod must also have lifting power to bring a fish up from the depths once he has sounded and become exhausted. Carbon fibre is the most suitable material because of the strength and lifting power which is available for its light weight. Hollow fibre glass is also suitable but because of its heavier weight can be tiring.

Reels

Large capacity reels are a must when fly fishing in saltwater. Where there is a possibility of hooking large fish, a large reservoir of line is a good insurance.

Another reason for using a large capacity reel is because it offers a relatively fast retrieve rate when full of line. This can be very important when fishing for fast swimming species. Some drag system is required and a simple click is enough for most species.

A star drag system can be a great asset when handling the larger species. This writer has settled on a wide spool reel which has a rim control. This reel holds over 400 m of line and has a single handle. Reels with double handles can be dangerous when a heavy fish is running and the spool is rotating.

Lines

Both weight-forward lines and shooting-head lines are suitable for saltwater fishing. In many instances long-distance casting can be an advantage and these lines will allow the angler to achieve good casting length. These lines also make casting easier when wading in the surf. Long casts can be made with the minimum of false casting.

The heavy forward sections of these lines also make for fast changing of cast direction when casting to fast travelling pelagics. Another less appreciated factor in favour of these lines is the fact that they take up little room on the reel allowing for extra backing. Use either sinking or floating line depending on where the fish are feeding.

Leaders

Leaders can take any form if anglers are not after records. In that situation use a leader of level monofilament. A wire leader is a good insurance against bite-offs from toothy species and to avoid line-wear during prolonged fights with large fish. If one is after records then leader lengths and makeup will be determined by International Game Fish Association Rules.

Flies

The most successful flies are light-coloured streamers which imitate small and sometimes large baitfish. Other fly types that can be used include shrimp and squid imitations that will fool some species which may not take streamer patterns.

Size of hooks used can vary from size 10 through to size 5/0. Any larger than this become difficult and dangerous to cast. Flies should be tied on stainless steel hooks.

Top water poppers tied with cork or balsa heads and long flowing tails are great attractors and should be included in the angler's tackle box. Poppers work best in agitated water such as around offshore islands and on surf beaches.

Fishing Techniques

One technique that will work on most pelagic species is the high speed retrieve. When fishing to visible fish such as in a feeding school, the fly should be cast to the edge of the group of fish, allowed to sink to their level and then stripped back toward the angler as fast as possible. Often pelagics such as kahawai, kingfish and skipjack tuna will rush a fly that is retrieved at speed after refusing a slower fly. If the retrieve is fast enough to skip the fly along the surface so much the better. It cannot be too fast.

Wherever school fish are found one should allow some casts to sink below the feeding fish. If the fish on the surface are not responding there may be another species at a lower level. This is often the case with yellowtail which will travel below schools of kahawai, blue maomao or trevally. In that situation an extra fast-sinking shooting-head is ideal.

For fishing shallow estuaries a floating line used in conjunction with a long leader is the best tool to prospect the likely feeding areas, and also keep the fly off the bottom when required. Floating lines can also be used with the poppers which are worked on the surface.

Fishing Locations

For the fish-eating species which are the easiest to fool with fly gear, one should fish in estuaries around rivermouths and harbour entrances, surf beaches and any area where there is white water around rocks. For the boat fisherman fishing offshore islands, watching tide rips and shallow reefs as well as watching for surface-feeding schools, will turn up fish. For bottom-feeding species, fish deep over any reefy ground or around any underwater obstruction such as bridge or wharf piles.

The controlled use of burley can draw fish to the saltwater fly fisherman. Using burley will attract some species that would be unlikely catches otherwise such as snapper, and cod.

It should be remembered that any fish will take a fly if that fly imitates the food that the fish is feeding on and if it is presented in a natural manner.

CHAPTER NINE

Famous Far North waters

Whangaroa Harbour – to which Kipling if he visited New Zealand now would surely award the accolade "last, loneliest, loveliest, exquisite, apart" which he once gave to Auckland, is the northernmost deep-sea fishing centre in the country. It also has weigh stations at Mangonui and Houhora Harbours further north, so its "territory" goes to North Cape and beyond it to the Three Kings Islands. Extended to the south to the Cavalli Islands, it has as fine a strip of big game fishing water as one would find.

Of the several sheltered harbours and numerous sheltered bays on this lovely Far North coast which faces northeast into the Pacific and directly toward the theoretic breeding grounds of the South Pacific striped marlin, Whangaroa is the best. The harbour entrance is narrow but deep and can be used in all but the very worst of weathers. Once inside the harbour the water, still deep and running away into numerous arms, often under high hills and cliffs, offers guaranteed shelter in beautiful surroundings. The outer part of the harbour belongs to boatmen alone. There are no roads to it.

The entrance to the harbour is called Kingfish Point, its fishing reputation won more than half

a century ago and, after a period of decline, now being re-established. The New Zealand kingfish is the southern yellowtail, a fighting fish for which New Zealand, although not Whangaroa surprisingly at the moment, holds several world records.

The beginnings of the game fishing club at Whangaroa are made a little hazy by the fact that the initial records went up in smoke after its first year with the burning down of the old Masonic Hotel. Alan Sanderson, the first secretary left a memorandum on the first page of the new minute book. He wrote down the following from memory (verified by other original members of the club):

"Elected honorary members:

"Captain L. D. Mitchell in recognition of his landing the first striped marlin to be weighed and recorded at Whangaroa, 10th February, 1925.

"Mr Zane Grey with whose party Captain Mitchell fished on the launch *Marlin*.

"Mrs K. Hoyt, the first lady angler to land a game fish at Whangaroa in company with her husband on the launch *Speedwell*.

"All fish subsequent to Capt Mitchell's during the first season were caught by Mr Stan Ellis on the launch *Matere* at times accompanied by

Out past the fiord-like entrance to the Whangaroa Harbour lie premier gamefishing grounds. Near the horizon on the right stretch the Cavalli Islands, scene of many an epic catch. Whites Aviation.

Mr E. C. Bromwich, and it is my opinion it is mainly to the aforenamed gentlemen that the club owes its existence."

Stan Ellis, having made his pile as a timber merchant in the King Country, had retired to concentrate on shooting and fishing and Whangaroa was his Mecca. He established his friend Cecil Bromwich as proprietor of the Hotel Marlin and engaged Eric Sanderson in the 1925–26 season to take him out, with makeshift gear — a tanekaha rod cut from the bush, a wooden reel and a benzine box for a chair. The mako he caught was the first game fish landed by a local European angler at Whangaroa. It spurred

him on to the formation of the club, the purchase of the hotel, the building of the wharf and gallows opposite it and the catching of hundreds more fish from the virgin waters.

From the small beginning the club grew fast. Interviewed by the New Zealand Herald in March 1927, after his second visit to New Zealand, Captain Mitchell said: "It was very gratifying to see the great strides which had been made at Whangaroa in catering for visiting anglers since last year, when I took the first two swordfish ever captured off there. The swordfish club now has a membership of 170. Since last December, between 20 anglers and 10 launches, over 76 game fish totalling in weight 15,500 lbs (7030 kg) have been captured on the Whangaroa grounds."

The pace did not last and the Whangaroa

93

Russell, with the headquarters of the Bay of Islands Sword-fish Club on the waterfront just to the right of the wharf and a scatter of islands behind leading to Cape Brett on the skyline. Whites Aviation.

Club went into one of the several periods of decline which have characterised its history. But after the Second World War, Bert Louden, the baker (one always knew, locals said, when he had been out fishing because the next day's bread was burned), with the local policeman, George Atkins, the postmaster, Percy Miller, and the garage proprietor, Ernie Brown, joined in one of its revivals. Bert Louden was president of the club from 1948 to 1952 when there were five charter boats associated with the club – *Lone Star, Valerie, Lady Alma*, (later *Tuatahi*) *Manaaki*, and *Zephyr*. Not since then has there been the same number of charter boats and – as other clubs have usually found – it is the

professionals, putting their experience to use day after day, who produce the fish in times when they do not actually fly on to the hook. It has taken yet another revival, culminating in building of club rooms (the first funds toward which were raised in local housie evenings), backed by a growth in the numbers of smaller runabout launches (about 100 now take part in the club's one-base contests), to produce the best fishing for 50 years and club membership rising to a record of over 700.

In the 1978–79 season, when 166 game fish were caught by the club, the number of marlin was 91 – the best season since 1929–30, really back to the good old days. And the recovery seemed to be confirmed in the 1979–80 season which produced 117 marlin in a total catch made up of 104 striped marlin, 7 blue marlin, 6 black marlin, 34 sharks, 41 blue sharks, 59 yellowtail,

11 hammerhead sharks, 1 thresher shark and 15 tuna.

The club recorded 118 striped marlin, 7 blue marlin and 4 blacks, plus 63 mako sharks, 29 blue sharks and 9 hammerheads in a total of 273 game fish taken in the 1980–81 season.

Records do not always go to the biggest boats. The biggest mako ever caught in New Zealand waters on 24-kg line was taken by Keith Gilbert on his 5.2 metre runabout *Medusa* out of Whangaroa, when fishing with his young son Grant, who acted as launchman while his father fought the fish. The mako had taken both skip baits and had then charged under the boat, spitting out one bait and being fought on the other line for three hours. Brian Shepherd and Keith Wilson came aboard from another boat to help to bring the fish to the gaff. But it was too big – 3.5 metres long – to bring on board. It had to be towed back to Whangaroa, very much alive, shaking the boat that was towing it from time to time, and still active when the Whangaroa wharf was reached, with about 50 people waiting there to see the fish come in. Writing afterwards in the club magazine, Grant said: "We couldn't stop the motor and tie up to the wharf as the shark was too lively, so we just went round and round in circles out from the wharf for about half an hour while the onlookers and experienced fishermen and the weighmaster thought of how to get it on to the wharf. When they had decided, the same two men who had helped to gaff the fish boarded our boat and put a choker rope around the shark and then threw the end of the choker rope to the wharf where there were many strong hands, about 20 in all . . . Dad was very pleased to see that it was all over and so was I."

The club has held world or New Zealand records in most classes of game fish over the years. Currently it has New Zealand records in only Pacific blue marlin and mako but this cannot be taken as a reflection on the quality of its fishing waters. Indeed many of the fish taken by boats of the Bay of Islands club come from

The record 389.18 mako – still a New Zealand women's record 31 years later –caught by Mrs R. Beaver, out of Whangaroa. Bingham Green.

around the Cavalli Islands, which are a good deal closer to Whangaroa than to Russell, and over which there has been rivalry – in earlier days not always friendly – since the two clubs started. One of the first moves of the Whangaroa Club was to issue a challenge for an annual fishing contest with the Bay of Islands Club for the heaviest game fish landed, "a dinner being given to the winning club by the losing club".

The limits of the club catches were set at the areas gazetted for each harbour area, which placed the Cavallis in the Whangaroa zone. Bay of Islands won the first contest; the records are missing after that but the Whangaroa Club has two menus of challenge dinners indicating that Whangaroa won in 1930 and the Bay of Islands in 1931.

The cup is still around somewhere – held by Whangaroa.

The rivalry did not end there, and one year when Zane Grey, the pride of the Bay of Islands, was fishing off the Cavallis, the Whangaroa Club authorised its president and secretary to hire a launch to take them out to the Cavallis and attempt to get Grey to weigh his fish in at Whangaroa or at least advise their club of his catches. And later the launchmen of Whangaroa, alleging poaching on their grounds, endeavoured to get the Government to declare illegal the fishing by Bay of Islands charter boats outside their limits – i.e. around the Cavallis. The Marine Department discreetly avoided taking sides by declaring as one area all the fishing zones of the Bay of Islands, Whangaroa and Mangonui harbours – a free-for-all which contributes to the special quality of fishing off this coast today.

The big game launch setting out from Whangaroa has several choices of a day's fishing. It can make for the North Ground off the end of Stephenson Island, a favourable area of broken bottom, and then turn out to the Ruahine Reef which comes up from deep water 3½ miles out beyond the island and then perhaps to the Outer Ruahine which is a deeper area of foul ground. The boat can then troll through a "hot spot", sometimes known as the "sixty", and perhaps associated with upwellings of current, which lies between the Ruahine Reef and the Cavalli Islands, and then on to the Taheke Reef, off the Cavalli Islands where Captain Mitchell hooked his giant black marlin.

Sometimes the whole triangle between Stephenson Island, the Ruahine Reef and the Taheke Reef is a hot spot, and during one national contest skipper Laurie Ross of Whangaroa counted 28 boats within a distance of a couple of miles, all pursuing game fish. About half that number of fish were caught, with many more lost.

One can go on over the North Ground right out to the 200-metre line and work down it until opposite the hot spot or the Taheke Reef. Out in

these waters in high summer, one comes on the East Auckland current with its deep blue water, carrying quietly down the coast its harvest of tropical and sub-tropical fish, large and small. The edge of the current is quite distinct – the waters do not seem to mix. And out here where the water temperature in summer can rise to 25°C, one comes on the occasional dolphin fish, dazzling both in its colours and its fighting qualities (it is superb eating too) and the occasional big leatherback turtle, which the boatmen leave in peace.

Even more popular these days than the day's big game fishing trip by charter boat is the three-or four-day charter which takes the fisherman as far north as North Cape and sometimes beyond; and as far south as the Bay of Islands, or even the Poor Knights. With good relations between the clubs now, one can courtesy-weigh any fish caught on neighbouring clubs' weigh stations. One advantage of such long trips – apart from the compulsory separation of businessmen from a telephone – is that fishing times can be regulated to the weather, and spots that the trawlers cannot get into can be explored for bottom fishing.

An American angler, Ed Perry, his wife Marion and his son, who went north for four days with Laurie Ross on the *Joanne* came back from an expedition which reached North Cape with four marlin, a mako shark, 30 kingfish and a whole load of snapper. Ed had the whole lot processed and air freighted home – for meals, and fish stories to accompany them.

The occasional trip even as far as the Three Kings Islands – some 35 miles on from North Cape – is also proving rewarding. On board the Whangaroa boat *Blitzem*, skippered by Ian Heaven, Mrs Francine Swales in October, 1975, caught a 37.19 kg yellowtail, a world record for 24-kg line which still stands.

This was a bonus for the club's jubilee year, 1976, a year in which another notable catch was made nearer at home, this time by an angler who had never rod-fished at sea before, out with a

John Burgess (standing) and Kevin Gilligan with the 137.43 kg broadbill John caught from the Tuatahi, *a notable and unexpected catch on 31 January 1976 out from Whangaroa.*

skipper who had never boated a billfish. John Burgess, of Auckland, was the angler and Kevin Gilligan, the skipper, and *Tuatahi* the boat. On the morning of January 31, 1976, they trolled kahawai baits without success, until at 2.40 pm something struck. After briefly surfacing 15 minutes later, the fish took the 60-kg line so deep that the boat had to be kept almost over the fish to hold line on the reel, and had to be run full astern at times even to manage this. This worrying fight went on for four hours before, as the sea roughened and started to break into the cockpit, the fish was found to be no longer running in the same steady sweeps and John Burgess found it was possible to gain line. It took two hours longer to bring to the boat, the

fish surging the last 50 metres to the surface to lie spent. Two and a half hours after motoring back to harbour in darkness the angler and skipper found to their great surprise that they caused something of a sensation – they had a 137.44-kg broadbill, not only one of the most difficult billfish for the inexperienced to catch, but the first of these fish to be caught by a Whangaroa Club member for 47 years.

The club has a reputation, perhaps because it has been so isolated from the mainstream of tourist traffic, for its friendly informality and unorthodoxy. Thus it is not unexpected to find that one of the two awards of the Old Man and the Sea trophy (for most meritorious catch) to go to the club should be awarded to a 14-year-old boy, William Bannister.

The other Old Man and the Sea Award to go to the Whangaroa Club had been five years before, when Barney Williams of Whangaroa hooked a 165.11 mako on the North Ground, fishing with 37-kg line from his 4.8-metre runabout *Emma J.* which had a 15-hp motor. The fish struck only three metres from the boat. It jumped and thrashed making it difficult to handle from the small boat and it took nearly two hours to work inside Stephenson Island, three miles from the harbour entrance. Here Bingham Green, who was the other occupant of the runabout, said that the savagely fighting fish was almost impossible to hold from such a small boat. As it continued to try to run for the open sea, it was worked, with a motor much less powerful than the fish, slowly (over $2\frac{1}{2}$ hours) to the harbour entrance, then towed up the harbour, a further three miles.

The fighting fish are clearly outside the Whangaroa Club's door and always have been, but the club has had only a small, moving population to give it support, and is somewhat overshadowed by the nearby very successful fishing at the Bay of Islands. A long succession of presidents from the days of Stan Ellis have battled with the problems of the club, including the problem of just keeping it going: L. M. Lane,

Fourteen-year-old William Bannister (Weight 47 kg) is dwarfed by the 310.71 kg black marlin which won him the "Old Man and the Sea" award for 1967-68. He and his friend took the place of an angler who did not turn up and went out in his father's launch, Lady Jess. *His line screamed out on the Ruahine Reef; the big fish jumped and then drove steadily out to sea for four and a half hours, broaching eight times before the fight was over.*

At first the sun shone so warmly that the young angler had a bucket of water poured over him to cool him down; then the wind blew up and the sea became a mass of white horses on top of giant waves. Through it all he fought with a harness so big for him that it had to be packed with a cushion. He had a box put under his feet because from the chair he could not reach the deck.

Back on shore he celebrated with a glass of lemonade and went home, very tired, to dream.

Dr W. J. Edginton, K. D. Dunbar, A. Sanderson, H. J. Clow, F. Slater, E. Brown, A. Louden, T. Roberts, F. J. Webber, Larry Moselin, Dawson Murray, Keith Johnston, Pat Vincent, Jim Harvey and now Laurie Ross. His wife, Judy Ross, the immediate past secretary, was one of the most successful of a long line of administrators of club affairs.

The most successful boats chartered out from the base were *Manaaki* and *Lone Star*, and there have been other well known names such as Fred Wilkins' *Sou'East*, which he brought up from its triumphs at Mayor Island and which is now based at Tutukaka. Harry Bannister's *Lady Jess*, Joe Miller's *Zephyr* and W. White's *Hazel* also fished with distinction. But there have never been as many as half a dozen boats for charter at Whangaroa, more often one or two, sometimes none – with occasionally one chartering for the club from Mangonui.

Currently two charter launches cater for anglers at Whangaroa, both of them operating in association with other bases. Laurie Ross now skippers *Maraqueta*, which works from both Whangaroa and the Bay of Islands, and Sid Gammon usually brings *Carousel* up from Tauranga for the late summer.

No mention of celebrated boats is complete without reference to the most unorthodox and one of the most successful of all, the *Waiataiti*, which won the big prize in the national contest of 1976–77 in competition with many sleek, speedy and often luxurious rivals. The *Waiataiti*, owned by Pat Vincent, the manager of a coastal farm at Mahinepua Peninsula, is a sheep barge about 7 metres long which has a fighting chair mounted above one of the rear pens. It has a speed of only about 6 knots forward and a wind-assisted reverse, which make the playing of double strikes – such as the one which helped it to win a national contest – a matter of agility between the anglers rather than adroitness in launchmanship. Its farm base is close to the Cavalli Islands and it is as familiar a sight on those grounds as any of its luxury rivals.

Whangaroa's tradition for unorthodox angling goes further even than this. The harbour is a base for commercial fishing as well as game fishing, particularly for commercial craft which work at Three Kings Islands and off the West Coast around the northern tip of New Zealand. Some of the commercial fishermen have joined the game fish club and troll lures from outriggers, orthodox and improvised, on their long hauls north. Laurie Ross tells how one such fisherman, while going up to Three Kings with a load of crayfish pots stacked high all over the boat up to the level of his deckhouse, was seen sitting right on top of the pile of pots playing a big mako, which he lost.

With all the successes of the other fishing grounds, the Bay of Islands remains not only the prestige big game fish area of New Zealand but, for the striped marlin which is the special gift of the sea to this part of the world, the most prolific.

Big game catches did not start in the Bay of Islands with Zane Grey, however much he may be regarded as the patron saint of Bay of Islands fishing. The bay was the scene of much good fishing well before he came here, encouraged by C. Alma Baker, a New Zealander who had amassed wealth in the Malay States and who remained dedicated to the interests of his own country, and who had interested not only Grey in coming but the Government in giving every assistance. Baker was a leading fisherman and designer of fishing gear himself and is honoured in a display in the Bay of Islands clubhouse.

The earlier European records of the Bay of Islands area emphasise the standards of the fish and fishing already there. When Captain Cook visited the area in November, 1769, he was impressed by, among other things, the huge nets of the Maoris in the bay. The Cavalli Islands were named by Cook because of the fish – perhaps the trevally, natural local schooling food of marlin – which were sold to his ship from canoes which went out to meet it.

The Bay of Islands was later to become the cradle of the new European settlement in New Zealand – and the present Russell (then Kororareka) was the homing ground of the rough sealers and whalers of the southern seas. It provided the first hostelries and stores, is still the site of the oldest Anglican church and the oldest Catholic mission building in the country. When the first seat of government moved from the Bay of Islands and the first newspapers and the first Anglican Bishop went south also, the town remained and the bay waited for its next claim to fame as an international game fishing centre – for the fishing, which had helped to sustain a large Maori population around the deeply embayed shores and on the many islands throughout the bay, continued to be good.

Long before organised angling became the rule around the rest of the coast, the Bay of Islands had its kingfish club (in about 1910) and it was one of its club members, Major A. D. Campbell, who caught the first striped marlin there in February, 1915, almost simultaneously with the boating of the second by F. P. Andrews (who was later a life member of the game fish club). The fishing gear then was only half as good as the tackle which Jim Whitelaw remembers from the late 1920s, and that was only half as good as it is today. Some idea of what the earlier game fisherman used is given in the first existing record of the Kingfish Club, its annual report of 1920 which sets out the essential gear as "One stout rod . . . the best is a tanekaha, made out of sapling: one seven inch Reliable or Nottingham reel, with ratchet and suitable brake viz, a leather strap attached to reel beneath rod; one 30 thread kingfish line of 200 yards or 300 yards; six spring wire or phosphor bronze traces; six No 9 Kingfish treble hooks, for mako a 12 ft piano wire or twisted steel wire is necessary; six heavy brass box swivels, two Moir Cartman kingfish spinners; one leather rod butt holder, one leather shoulder strap to attach to rod; one sheath knife."

Before Zane Grey appeared on the scene, the Bay of Islands had already been "found" by many overseas sportsmen. In the first season that Grey and his party fished there 20 launches were chartering for game fishermen, and Grey shared the grounds with 46 other successful overseas anglers – from England, Ireland, United States, Rhodesia, Malay States and Australia – and about the same number of New Zealanders. Some of these anglers were already old timers on the grounds. However, Jim Whitelaw credits Zane Grey with changing the whole picture of the sport with his new gear and new ideas, and ending a lot of the loss of fish due to tackle being inadequate.

Grey quarrelled with the New Zealand habit of drifting for fish instead of trolling; with using a "barbarous" triple hook instead of a single one; with the old-fashioned reels they used and with the custom of placing the reel below instead of on top of the rod. "It is impossible to fight a great game fish with reels and guides underneath the rod," he said. "I mean *stop* him and *fight* him. In order to do that an angler must have a short strong rod and a heavy reel with adequate drag and powerful line. Reel and guides must be on top because if they are not the angler cannot brace his feet on the boat and pull with all his might."

Grey showed what he meant in boating a world record striped marlin of 204.12 kg ("bronze-backed, silver bellied, wide and deep and long, with vivid purple bands") when fishing on an excursion south to the Poor Knights Islands. Just before, he had lost, after an hour's fight, what he described as the largest striped marlin he had ever seen and one which almost dragged him over the gunwale.

Laurie Mitchell used the same technique in catching the black marlin which held the world record for 26 years, and for more than 50 years the New Zealand record, while fishing off the Taheke Reef near the Cavalli Islands. It was a fight which lasted four hours against a fish that felt as "solid as the Rock of Gibraltar" and took the launch 10 miles out to sea. The old battle scarred marlin half flooded the boat with its struggles at the end, when three men had to lie down in the cockpit to hold it. During the fight another black marlin, fully as large as the other one, charged past, perhaps its mate and perhaps trying to help it free.

Even without counting the 107 fish caught by Grey and Mitchell on that first visit, the 1925–26 season was the best ever at the Bay of Islands and the best for a further 10 years, so the time of the visit which produced the *Tales of an Angler's Eldorado*, which placed the Bay of Islands on a world fishing pedestal, was well timed.

Grey returned twice more to New Zealand fishing waters to fish and in particular to confirm what he had at first doubted, the place of the mako as a premier game fish. Writing in the *New Zealand Herald* in March, 1926 he said: "I have caught 10 mako to date and the Captain (Mitchell) about the same number. Up to 400 lb the fish is immature and sometime yielding. The large mako are torpedoes. Captain Mitchell hooked one yesterday we estimated to weigh 1200 lb. It leaped prodigiously and made incredible runs, finally biting the leader through. This mako was truly terrific – the most wonderful fish either of us ever saw on a line."

And with a further tribute to the black marlin – "three outwitted me and escaped me", while the fourth "punished me severely" though he captured it – he pronounced the New Zealand waters "the most remarkable in the Seven Seas for magnificent game fish". Not many areas could continue to live up to that sort of reputation over half a century, but year in and year out, through lean times in fish numbers and through good, the Bay of Islands has continued to provide consistent big game fishing of the highest class, with a stream of world records which continues to run today.

There have been some good women anglers fishing out of the Bay of Islands, including Mrs Eileen Brownson of Auckland who caught a 383.74-kg black marlin in 1950, still the New Zealand record, and the second longest surviving record on the books. She later also caught out of

100

Another recent Bay of Islands world record: Mrs Lola Fuller with her 174.63 kg mako caught on 23 March 1980 on 15 kg breaking strain line from Lucky Strike. Graeme Townsend.

Whangaroa a world record 389.18-kg mako – another which still stands as a New Zealand record. She was praised by Les Blomfield, with whom she once landed four marlin before lunch, as knowing "more about catching fish than most men will ever know".

Mrs Kathleen Hassall of the Otehei Bay Fishing Lodge, which grew on the site of Zane Grey's camp, had three world records, her biggest a black marlin of 246.07 kg caught in 1952 on a 37-kg line. And more recently Miss Kura Beale has made many notable catches of marlin, yellowfin tuna and yellowtail, and held several world records, one of which was for a yellowtail of 36.74 kg on a 37-kg line.

An angler whom Jim Whitelaw, when on the *Pirate*, had cause to remember was A. G. C. Glassell who used to spend $1000 to freight his gear out from Texas and had his own photographer who was kept standing on top of the boat all day so that no picture opportunity would be missed, rain or fine, and who was roped to the mast if the sea got rough. On one occasion it is recorded that when Glassell caught a fine striped marlin the photographer had the shot developed, printed and hanging up in the cabin of the *Pirate* within 10 minutes.

Glassell once fished for 28 days on end with Jim Whitelaw trying for a black marlin. "We would start from the Sisters in the morning," says Jim, "go around Piercy Island, back to Bird Rock and back to the Sisters; and then around again, all day long for four solid weeks." On the 28th day Glassell hooked a black of about 180 kg to 220 kg but lost it when he braked too hard, so Jim (with another booking coming up) passed him on to Leon Warne with whom he managed at last to fulfil his ambition.

One of the earliest records set in the Bay of Islands still stands – it is for a 305.27-kg broadbill swordfish caught by Huntingdon White-Wickham who used to book a cabin for the season in Deep Water Cove, the first outer fishing base in the bay, and one only gradually supplanted when Zane Grey went off to establish his own base at Otehei Bay on Urupukapuka Island. Fishing from Harold Vipond's *Ozone*, he caught another world record, in 1931, a mako weighing 361.97 kg, which was not beaten until, 12 years later, B. H. D. Ross caught his 453.6-kg monster off Mayor Island.

The organisation of fishing in the Bay of Islands has run a more even course than in most of the other fishing centres – it managed to survive through the war years when other clubs went into recess, sometimes for a good deal longer than the war lasted. Although only four fish, three striped marlin and a mako were caught in 1941–42 in the depths of the war, the club ticked over, and even in the Depression years the club maintained its reputation for record fish. After the first Kingfish Club had lost some initial momentum, it was restored in 1920 and, with marlin and sharks the more exciting game by now, changed its name to the Bay of Islands Swordfish and Mako Shark Club in 1924 – the "mako" part of the name being dropped later.

Present membership is about 600, and last year the club offered seven tournaments at intervals through the year as well as several long-running contests.

But the real test which the Bay of Islands has continued to meet has been in the catches made, switching species when some were scarce. From the day the Bay of Islands Swordfish Club was formed from the Kingfish Club in 1924 until the end of the 1979–80 season, 16,877 game fish had been weighed in with the club at its stations, originally including Deep Water Cove and later Otehei Bay but now at Russell and Paihia only. More than half of these fish were striped marlin, with catches fluctuating to a peak year of 536 in 1948–49, then slowly falling away to 36 in 1969–70 and then coming back up again to 387 in 1979–80.

The first blue marlin caught (or identified) in New Zealand waters was caught off the Ninepin by Des White from the launch *Lorna Doone* in February 1952. It weighed 171.46 kg and was not considered of sufficient importance for the club's booklet, but interest grew in this vigorous fighting fish as more and more were caught – no fewer than 10 in the 1962–63 season, when the biggest was a national record of 343.83 kg for Bruce Ashley and the average was 231.33 kg. The weights were moving up and expectations that even bigger blues were around were fulfilled in 1968 with R. Greig's 461.31-kg fish – the biggest billfish ever caught in New Zealand waters.

The most consistent, although usually lower catches, have been of mako sharks, of which 3,177 have been caught since 1924–5, with the figures of the last few years averaging nearly 80 in a season (December through to May). A total of

475 black marlin is spread over this same period but blue marlin, which may not have been recognised as such, are in the record book only in the last 30 years – a total of 139. The best years of yellowfin tuna, where more than 100 were caught, were in the mid 1960s; and of the yellowtail, in the decade up to 1978. These were years when marlin catches were down and the catches reflected the versatility of the fishing available – the giant yellowtail are always about, and the yellowfin tuna can be counted on, as pelagic fish, to come back, overseas fishing fleets permitting.

Today the fishing for the big game species starts usually on a line just outside the mouth of the bay, to the seaward of both the Ninepin and Red Head. Gone are the days when all the marlin one wanted could be picked up off Bird Rock and Piercy Island. Gone, too, are the days when big blacks could be caught even further inside the bay.

Mervyn Arlidge had his best ever catch in about 40 years as a skipper around about Red Head – a black marlin of about 400 kg – but that was in the days when between Piercy and Bird Rock occasionally half a dozen boats drifting all got a fish on at the same time. There would be marlin jumping all over the place, with the anglers not knowing which fish was theirs. No wonder not all the fish were caught, particularly when there was the anxiety, that trolling boats of today do not have, of hoping the engine would start when a strike came. The float would give a jerk, and under the water it would go. Before anything could be done, the fish would shoot up on the other side of the still stationary boat; and someone would have to run around the boat with the rod, passing it around the stays to the mast, before the launchman dared to start the motor.

But while inside the bay offers few big fish today, especially with the diminution in the schools of kahawai and trevally which used to entice and keep them in close, outside the bay the fishing is as good as it ever was. Admittedly up

A record since broken: Phillip Bryers with his 167.83 kg striped marlin caught on a 24 kg line from the Lady Doreen *out of the Bay of Islands in 1979. Klaus Rober, of Tahiti, took the record the following year.* Graham Townsend.

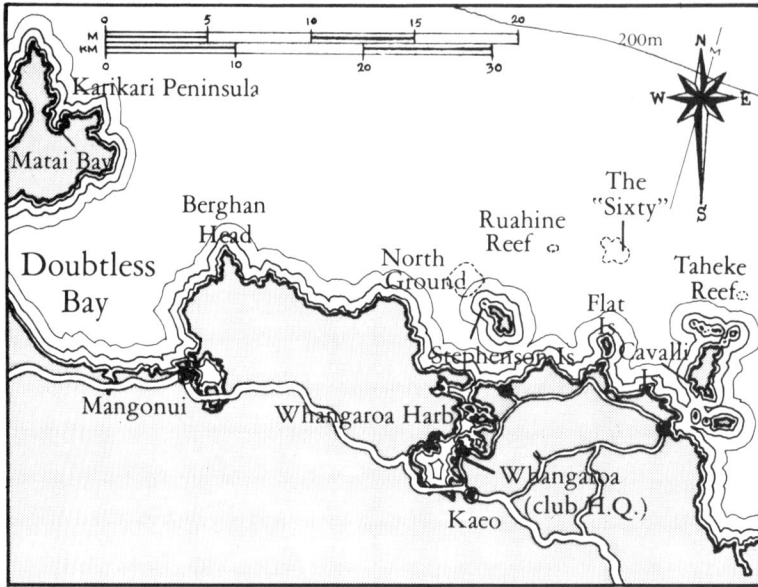

Map 1 *The fishing waters of the Whangaroa Big Gamefish Club.*

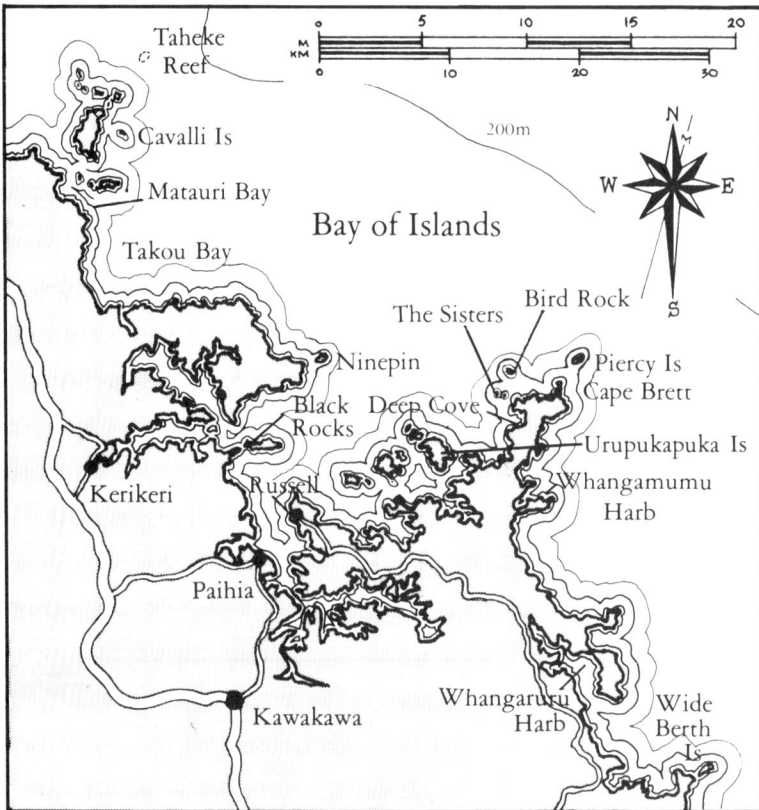

Map 2 *The main fishing waters of the Bay of Islands Swordfish Club.*

to 40 boats now fish where there were in the old days a maximum of ten but an average of two good marlin a day over a six-month season is very good fishing. The tournaments help the numbers by drawing in more boats and anglers for a period and in the 1979–80 season the Air New Zealand International Bay of Islands billfish tournament saw 69 striped marlin and 6 makos caught between 51 different anglers and 26 teams in five days – including a new record 183-kg striped marlin on 24-kg line boated by Klaus Rober of the Moana Club de Huahine, Tahiti. The fishing outside the bay on these occasions ranges up and down the coast for an easy run of about two hours each way – past the Ninepin to the north east across Takau Bay (which often produces a good fish) to premium waters to seaward of the Cavalli Islands, where lies the Taheke Reef, the happy hunting ground for so many anglers seeking the really big ones.

It was off the Cavalli Islands that Mrs Margaret Williams caught her 181.89-kg world record striped marlin on 24-kg line off the *Freelance* in 1970, and here in 1977 that Phillip Bryers caught two world record marlin – one in 1967, a 167.83-kg world record for the 24-kg line class (since beaten by Klaus Rober), and the other his 189.37 kg on 37 kg an all tackle world record, which still stands.

Fishing from the Bay of Islands usually does not end at the Cavallis, although this is the limit of the easy one-day fishing outing, because there is often a "hot spot" for big fish between the Cavalli Islands and the Ruahine Reef and the outer Ruahine grounds, which lie almost directly out from the entrance to Whangaroa Harbour, past Stephenson Island which also has its good north ground.

South of Cape Brett the fishing is not usually as plentiful although good catches have been made around Cape Brett, and Tutukaka fishermen often find it worthwhile to come up past the Wide Berth Islands to these home waters of the Bay of Islands Club.

The very size of the Bay of Islands – it is 10 miles out from Russell to the outer limits of the bay – encouraged fishermen in the earlier days of slower boats (and when even then, with boat charter rates of £6 to £7 a day, petrol price was a major cost factor) to look for bases nearer to the fishing grounds. The most popular of them was Deep Water Cove, only a few minutes from the fishing grounds then centred on the area between The Twins or Motutara, Bird Rock or Mahenotapuku, and Piercy Island or Motukokako. In the cove there were cottages for anglers and good sheltered anchorage except in strong westerlies. But after Zane Grey opted for his own base in Otehei Bay, Urupukapuka Island, his devotees moved in after him to establish the Zane Grey Sporting Club there. It was later developed into Otehei Lodge, a well-appointed fisherman's hotel, but the central building was burned down a few years ago leaving the outer bay without special accommodation for anglers. However, Russell and Paihia are now among the best areas in the country for tourist accommodation, and the range and speed of the modern launches (which have continued to improve since the diesel engine first made it possible to venture further out from the bay and troll for less than the cost that it used to take to drift) makes the journey out to fish from the head of the bay not as time-consuming as it once was.

The fishing now also tends to be further out and closer to the 200-metre deep line where it runs about 10 miles further out to sea, or even deeper for such fish as blue marlin or maybe the elusive dolphin fish. The blue water here in summer usually comes in close to the mouth of the bay – and has been known to come well into it almost to Black Rocks – and that, as all fishermen know, is striped marlin water supreme.

The charter launch skippers of the Bay of Islands area have their own association handling bookings for a fleet of fifteen craft, all with flying bridges, refrigerators, and comfortable to live aboard as well as efficient to fish from. Standard day charters are from 8 am to 5.30 pm and the launches also cater for live-aboard cruises, bookings for which make up about half of their time at sea. These boats and their cheerful skippers are listed in the appendix. Most of them are relatively new but old fishing boats – like old soldiers – seem never to die.

Several of the veteran boats of the game fishing fleet are still in the bay, although some have been renamed and most partly rebuilt. They include Francis Arlidge's *Alma G*, and Mervyn Arlidge's *Alma G II* (at first called *Zane Grey* when that angler was chartering it, but both eventually sharing the name given for a young cousin of the Arlidge's, Alma Green); the *Manaaki* and *Otehei* (the *Otehei* is now fully restored and back for charter) built for Randall Elliott; Les Blomfield's *Avalon* (he won the Old Man of the Sea Trophy in 1974 after catching at the age of 78 an 81-kg striped marlin, after 55 years association with game fishing in the course of which he boated about 1000 marlin); and Jim Whitelaw's *Pirate* which he took over from Otto Sommer after the Second World War.

While nearly all these boats have by now been retired from chartering, a much more recent and also famous boat the *Lady Doreen* is going strong. Now with Bruce Smith as skipper, the *Lady Doreen* was originally built and for a long time run by Snooks Fuller. A member of the long-established boating company in the bay, he designed the launch on the back of his exercise

books while at school and helped build it with his father and Wally and Bert Deeming at the age of 18. The boat with its four chairs has many good fish to its credit. Since he sold it six or seven years ago Snooks Fuller has bought another boat, the *Lucky Strike*, for himself, and has been using its tuna tower to do photography of game fishing while his wife Lola tags fish and gets women's records. One of these world record fish, a striped marlin of 136.53 kg on 15-kg line, was caught on a live bait with a nylon trace well outside the line between Karikari Peninsula and the Cavalli Islands when the *Lucky Strike* was on the way back from a trip to North Cape. Hooked in the corner of the mouth, the fish jumped at first and then went deep. When boated it looked a good but not an exceptional fish, and it was put on the back of the boat. There it remained for two-and-a-half days, while two other marlin were caught and put on the boat and two marlin and a mako were tagged and released. Only when it was weighed in at Paihia was it realised it was a record fish.

Since then Mrs Fuller has caught a world record mako of 174.63 kg on 15-kg line off the Cavalli Islands – a fish that jumped at the bait, came at first easily to the boat but was not subdued for an hour and a half.

Mrs Fuller also holds New Zealand 24-kg line records for black marlin (159.66 kg) and blue marlin (160.11 kg).

CHAPTER TEN

Tutukaka to The Barrier

At Tutukaka, a picturesque bay further down the Northland coast, a big game fishing base has been established at the point of greatest advantage. Its fishing area starts within minutes of leaving the clubhouse and extends into very special waters, for here the East Auckland Current swings directly on to the Poor Knights Islands, 14 miles off the coast, giving this group a unique marine environment.

The waters around the islands have recently been given a special protective status as a marine park, but this does not affect the big game fishing. None of the waters now protected completely have been fished for years by game fishing launches except perhaps for bait — which can now be sought elsewhere — and game fishermen are among those who support the protection given to the islands' marine environment.

The Whangarei Deep Sea Anglers Club did not always, as its name suggests, have its headquarters at Tutukaka. The club was formed in the neighbouring city, 28 kilometres away by road, on August 1, 1944. It reflected an enthusiasm which was growing for fishing, not around the Poor Knights at that stage, but at the Hen and Chickens, another island group just to

the east of the entrance to the Whangarei Harbour, and, outside them, the Mokohinau Islands. Prominent among the early anglers were Les Waldron and Arthur Byles, who put into practice out of Whangarei the fishing methods established in the Bay of Islands. The local club was established at a meeting held on August 1, 1944, with Les Waldron the first president and the Hon A. J. Murdock, M.P. as patron.

For several years the club rarely fished further afield on its one-day excursions than the Hen and Chicken Islands, about an hour's run from the harbour, although several groups of launches made longer forays down to Great Barrier Island. On one of these trips the new club president raised 16 marlin in two hours between the Hen and Chicken Islands and the Mokohinau Islands, but they were not really interested in bait and he hooked only one and then lost it. Dr Harold Pettit in the meantime proved that there were good fish about which would bite by landing for the club a black marlin of 347 kg.

The club consolidated at Whangarei for about six years, in the course of time establishing a headquarters at the Parua Bay Hotel, about halfway out to the harbour entrance and building a wharf there with the aid of members' finance and labour. When the club established a weigh station Percy Wilson, the hotel proprietor, became the weighmaster and he also had a radio listening set installed in the bar so he could hear when a fish was due in. He was later accorded life membership for his services. The club had a second weigh station at Urquhart Bay, just inside Whangarei Heads. With the purchase of a set of good deep sea gear, a roster was arranged of private launches to take out fishing parties. The club started off each season with a one-day fishing contest.

At this stage the club was as concerned with snapper fishing as it was with game fish, and it was not long before different needs drew the two interests apart. The Hen and Chickens rarely provided exceptional game fishing, and Arthur Byles, among others, cruised about in his launch *Ranoni* for new grounds to the north of the harbour entrance.

Some success at Whangaruru (three marlin before lunch), and the Poor Knights brought a reminder that the coastline handy to these grounds offered an alternative base at Tutukaka, where there had been an earlier club. The Tutukaka Deep Sea Fishing Club had made some worthwhile catches from its formation in 1936 to its close-down at the start of the Second World War. (Dick MacKenzie who was to be weighmaster for the Whangarei Club at Tutukaka and later a life member, had run the only charter boat there, the *Zita*, from the Tutukaka guest house.)

As a first move, the Whangarei Club established a weighing station at Podjursky Bay at Tutukaka, and in 1952–53 Arthur Byles fished from there. His fishing companion, Cecil Hewlett, brought in the first marlin the club weighed at Tutukaka, a striped marlin of about 118 kg. Les Waldron also began fishing out of Tutukaka the following year and little by little all the Whangarei deep sea anglers followed suit. The break between the two groups of Whangarei anglers became official in 1955. Tutukaka became the Whangarei Deep Sea Anglers Club base, and

the only fishing contact maintained with the city was a weighing station there for launches returning home after the fishing season. Ivon Watkins was president and Rob Dinsdale secretary of the new independent club, R. S. (Dick) MacKenzie became weighmaster and the guest house of the Going family housed the club's radio station.

In 1954 the wharf and all facilities were moved from Podjursky Bay to the present location and a weigh station was established at Whangaruru, with Skip Ewan weighmaster. From an initial membership of about 50 – with a new jetty and small clubhouse at the new base, and with one charter boat, the *Rongotai* – the club grew rapidly in strength. When the first year's catch of 28 fish rose to 41 in the second year the membership rose to 300. In no time the small clubrooms became so crowded that a member commented that it was impossible not to meet everyone else in the club.

All it needed was tradition to match the older fishing venues to the north, and the club soon set about establishing that. Perhaps the starting point occurred on January 17, 1957.

On that day a new twin-screw, four-chair charter fishing launch the *Kitty Vane*, which was built for Hugh Going in a shed behind the guest house, brought in a broadbill which established a notable series of firsts. Pride of place in the present clubrooms is still given to a cast of the 128.36-kg fish. It was the first billfish caught from what was to become a celebrated boat, the first game fish caught by the angler Eric Brown, who was out deep-sea fishing for the first time. It was the first billfish caught by the club for the season and its first broadbill ever.

Caught on the drift off the North Reef of the Poor Knights, it was one of a double strike, and the second fish, although not seen, was believed by those aboard to have been another broadbill. The fish boated was only the third broadbill to be caught in New Zealand waters since 1928.

In the following season, fish caught by the club rose to 101 (76 of them to the *Kitty Vane*)

Tutukaka, home of the Whangarei Deep Sea Anglers Club (clubhouse, centre foreground), looking out over the club's southern waters, Whites Aviation.

and membership to 500. The club blossomed as the fish continued to come in – 90 in the following season; 181 in the next; then 213, and, after a poor season for marlin (but yielding two big blacks, one of them of 307 kg, caught by another Eric Brown, which jumped 23 times and took nearly 6 hours to boat), the fish numbers were back up to 240. Membership soared to 1,500 with increasing catches in 1960–61. When the inevitable lull in fishing occurred the club, having little else to offer, lost membership. It took up the challenge to provide a base second to none in all respects.

The Northland Harbour Board dredged the harbour to reclaim two sections of the foreshore along with the building of a new breakwater running into the harbour from what was known as Bell Rock. Incorporated in this programme was the installation of two floating pontoons, a floating marina and pile moorings for the launches. With the inclusion of a boat ramp for trailer boats, weighing and refuelling facilities, Tutukaka is now the envy of other game fishing clubs for its excellent facilities and sheltered harbour. The centre-piece is its new clubhouse, adjacent to the end of a new jetty, where fishing launches can come right up under the clubhouse windows. With a membership of about 1,600 well catered for, and fishing itself on the up-and-up again, the Whangarei Club's base reflects many people's idea of what good sport-fishing is all about.

The customary fishing grounds of the club are set – like those of the other clubs on the coast –

Some of the 18 striped marlin and two mako sharks which were weighed in at Tutukaka on 20 March 1975, from a "hot spot" between the Sugar Loaf and the Hen and Chickens.

by the distance a boat can comfortably cover to provide four or five hours of concentrated fishing before needing to turn back to reach base by the end of the day. For Tutukaka these limits are roughly the Wide Berth Islands to the north, the Taiharuru Reef (better known for yellowtail than for marlin) in the south, and the Poor Knights Islands (and a few miles beyond them on good days) to the north-east. The Hen and Chicken Islands are just too far off for day-fishing and are rarely patronised (probably much too rarely) except by passing boats.

A fishing trip can always be stretched from anchorage to anchorage along the New Zealand coast, and there are several safe stopping places to the north of Tutukaka to over-night – at Mimiwhangata, in Whangaruru Harbour and off the old whaling station in Whangamumu – from which one can fish the following day up to Cape Brett and around into the Bay of Islands. Offshore the picture is not so good. The Poor Knights offer an uneasy anchorage because of the sheer coastlines and the very deep water. A night spent in the shelter of one of the big caverns there is too eerie an experience for most.

However, for good fishing it is not always necessary to go far from Tutukaka's small, safe, all-weather harbour. Good fish have been hooked right at the harbour entrance, one by a small boat owner who was coming in to port with his baits still out because it was too wobbly to bring them in – but not so wobbly that he could not go out again with the strike to bring his fish aboard.

Harvey Franks, who skippers *Lady Margaret*, one of the eight surveyed charter boats at Tutukaka (the others are *Kitty Vane, Sou' East, Norseman, Lady Jess, Marco Polo, Matira* and *Waimana*) hooked the biggest fish he has ever boated a quarter of a mile from the harbour entrance, also on his way home. His boat was then the *Ruth*, and the fish a 342-kg black marlin. In good years marlin can be seen finning near the reef just outside the harbour where the launchmen catch much of their bait. A boat coming in early once struck a school of marlin about half a mile off the entrance, getting seven strikes and catching one fish.

Many boats, therefore, setting off for the more proven grounds further out, put out baits, or at least lures, as soon as they clear harbour. Of the many favoured fishing areas further out, the first reached is the Middle Ground or the Rip about 2 miles straight out from the harbour, where a series of strong coastal currents seem to carry fish with them; the Hot Spot about five miles south-east toward Taiharuru Reef; the Sugar Loaf about 8 miles straight out to the east from base; and the Pinnacles, one mile further on to the north-west. The Sugar Loaf and Pinnacles are bare rocks housing a large colony of gannets, but the Sugar Loaf rises sheer from about 100 metres deep and the Pinnacles lead on to broken ground suggestive of lurking black marlin.

The Poor Knights Islands themselves, about 14 miles out, are best fished beyond their northern tip where the warm current wells up from the 200-metre line and many good fish have been taken there. Named in a whimsical mood by Captain Cook, the Poor Knights are a small group of very steep rocky islands of a total area of about 195 ha. They are penetrated by caves, tunnels and natural arches, some of them navigable, often breathtaking in wild beauty. Birdsong drifts down from the top of the cliffs, where the land is rich in vegetation and relatively undisturbed forest. Below the boat, the water is hundreds of feet deep and teems with reef and coral dwelling fish, and rare species brought in by the warm current which strikes directly on to these islands.

Reserves and sanctuaries within the Hauraki Gulf Maritime Park, the islands are the home of the Poor Knights Lily (*Xeronema callistemon*), are the only known nesting place of Buller's shearwater, and carry a population of the protected tuatara lizard. Apart from the strict protection given to the islands and restrictions on landing there, the waters around them have also been given marine reserve status. Big game fishing trips from Tutukaka used to include an almost obligatory scenic cruise along the coasts of the Poor Knights, and it is no less worthwhile today. Game fish were earlier found close to the islands, but the need to search for them these days takes charter boats straight to the North Reef and beyond. The main visitors to the island waters these days are the scuba divers who find there an underwater paradise for observation and photography.

There was once a Maori population of several hundred on the Poor Knights but they were attacked and almost exterminated by a raiding party from the mainland when their chief Tatua was away with most of his warriors.

Gone, too, are most of the schools of kahawai and trevally which used to cover wide areas and always brought hope that a bait trolled through them might yield a bigger fish feeding beneath. Intense commercial fishing close to the coast is blamed for this disappearance. But one may still see dense balls of smaller fish herded together so tightly by predators that the top fish are lifted above the surface, and occasionally see a striped marlin turn to chase, skittering across the surface, an ocean piper making an escape dash. The agility of the huge fish, twisting and turning, makes this one of the most remarkable sights of the sea.

Some fish are caught out from Tutukaka on the drift, but none of the islands offer enough shelter to make drifting here comfortable for the average angler on the average day, so most launches still tend to troll – usually with two baited lines well back on outriggers with two shorter lines in between, one at least of them carrying a tuna lure.

If the fish seem harder to get, it may be because more people are trying to catch them. John Going, skipper of the *Kitty Vane* since 1971, says he hardly goes a day without seeing a game fish in the main part of the season – from January until early May – although the season seems to be getting later and he sees more marlin in April than he does in February or March. He recalls a recent day when he approached what he thought was a school of porpoises to find that it was a school of striped marlin, leaping and feeding on the surface, and another day when he saw "nothing but marlin" down near the Hen and Chickens over an area about twice the size of the surface of the Tutukaka Harbour.

"To see all those tails going through the water was unbelievable," he says. "I never thought I would see such a thing." As usual, while on the surface they would not bite, but later eight out of the nine boats which came to the area were playing fish. Perhaps this phenomenon of schooling marlin comes before a storm. Other evidence suggests this, and a howling south-easterly came up shortly afterwards.

Tutukaka also knew another day when striped marlin were not only around in numbers but were taking baits. It was one of the working-bee days for members on the new Tutukaka clubhouse. The charter boats were already out past the Poor Knights when some of the members, finishing their labours at lunchtime, went off down the coast in their boats in the afternoon to try their luck. Their cries of success across the R/T brought the charter boats pell mell in from the blue water to join them in a bonanza of 18 marlin only 5 miles from base.

The current and previous world all tackle records for thresher sharks – among the few fish for which New Zealand holds this honour – both have been won from Tutukaka. Mrs Dianne North, of Whangarei, the current holder, is the

first to admit that there is a lot of luck in big game fishing since the thresher shark she caught off Tutukaka on February 8 weighed in at 363 kg, the only all tackle record for a big game fish (excluding bonito and skipjack) held by a woman at the time.

Dianne's only previous success in game fishing was a 19 kg yellowtail caught out from Whangaroa, although she had watched and waited while other game fish were played and boated. So when something took a bait from Garth Marsland's launch *Maestro* during a ladies weekend tournament run by the Whangarei club, and it was her turn with the rod, she had a big fish on for the first time.

The fish immediately went deep, for the first of several times; and it took all the angler's strength, applied with the advice of experienced anglers aboard, to bring it alongside 3¾ hours later. Dianne recalls not only how cramped her hands became, but also seeing the drum of the spool through the last turns of the line on it, so much did the fish take out.

The *Maestro* had gone out from Whangaruru on the morning of the catch and the fish was struck (on a trolled kahawai bait on a 37-kg line) about two miles north of the Poor Knights Islands. The fish ran toward the land and was boated near Matapouri after being fought for about 14 miles. The previous all-tackle world record, also caught on a 37-kg line, was held by Brian Galvin, with a 335.2-kg thresher caught on February 17, 1975, from John Going's *Kitty Vane*.

In keeping with its fruitful and spectacular fishing area, the Tutukaka club fittingly leads in the field with successful nominees for the Old Man and the Sea trophy, awarded each year since 1959 for the season's most meritorious catch. It is an award interesting to all for the unusual feats that it rewards.

The first winner of the trophy, J. R. Price was from the Whangarei Club (he won it for his catch – a 109.77-kg mako shark on 24-kg line on March 3, 1959 – the result of a 3¼ hour fight),

Jan Going with her 224.50 kg mako – a world, New Zealand and Whangarei club record catch – taken from John Going's Kitty Vane.

Fred Bogun of Mt Maunganui with a 304.37 kg thresher shark he caught off Mayor Island.

'A big bluefin tuna caught from a fishing trawler off the West Coast of the South Island by Roy Woolley of Christchurch'

Rita Hague admires a New Zealand record yellowfin of 75.50 kg. The angler, W. A. Cawthorn, used 24 kg tackle fishing from Pearly Shells. D. Hague.

and so was the second, although Mrs Dorothy Martin of Hawaii, was actually fishing for her home country at the time. Fishing with her husband, Roger, in the world contest of 1960 out of Tutukaka, she hooked, played for two tense hours and finally boated a 139.25-kg striped marlin on light 24-kg line.

They were on their way out from Tutukaka in the *Kitty Vane*, then owned by Hugh Going, trolling tuna lures on the way to the Poor Knights. One tuna was caught and three lost before a marlin took a spirited interest in one of the lures. At its third lunge at the lure, the marlin got the small hook jammed around its bill. Unhurt but annoyed, the marlin roared about trying to shake off the hook, causing the rod bucket to break and threatening the line at every moment. Only in the lee of the Poor Knights would it be finally brought to gaff.

Alec Stevenson, of Auckland, won his award for determination too. A paraplegic and double amputee he had gone out from Tutukaka year after year in the *Ruth* and then the *Lady Margaret* after getting the fishing bug in 1960 when he saw his brother-in-law bring in a mako. After nine years he brought in a blue shark, but it was not rated as game fish then and, in any case, Alec wanted a marlin.

His first real game fish came after 15 summers – an 18-kg yellowtail caught in 1975. A 47-kg mako followed the year later but not until January 1977, and on his birthday, did he catch off Whangaroa, his first marlin. This was not the fish that won him his trophy, however. He had to perform a much more difficult task for that, seated in his wheelchair, which was fitted with a socket in front for the butt of his rod, and which, when he got a fish on, had to be lashed to the side of the boat to prevent it from being dragged around the cockpit.

In home waters again, 5 miles outside the Pinnacles, on February 19, 1977, he hooked another striped marlin of 126.32 kg this time. In the fight that followed, the trace wrapped around its tail. It dived to the bottom and died. Only

someone who has fished for 17 years for a second marlin will understand his determination to have it up. In a lumpy sea – that did not worry him, he says, the spray helped to cool him down – he heaved with his arms and fingers alone, without any of the leverage an angler usually gets from his legs, for an hour and 10 minutes, inch by inch, to bring the marlin to the boat. Since then Alec Stevenson has caught another striped marlin, and his 182-kg black marlin caught in the 1980 national championships was the heaviest for his club that year, but the award winner was his hardest fish.

Two of the other Old Man and The Sea trophies which have gone to the Tutukaka Club illustrate how fishing families contribute to clubs.

Laurie Going, then aged 82 and the club's active weighmaster won the award in 1975 for his skill and endurance in successfully boating a 167.07 kg striped marlin from *Hooker* – a new Tutukaka boat launched that season by Hugh Going. The veteran not only fought the fish, he insisted in helping to boat and tail rope it.

And on December 22, 1979, his grand-daughter Jan made a catch which won her the 1980 award. It was a day when the family could go fishing, for there were no bookings for her father's charter boat, the *Kitty Vane*. They had trolled out past the Poor Knights; the only incident coming when one of a school of big manta rays was foul hooked, and took an hour to bring in so that the skin could be slit and the hook freed. The party watched the huge fish, three metres or more across the fins, skip away across the sea like a frisky sprat as they turned in past the north end of the Poor Knights. There a mako jumped from the water and crashed down on the bait. When Jan struck the fish a minute or so later, it shot from the water again, not more than 10 metres from the boat, clearing the waves by three or four metres. And then jumped again, and again, with spectacular leaps. It swam away with the 24 kg line, and, when played back to the boat, jumped again, within the length of the

Alec Stevenson — determined wheel-chair angler and winner of the "Old Man and the Sea" award — with his wife.
Northern Advocate.

double line. It went on fighting and leaping, once going down very deep. The next time it came close to the boat John Going decided it was time to bring it to gaff before it could go deep again – in his experience makos rarely survive a second dive and the line was too light to bring up dead what was clearly a big fish. When boated it "luckily did not perform too much" but proved too heavy to bring aboard and had to be towed back to Tutukaka. There was time then to reflect on some good angling and some good luck – for there were, on inspection, only two wires left unbroken on the stainless steel trace. The fish weighed in at 224.50 kg – a club, New Zealand and world record.

Tutukaka is one of the leading areas in New Zealand for the tagging of billfish. Tutukaka boats *Hooker* and *Anakiwa* along with *Lucky Strike* from Bay of Islands have tagged 38 of the 49 marlin tagged to date.

The more tagged, the more learned. A black marlin which had been tagged off Cairns, Australia was caught by Ron Dazeley from Sid Pritchard's launch *Katoa* off the Elizabeth Reef on April 30, 1975. It was the first tagged black marlin recovered in New Zealand waters, the longest time out for any black marlin tagged off Cairns (954 days) and the greatest distance recorded to date for any black marlin (about 3,220 kilometres). The tag and Mr Dazeley's reward – an American $1 note – are on display in the clubhouse.

In the season 1976–77 eleven fish were tagged at Tutukaka – two striped marlin; and in 1979–80 twenty-four fish were tagged – 16 mako, 3 hammerheads and 5 striped marlin.

One of the most successful ventures of the Whangarei Deep Sea Anglers Club was the establishing of its One Base Contest. The first contest was held from March 17–21, 1975, when 36 teams competed and 35 fish were caught. The highlight of the contest was on March 20 when 18 marlin and 2 makos were caught in what is now called the "Hot Spot" due to this day's successful catch.

Since 1975 the Whangarei Deep Sea Anglers Club's One Base Contest has grown in popularity as an annual event. It was originally designed as a "fun" contest to draw together members from other New Zealand clubs (overseas anglers were and are very welcome to participate) to foster a better relationship and to compete in the same conditions from a single base; this aim has been achieved. In the 1979–80 contest 93 teams entered with 51 fish caught, making it the largest (and still, the club claims, the friendliest) contest in the Southern Hemisphere, as well as producing, over the years, several New Zealand and world records for anglers competing in this contest.

It has long been known that there are game fish at the mouth of the Hauraki Gulf, entrance to the Waitemata Harbour and Auckland, the largest New Zealand city. There, although the continental shelf is further out, a tongue of warm water from the East Auckland Current comes inside Great Barrier Island and keeps the game fish within striking distance of the coast. Marlin have been seen several times near Tiritiri Island. Until well after the Second World War, however, in order to own a launch big enough to make excursions far enough out into what can be notoriously turbulent waters one needed to be a successful businessman, and most Auckland big game fishermen in this category had earlier established an attachment for one or other of the long-established clubs of the North or of the Coromandel-Bay of Plenty area.

Those who took their launches up to the Bay of Islands, however, were conscious that on their way home again the only place to weigh in any fish caught was at Parua Bay in Whangarei Harbour or, at a later date, at Tutukaka; and even in fishing around the Hen and Chicken Islands it was not unusual to chase a fish well south of Sail Rock.

Zane Grey's historic party, during its second visit to New Zealand, did some fishing off the entrance to the Hauraki Gulf on its way from the Bay of Islands to try the Bay of Plenty in 1927.

Near Arid (or Rakitu) Island, off the east coast of Great Barrier Island, R. C. Grey (brother of Zane Grey) hooked a big mako, estimated at more than 180 kg which jumped "30 feet if an inch" before getting away, and Captain Mitchell caught one of 145 kg.

Big fish continued to be sighted in ensuing years in the area outside the gulf, as far north as the Mokohinau Islands, south to the tip of the Coromandel peninsula and out to Great Barrier – even not far out past Kawau Island itself. A few marlin were caught, some by local effort but often by larger launches dropping a bait on their way to, or home from, their traditionally preferred fishing spots on the established northern and southern grounds. Several of these fish were brought in to Kawau Island, a popular boating venue, where once Sir George Grey, governor of New Zealand had his home (known as Mansion House) and which is now part of the Hauraki Gulf Maritime Park. The spark of interest, thus continually fanned, kindled a growing interest in seeing what more organised fishing in the area might produce.

W. E. Wagener kept interest alive with a 165-kg marlin a couple of years later, and finally, after a group outing, while several launches were gathered in Mansion House Bay, discussion got to the stage of deciding to do something.

Arnold Baldwin recalls that on the way south to Kawau Island in *Valsan* various earlier discussions were revived. He thought, "Well, let's get organised, and have a meeting ashore for 9 pm. *Nana* (Claude Edwards) came around from Two House Bay, the *Nerides* (Colin Mason was in the crew) was tied to the jetty and we probably had 15 or 16 people ashore. The club was formed, on the spot." Thus on the evening of Friday, March 10, 1961, with Arnold Baldwin in the chair, a group of anglers resolved to form the Kawau Island Deep Sea Fishing Club, covering "the Hauraki Gulf and areas adjacent to Kawau Island, Great Barrier, Little Barrier, Mokohinau, Cape Rodney etc."

Claude Edwards was elected founding president, with his wife "Bub" as secretary, with Arnold Baldwin offering to be her assistant.

It was from Claude Edwards' *Nana* that the club's first recorded game fish was caught on December 20, 1961 – the fish a modest 47.62-kg mako. The first thresher was weighed in about a week later, but it was not until just before Christmas the following year that G. Spencer, fishing from the *Estalena*, brought in the club's first marlin, of 136.09 kg. By the second season the club catch had surged; 128 fish, including two national women's records one of which, a 54.43-kg yellowfin tuna, was caught by Mrs A. Williams in her first attempt at game fishing, with no harness and sitting on a benzine box. The other was an 83.46-kg mako caught on a 15-kg line by Mrs Gloria Spencer, who was later to set other records including a 149.23-kg hammerhead.

In its first national contest in 1963, a club team of Colin Mason and Ralph Drake caught five makos in one day. On another occasion Ralph caught a 259.45-kg thresher from Colin's *Masonia*, which had a second in the world championship. The following year in a world contest held in New Zealand, N. Fairlie's team was second in the billfish-shark section; and G. Dawson's and R. Harnish's teams were first and second in the tuna section. Peter Henley caught a world record kingfish which he brought in late on a Sunday night, knocked up Arnold Baldwin and persuaded him to take the fish in the back of the car to be weighed. They dragged in a policeman from his beat to accompany them as witness. The club was well away.

They were great early days. The club has never had a membership much over 500 – in 1980 it was 330 – but Colin Mason recalls annual meetings at Mansion House, in the days when Kawau was really going, when a combined meeting and dine and dance would draw 350 people out to the island.

Older members of the club also recall the initial excitement of finding and catching the fighting yellowfin tuna. Frank Petersen, later to

Beyond Kawau Island and Takatu Point (middle distance) lie the home waters of the Auckland Gamefishing Club. Little Barrier Island rises steeply in the centre background, with Great Barrier Island sprawled along the horizon to its right. In the foreground is part of the Mahurangi Peninsula. Whites Aviation.

be one of the club's vice-presidents, had been catching them on a spoon made from an old wooden handrail in 1959, before the club was formed and now he boated, with his party, three at Little Barrier on the first day (in water that was clean and blue and running at a temperature of about 19°C) and nine more the second day.

Although yellowfin then faded from the Auckland scene – the blame equally proportioned between the depredations of off-shore long-liners and a possible trend in water temperature – yellowtail, which were always the largest catch numerically, have continued to be

caught, up to record size. A light-tackle expert, Dr G.B. Tetro, added to the club's many meritorious catches in December, 1972 with a 17.23-kg yellowtail on a 3-kg line in the Rangitoto Channel.

The club has never caught many marlin in a season, and a moderate number of mako and other sharks (and the only mako landed in the gulf area was caught in a net at Hadfield's Beach, halfway out along the coast to Kawau) but this reflects not so much an absence of fish as a lower fishing effort than other clubs out in waters where the fish are to be found. When, as in the national competitions, boats go out in numbers, the fish are caught. In the 1974 national contest, a team from Kawau was second to the Bay of Islands in the billfish section, and another team was second to Whakatane in yellowtail, while the then club president Leo Collins and the present

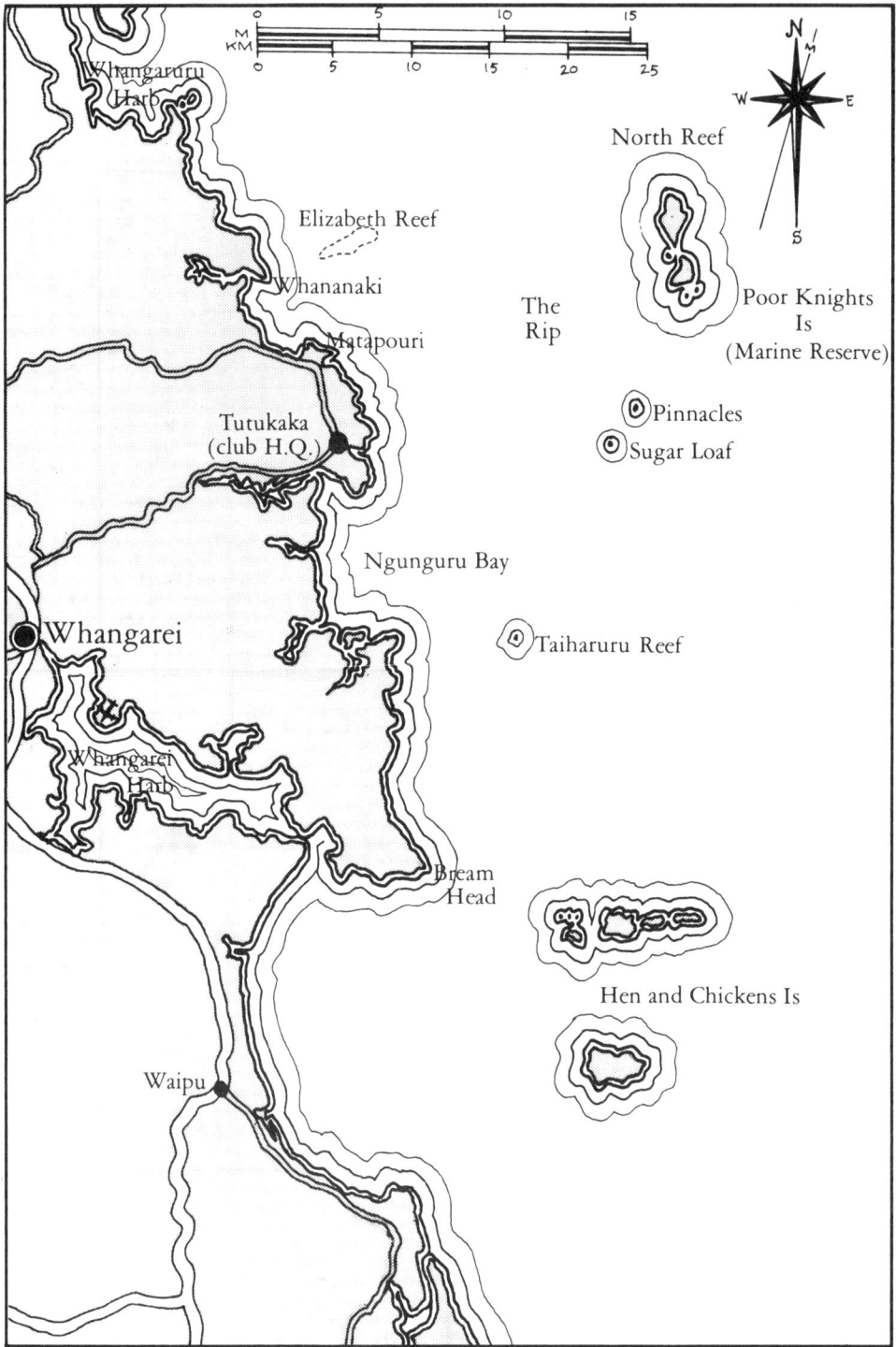

Map 3   *The home waters of the Whangarei Deep Sea Anglers Club.*

president Jack McMahon scored the most points in all sections.

A notable session for members of the club in another national contest is described in the club magazine by Jack Bennett. He was fishing with other club members off Groper Rock in the Mokohinau group early in 1977. It was 12.45, nearly lunchtime: "Action, the 12/0 reel with 800 metres of 80-lb line (37 kg) started to scream, not stopping until about 200 metres of line was left on the reel. By this time Keith (Bennett) was in the chair all ready to go and I was stoking the *Kalamera*, frantically trying to catch up to the fish. This was the beginning of 5¼ hours of really dour struggle between Keith and the fish. At first, by the speed of its travel, I thought it must be a billfish, but after about an hour I realised that it was probably a thresher. For the first two hours the fish led us, and Keith would make line and then lose it. Finally the fish became tired and seemed quite content to be led at trolling speed. Keith could finally hold the fish up at about the 20 m level, but it refused to be pulled any further into the lighter water. After five hours both fighters were exhausted. We recovered Keith a little with a rum, and he applied more brake and vigorously pumped his rod, gaining half a turn at the time. As soon as he had the fish moving, he kept the action going and ever so slowly the fish came to the top. I have never seen so much strain applied to rod and line. When the trace came to hand . . . I gaffed the fish, and at the same time I gashed my forearm on the underneath of Keith's reel as he stood beside me. This mishap caused us to go right back to Fitzroy where the district nurse very expertly inserted six stitches in my arm at 10.50 pm."

The anglers took the thresher with them back to port and Keith, who had collapsed after playing the fish, was well recovered when the fish was weighed in the next morning at 238.14 kg. It won the angler an armful of trophies and the award for the heaviest game shark caught on a 36-kg line in the 1977 New Zealand Open Game Fishing Contest.

Gerry Dawson, a life member of the club who looks back nostalgically to the days when there were schools and schools of trevally before purse seiners scooped them up, has fished happily for years with friends from his launch *Waitanguru*. The biggest fish ever caught from it was a 277.14-kg blue marlin, caught by F. Peterson near Mokohinau early in 1966.

As so often on the New Zealand coast, fishing out of the Hauraki Gulf is a bonus to the enjoyment of splendid boating waters. These waters are as spread out as the Auckland urban area and the Auckland club itself (the name was changed in 1978 from Kawau to give the club a closer association with the city). The centre of the fishing area is a triangle between the northern end of Great Barrier Island, Little Barrier Island and the Mokohinau Islands, but Auckland fishermen feel they are on home ground up as far as the Hen and Chicken Islands (the southern waters of the Whangarei Club) and around the tip of the Coromandel peninsula to the Mercury Islands, home preserve of the Mercury Bay Club. They also fish as far out to sea beyond Great Barrier Island as motor yachtsmen care to venture, as well as right into the Hauraki Gulf, past Kawau to Waiheke Island and down the Firth of Thames.

There is plenty of good shelter on the mainland coast. The multitude of good anchorages and trailer-boat launching areas is one of the reasons why the club operations are so widespread. However, only Great Barrier Island, and then only on its south-western coast, offers confident shelter once the mainland is left behind. There is no comfort in a blow around the Mokohinau Islands, nor the Hen and Chickens, and Little Barrier is not much better. The water as far as Great Barrier being fairly shallow – the 200-metre line runs well outside it – an area which is inviting to boats in good weather can become very rough in short time when the weather turns bad. Even the Great Barrier anchorages do not tempt many fishermen

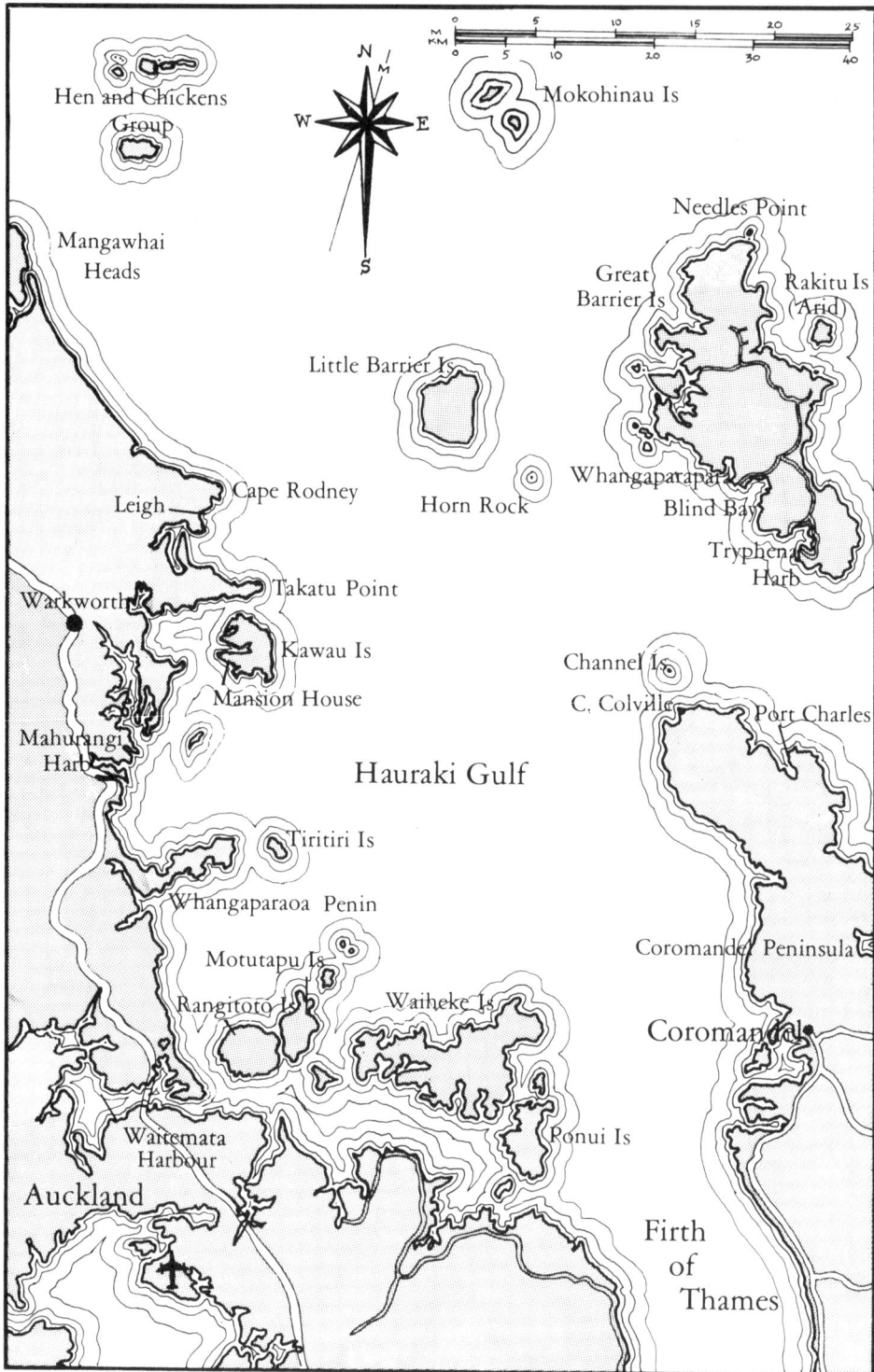

Map 4   *The Hauraki Gulf and the main fishing waters of the Auckland Gamefishing Club.*

out who can spare only a weekend, because a launch party which sets out on the five- to six-hour journey to Great Barrier on a fine Friday afternoon cannot always be sure of being able to cruise home in comfort on the Sunday.

One of the more popular departure points for the area is the Sandspit, on the coast opposite Kawau Island. The Sandspit is a little over an hour by road from Auckland, offers good pile moorings, and is only a short distance by sea from Takatu Point, where the big game fishing grounds open. All the islands then in view offer good fishing prospects, with extra points of angling interest around Simpson Rock, which stands 6 m out of the sea between Little Barrier and Mokohinau Islands, and Horn Rock, south-east of Little Barrier, which breaks only in a swell.

Little Barrier itself is a bird sanctuary. From the heights of the island, named Mt Many Peaks, where the bush has recovered some early minor logging and is unmodified by any introduced browsing animals, many native birds call down, including the handsome stitchbird, now to be found only here.

Great Barrier Island offers not only good fishing waters but a beautifully indented south-western coast where there is good shelter,

particularly from easterly storms; in charming Port Fitzroy, where bush-clad slopes run down to the water's edge, you're safe from almost anything the weather can produce.

The Mokohinau Islands are a picturesquely craggy group of rocks, not notable for easy anchorages but formerly the site of one of the club's weighing stations, when the lighthouse on the main island was manned. Cuvier Island, off the tip of Coromandel Peninsula is reverting to natural bush; and a colony of rare birds, the North Island saddleback, has been introduced there in an effort to ensure their survival. Many of the islands of the gulf and some areas of the mainland are part of a Hauraki Gulf Maritime Park which will safeguard the attractions of the area for all time.

Auckland club membership comes from all along the coastline fronting this fishing area and from as far as Wellsford to the north and Taupo to the south. Indicative of its local spread is the number and location of its weighing stations — on Great Barrier Island (at Port Fitzroy and Whangaparapara), at Kawau, on Waiheke Island (Orapiu), at Mangawhai Heads, Arkles Bay, Leigh, the Wade River, Takapuna, Howick (Half Moon Bay), Maraetai and on the Auckland waterfront itself at Westhaven.

CHAPTER ELEVEN

Mercury Bay to Mayor Island

The winding Tapu-Coroglen road over the Coromandel hills never did discourage the really keen angler on his way to Whitianga, but it helped to give the place an out-of-the-world isolation. It is a charm that Whitianga has been able to retain even now when a tar-sealed route via Kopu provides a good driving surface all the way to the end of the wharf, where the Mercury Bay Gamefishing Club has its comfortable and convenient headquarters.

There is hardly a feature on any part of this coast which does not have a link with the British navigator-explorer Captain James Cook, and it would hardly surprise – such is the largely unspoiled atmosphere of this place – to look out to sea from Whitianga and catch a glimpse of the sails of the *Endeavour* sailing into Mercury Bay again as the ship did on November 4, 1769: "My reasons for putting in here were the hopes of discovering a good harbour and the desire I had of being in some convenient place to observe the transit of Mercury, which happens on the ninth instant, and will be wholly visible here if the day is clear. If we be so fortunate as to obtain this observation, the longitude of this place and country will thereby be very accurately determined."

The longitude was so determined from a headland above Cook's Beach, just around from the present town, accurate to 11 minutes. If one traces back the original of the name Whitianga itself, it derives from an earlier navigator still: it means "crossing place of Kupe", who by tradition captained the historic canoe Matahoura which is said to have arrived here in 950 AD.

In 1924, E. E. Chadban – or Chad – was proprietor of the Whitianga Hotel and a keen big game fisherman who had helped in setting up the sport at Mayor Island.

So Chad was fairly sure what had been seen by a crayfisherman who talked in his pub one day of a giant piper which had come up alongside his boat. With a party of three boats he set out the next weekend to put his hunch to the proof, not in a way of which the purist might approve, but effectively enough. Not having any game fishing gear, the party trolled kahawai baits on hapuku lines and when they had a strike, tied the end of the line to a drum. When the lines were hauled up later with the tired-out fish, the party had a striped marlin and a mako shark.

Such a result, with Chad's enthusiasm, was enough to fire interest in forming a game fishing club. A meeting was held in a fish and cargo shed

The clubhouse of the Mercury Bay Gamefishing club sits on the end of the Whitianga wharf in the centre of this Whites Aviation photograph. The main fishing waters lie straight out. Captain Cook's observation point for the transit of Mercury was on the point beyond the wharf.

at the end of the wharf where the clubhouse is still today – one storey up – and a club was a going concern in time for the start of the 1925 season.

Chad was fittingly the first president of what was called the Mercury Bay Swordfish and Mako Shark Club. He held the post for 10 years until he went away to make his mark again in the Bay of Plenty. Archie Wells was the first secretary. A gallows was built on the beach. Chad himself caught the first striped marlin of 136 kg for the club on February 26, 1925. Tom Cannon, the local policeman and a member of the first committee, caught the other of the club's first two fish that day, a 145 kg mako.

Among early visitors were A. D. Campbell and, inevitably, Zane Grey, with Captain Laurie Mitchell. In Francis Arlidge's *Alma G* and Peter Williams' *Avalon*, the latter briefly tried the Mercury Islands in February 1928. The following year Grey was encouraged enough to come back and with three launches, the same two Bay of Islands boats and the local *Dauntless*, they caught 110 game fish in 11 weeks – including 43 striped marlin, a black marlin, 63 makos and a hammerhead.

The year 1932 marked the end of club fishing from Whitianga for 15 years. The Depression and later the Second World War were to put such pleasure out of the mind for most of those who, local and overseas, had built up Whitianga's reputation.

The story of the long, arduous and unorthodox battle with a 419-kg black marlin from the *Ronomor* in 1947, which sparked the

resurgence of the club into even greater success is told elsewhere in this book. The club had a new name, the Mercury Bay Gamefishing Club. Its prime mover and first president was again the local hotel proprietor, this time Roy Dale.

The club not only had only five presidents in its first 23 years (the others being Messrs K. Peachey, H. Madill, A. Black and M. A. Cruickshank) but for 21 of those years had the same secretary, Mr J. P. (Jack) Crawford. He was also a foundation member of the New Zealand Big Game Fishing Council, its president for two terms (1964–65 and 1969–70) and became one of its life members.

Several boats set up for charter, the membership climbed with the good years, at one stage topping 1,000. The types of fish caught as well as the numbers varied with the season. The clubhouse was still in the cargo shed at the end of the wharf – often half full of bales of wool, providing seating for the members. Later the new clubhouse was built on top of the old.

Quite apart from the bigger game fish, there were yellowfin tuna off Whitianga before they became more plentiful further south. They used to appear in a run about January and come back again in April. When they were about, the sea would be thick with them. M. A. Cruickshank, a former president of the club, remembers a day when his boat had a triple strike of yellowfin: not that the triple strike was unusual then but landing all three was. It was a great battle, the tuna keeping all three anglers on their feet, with

ABOVE: *E. E. Chadban, who helped to get game fishing going in Mercury Bay as well as at Mayor Island, with the first two fish taken when the Mercury Bay club was formed in 1925. The fish are a striped marlin caught by Chad and a mako shark caught by Tom Cannon, the local policeman.*

BELOW: *The first two marlin caught on rod and line at Mayor Island and the man who caught them – Colonel Calthorpe (holding rod). The man on the left is believed to be Billy Edwards who, as skipper of the* Hokemai, *helped to establish the sport on the island. The date is some time in 1922.*

Zane Grey's fishing camp in Whalers Cove on Mercury Island in 1929.

much agile ducking and diving around the cockpit as lines crossed and recrossed.

Don Ross, who was one of the first actively to fish for the tuna, recalls that he did not know what they were at first. But an Australian out on his boat said: "Those are tuna, you should have a go at them." It was soon found, however, that our small reels were no match for tuna. The reels would fly to pieces, the monofilament line used tightening on the spools until the pressure burst them apart. Even when heavier gear was used, making it possible to fish the same school over and over again and to catch what was hooked, the reels would smoke with the fast first runs of these exciting fish. And there was the day of the big blue-fin, the cast of which hangs on the clubhouse wall; the story of that is told elsewhere, too.

For the angler, Whitianga and the Mercury Bay Club have features which make this an all-round venue. The base itself has access in almost all weathers to the fishing grounds. A shallow bar has only in rare memory made it difficult to get in, even at low tide. The wreck which gave Buffalo Beach its name was unusual – H.M.S. *Buffalo* was standing off the shore in 1840 with kauri spars when it was caught by a storm and driven ashore. But to the smaller craft the only problem that arises is caused by the strong current off the wharf when the harbour fills and empties with the tides through its narrow entrance.

Out to sea, the fishermen are soon into likely

Zane Grey surveys the Whitianga waters from the foredeck of the Frangipani.

waters, which are, however, shallower than those on many grounds at first, and are dotted with more islands and more foul ground than usual. Much of the fishing is done in 60 to 100 metres of water, with banks only 20 metres down. The 200-metre depth line is out past the further islands but within reach of them and the shelter most of them offer in emergency.

To the north lie the Mercury Islands, with Ohena Bank and Island, Lou's Rock, and Whale Rock on the way there – all interesting fishing spots. It was at Ohena Bank that Bruce Fisher hooked a black marlin with a kingfish bait and fought it for more than 10 hours before losing it. And right over Lou's Rock, Jack Jackman sighted a broadbill when with skipper Bert Chaney in the *Ronomor*, and lost that, too, after the fish performed magnificently, and charged the boat several times before finding a weakness in the line and breaking free.

Off Whale Rock two Hamilton anglers, Bill Glover and Jack Maxfield were startled to have a 136-kg mako deliver itself into the boat with a flying leap immediately on being hooked and there wedge itself so tightly that, although still very much alive and kicking, the anglers were able to secure it without much damage to their 5-metre runabout. A similar catch, with a mako in the cockpit, was made in Roly Smith's *Marlin*, although this time the fish did not leap aboard but thrashed its way into the boat while being hoisted ignominiously by the tail with a block and tackle, after giving the quite wrong impression that it had no fight left in it. Roly Smith fell overboard and three anglers left the cockpit just as rapidly for safer parts of the boat until Roly could clamber back aboard.

North of here, around the Mercury Islands themselves are three fruitful areas, the inner and outer banks near Red Mercury and Ecklands Bank further out, with Richards Rock in-between. It was close in at Richards Rock that the big bluefin tuna of 235.64 kg, which set a New Zealand record, was hooked by Jack Jackman in 1967, and where an earlier club

president Arthur Black picked up a huge black marlin which took him out to sea for four hours at a steady, undeviating 3 to 4 knots before it was attacked by a shark and the line went dead. The three banks are noted for many varied catches.

Some anglers, and one of them is Nelson Tye, a former club president and skipper of the *Lady Clare*, prefer the southern waters, down past picturesque Castle Rock toward the Alderman Islands. It was in this area that Nelson's boat once caught five marlin in six days. The Aldermen lie about 19 miles from Whitianga and make either a good turnaround point for a day's fishing or shelter for a quiet lunch aboard on the way down to Mayor Island, to enjoy the fishing waters and the hospitality of the neighbouring Tauranga Club.

Like most clubs around the coast, Whitianga has faced a period when fishing has fallen off from the bumper early years, when trailing a line or deep drifting brought almost certain success. Boats have been going further out to sea to search for blue water and the big fish that go with it. New ways of attracting fish to the bait have been tried – by trailing a rattle of coconut shells for instance, or fishing at night with a bright overhead light.

Don Ross has turned to the idea of deep trolling with heavy lead weights keeping the bait from 20 m to 30 m down and says this seems to catch more fish, although so far smaller ones as a rule. Catches have not all been game fish – they have included grey nurse sharks, shovel nose sharks and a couple of crayfish pots off the bottom.

But then Don is used to the funny side of fishing (he would like to write a book about it). He recalls for instance the keen English fisherman who had fished all over the world, had never even had a strike and looked to Whitianga to fill the aching void. The day passed uneventfully until, the sea freshening and the boat rolling, the angler called excitedly that he had a strike. Now happy at last, he fought with tight line against the heavy drag, making no progress and finally getting back his bait, untouched it seemed. Back at port Don found that the heavy motor tyre he used as a fender had slipped off the deck, presumably when the weather roughened and the angler got his "catch". His first doubts about the "strike" became a certainty. "But the bloke was so happy, even at the thought of hooking one at last," says Don. "I didn't have the heart to tell him."

Around Mayor Island between 1945 and 1950 a boat could confidently hope for the limit of four striped marlin in a day; at one stage 63 were caught in three days, and a single launch, the *Sou' East*, boated 106 striped marlin, plus other big game fish, in 60 days. In the best season, the local club weighed in 745 striped marlin, four black marlin, 27 mako sharks, 11 thresher sharks and one hammerhead. Recent years have seen nothing like these exceptional catches – the usual total is about one quarter that of the bumper early years, with the accent moving away from billfish to sharks – the catches of both are now about equal. But by other than Mayor Island standards the fishing is still good and, in its continuing favour, the number of really big fish is being maintained. And there is still the major draw of Mayor Island itself.

Out in the centre of the Bay of Plenty, 23 miles north of the port and city of Tauranga, and a three hour launch trip from the club offices on the city waterfront, Mayor Island was rich in tradition long before the big game fish club built its own traditions and set up its fishing lodge there. Essentially the island is the jagged rim of a large extinct volcano, sloping inward to twin smaller lake-filled craters, and on the outside falling away steeply to the sea. In 1922 an English visitor, Colonel Calthorpe, boated the first two striped marlin to be taken in those waters by rod and line. He caught a third one the following day.

Two parties taken out the following year, including the indefatigable A. D. Campbell, caught 18 marlin in one weekend. More and more fishermen came, local and overseas, and a

group of charter boat skippers, Arthur Fletcher and Barney Hilditch (*Naomi*), Charlie Millet (*Virginia*), Chad and Fred Wilkins (*Kingfish*), and Curley Steedman (*Dauntless*), in that order, started the golden years of Mayor Island fishing.

In 1943, fishing from the launch *Renahau*, owned and skippered by Joe Barney, with Curly Steedman as mate for the day, B. D. H. (Doug) Ross hooked and brought in a huge mako. The shark had earlier bitten off the tail of a striped marlin being reeled in by another member of the party and had charged and put some toothmarks in the stern of the *Renahau*, just below where Curly Steedman was standing at the rail, his bare feet a foot from the water. It greedily took an offered bait. The mako took only about an hour and a half to get to the boat again, but the eight men could not get it fully aboard and it was towed back to Tauranga half in the water. There the scales swung around to their limit of 1,000 lb (453.60 kg), but the mako was obviously heavier than that – perhaps a good deal heavier because the fish, caught on a Sunday, was not weighed until the Monday.

It was, however, a world record fish, beating the record set 12 years before by Huntingdon White-Wickham off Cape Brett with a fish of 798 lb (361.97 kg).

The Tauranga Big Gamefishing Club was formed in 1923 with A. J. Mirrielees as first chairman. John Mowlem, who had contributed so much to early fishing including the first two charter boats, the *Naomi* and *Virginia*, also took a lead in establishing the first (and then modest) accommodation on Mayor Island, where anglers had so far been content to rough it in tents under the trees. One of the first parties to use the new bach was the American deep sea study group which came in 1938, led by Michael and Helen Lerner – a visit which was to prove a forerunner to the setting up of the International Game Fish Association in June, 1939, with Mr Lerner as founder.

As with other game fishing clubs, Tauranga's membership has varied with its fishing success,

Des Benson of Nelson with the night's catch of bluefin tuna taken by rod and line from a fishing trawler off the West Coast of the South Island on 4 August 1980. The fish ranged in weight from 75 to 133 kg. Only physical exhaustion kept Tony Haultain and Des Benson, the two anglers involved, from catching more.

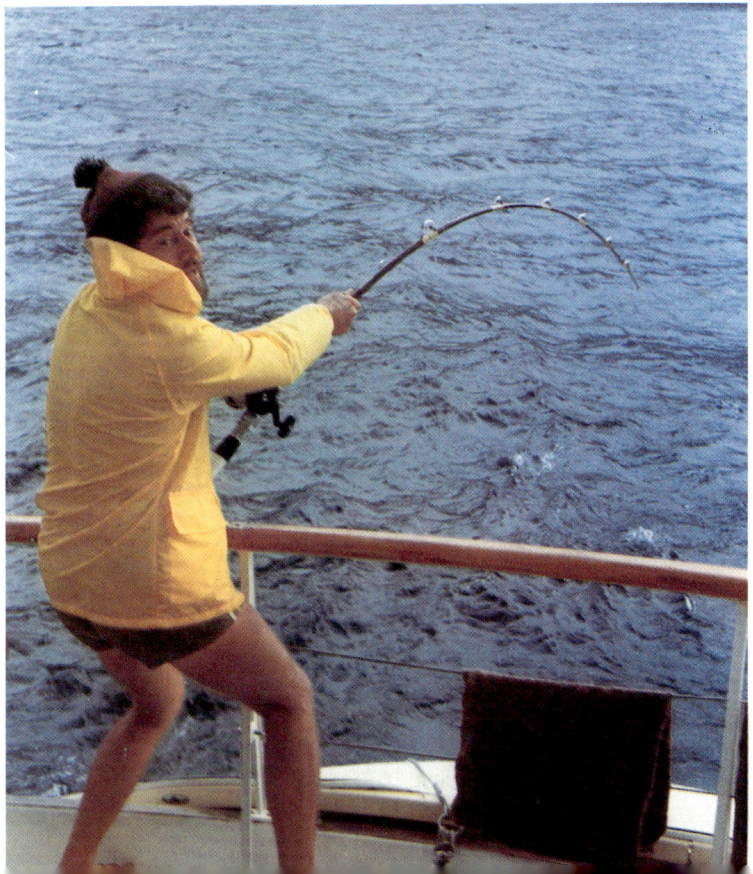

Don Hague, over-awed by the power of a yellowtail on a 10 kg line at the Three Kings Islands, fishing from the late Ian Heaven's Blitzen. *R. Hague.*

Something of the colours of a dolphinfish (mahimahi) are captured in this photo of one caught by J. R. Bloomfield at Waihau Bay.

Kahawai and saltwater fly fishing gear. Gary Kemsley.

Some saltwater flies and a popper. Gary Kemsley.

Outward bound from South East Bay, Mayor Island, for a day's fishing in the late 1940s. The boats are: foreground, right to left – Maharatia, Sou' East, Renehau; *back, right to left* – Galatea, Dauntless, Virginia, Hukarere. National Film Unit.

reaching a peak of 2,043 members in 1968, and 1,142 in 1980, but it has maintained a good fleet of game fishing charter boats. The fourteen boats now available out of Tauranga are the *Balsona, Carousel, Intrepid, Judith Aimee, Leeway, Luana, Masquerade, Ma Cherie, Marline, Ruth, Sabra, Taiho, Taimarino,* and *Waimarie II.*

Big fish can be caught in Tauranga Harbour itself. Alan Bonner got the club's Wooden Spoon one year, as well as a trophy for the most meritorious catch of the season, for his exploits with a 185.97-kg bronze whaler, foul-hooked and caught on a light rod. The fish had towed his 6-metre runabout all over the place and finally into shallow water where Alan jumped over with a looped rope to secure it. The shark whipped around on him; he left the water again at speed. He finally towed the shark to base and was later given his Wooden Spoon award for trying to catch a fish with his bare hands.

The harbour entrance, which becomes difficult only in a heavy north-easterly, is a good light tackle area, and Karewa Island about five miles north has known some celebrated big catches. I boated a broadbill off Karewa Island. It was my first in 36 years' association with big game fishing and the first in the Tauranga club's waters in 10 years. The angler was a Canadian, Leo Leavitt, fresh from the prairies of Alberta, who had never been out in a boat before. The

Rock formation in the aptly named Cathedral Bay, Mayor Island. J. F. Louden.

broadbill took only an hour and a half to bring to gaff but in that time it took my launch *Sou' East* seven miles and surfaced twice, without revealing its identity until the final gaffing.

A good many game fish have been, and are still being caught, between Tauranga Harbour and Mayor Island, but essentially this is a result of trolling to and from the heart of the fishing grounds. The core of the fishing is done at Mayor Island from charter boats based at Tauranga, and booked usually for several days out on the grounds, using the island as a base. The anglers sleep ashore at the lodge and have their main meals there while the skippers, usually with a spare hand, stay aboard, because South East Bay is

open to the winds from that direction. A sudden decision may have to be made in the middle of the night to leave for North-West Bay if the wind shifts.

If the club activities revolve around Mayor Island, it is the clubrooms there which are the hub. The club has built a facility in South East Bay which provides all that a visiting angler would want. It has many of the facilities of a hotel, with enough comfortable beds in neat cabins for well over 100 people, plus staff; a dining room that will seat more than 200 people on special occasions, and a well appointed lounge and bar. It is, in good years, the closest base to fishing grounds in New Zealand and maybe in the world, for the launches can put over their lines as soon as they have cleared the other boats,

130

When Prime Minister of New Zealand, Sir Sidney Holland did some keen fishing. He is on the left in the photograph alongside Fred Wilkins; his is the right hand fish, being weighed at South East Bay, Mayor Island.

and have often hooked big game fish right in the entrance to the bay. An airstrip to bring the base within a few minutes of Tauranga, and make it more readily accessible from other centres, is about the only other facility it should have. I foresaw the necessity nearly 20 years ago and tried hard to get approval from my committee to establish one.

At present it takes boats from Tauranga about three hours to reach the island, trolling for part of the way, and then putting in half a day's fishing off the island before landing the anglers at South East Bay for dinner. In the morning, angling can begin straight after breakfast.

Mayor Island is roughly circular in shape and approximately 2½ miles in diameter. The north to north-north-west sector is exposed to the southerly set of the East Auckland Current and thus in effect acts like a drift fence or barrier, causing slow eddies. In addition the 200-metre depth line, after curving inshore south of the Aldermen, turns sharply seaward again a little north-west of Herbie's Hole about a mile offshore and continues to seaward until a little more than a mile clear of the island before curving away again to the southward. This effect creates a plateau with an average depth of about 50 to 60 metres about a mile wide and three miles long parallel to the barrier section of the island, and dropping off very sharply indeed to depths of more than 200 metres.

The drop-off, an almost cliff-like feature of the

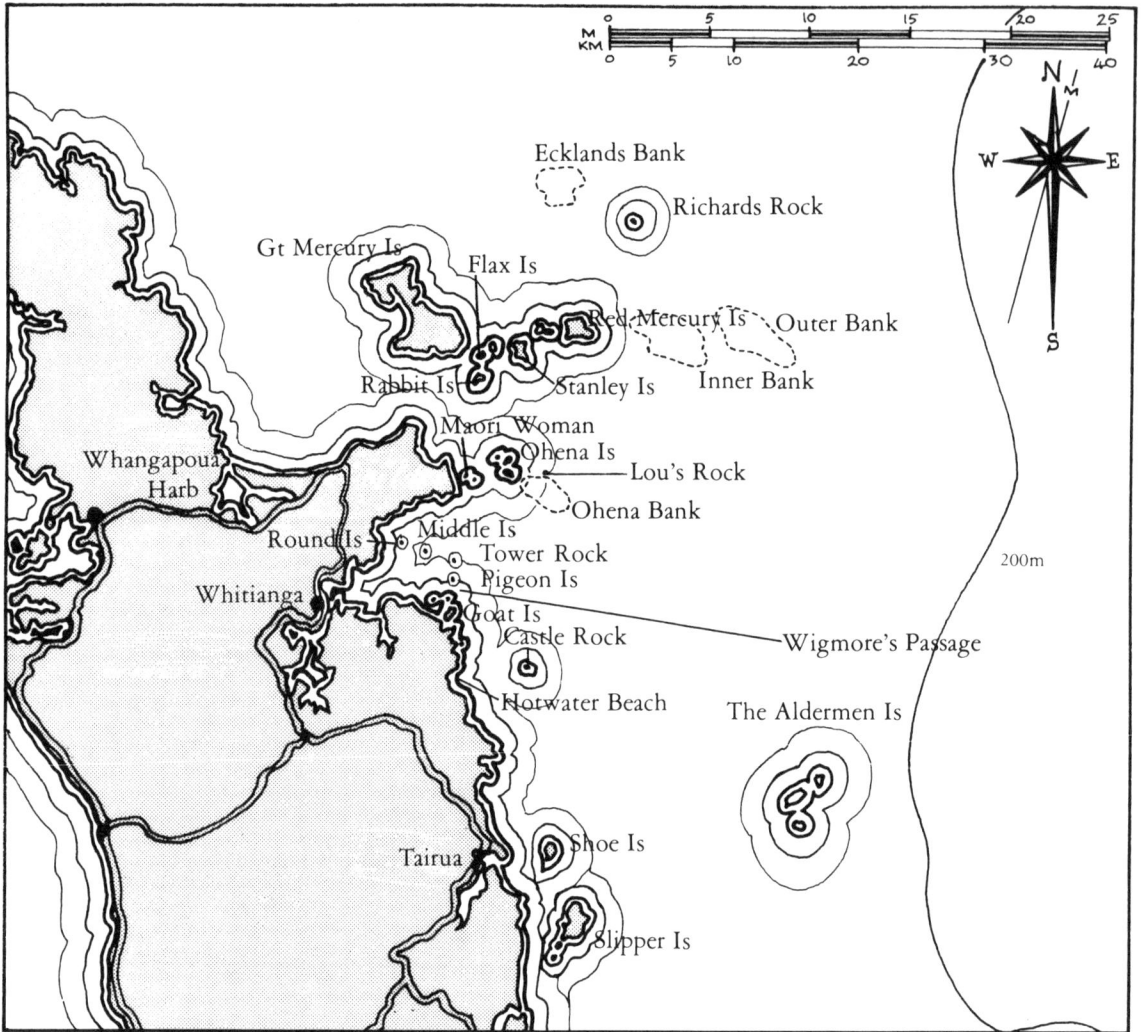

Map 5 *The Mercury Bay Gamefishing Club's island-studded waters.*

bottom, creates food-carrying upwellings which are held on the plateau by eddies long enough to attract and support a large population of indigenous and travelling fish. The glamour spot of this system was the Bait Pond, where a short reef projected from the cliff-fronted foreshore, trapping feed and causing a near-permanent population of kahawai, trevally, snapper and kingfish in crystal-clear water about three to four metres deep. There one could almost always catch fish, and watch them take the bait.

It is perhaps of some significance that in spite of the activity of the Japanese offshore for many years, it was only after a few seasons of intensive gill netting by local boats that the plateau and its Bait Pond lost its unique population. This may indicate that Mayor Island's supply of marlin may not have changed any more than the other grounds on the north-east coast. Rejuvenation of the populations of small fish may re-establish previous patterns.

Off North West Bay has always been a good fishing area and was the "hot spot" in 1978. Jill Gray, one of the professional skippers working out of Tauranga in the tradition of her father, Bob Gray (and one of the few women skippers

New Zealand game fishing has known) has a soft spot for the area. Here it was, just after she had got her ticket that, when fishing for fun with a friend, Miss Robyn Davis, they boated an 82.10-kg striped marlin. Although small by later standards, it provided a most interesting afternoon's fishing. She says they were trolling a small kahawai when the fish came up out of the blue, grabbed the bait and took off. The boat did not have a fishing chair, only a board with a gimbal on it, and Miss Davis, who was on the rod, had to sit on this on the engine box.

As the marlin tail-walked, the reel, which did not have a backing plate, started to come off the rod and had to be lashed on again with line. When the fish was brought to the boat, the gaff broke and Miss Gray was hauled over the side, to be grabbed by the ankles by her friend and dragged back again. Between them they then got the fish on the boat.

At Herbie's Hole, just to the north again, the feature is a cave named after H. W. (Herbie) Burch, one of Curly Steedman's early charterers in *Dauntless* and later owner of *Maharatia*, skippered by Curly after the Second World War. Herbie caught his, and Mayor Island's, first broadbill (270.32 kg) there while drifting on *Dauntless* on March 13, 1937.

A good fish taken in recent years off the nearby Bait Pond was a 340.30-kg blue marlin caught on 60-kg line by Brian Anson in the *Ruth*. The fish struck about a mile off the shore and immediately ran off with more than 800 metres of line. A marvellous series of acrobatics kept it on the surface all the way. Then it settled to a series of sudden dashes which took the launch backward a distance of about 10 miles toward The Aldermen. The fish at times dived deep, with 500 to 600 metres peeled from the reel and angled steeply down. As the fight went into darkness, it was possible to see the fish by its phosphorescence up to 30 metres below the boat. The fish took 4½ hours to fight.

Near the northern end of the island the Maori Chief, a rock the pinnacle shape of which

suggests its name, has been the scene of several record catches including a world record blue marlin of 373.31 kg hooked by Alec Nicol of Tokoroa on February 27, 1972, (beating one of 295.74 kg caught by G. A. Wooller in the Bay of Islands in January, 1965). The angler was fishing from his own 8 m trailer launch *Restless*, trolling a kona lure on 37-kg line when a huge fish broached, sending spray 5 metres high as it fell back. It proceeded to leap 14 times more during the 2½-hour fight that followed.

Both the present and previous world records for thresher sharks caught on a 60-kg line were also set in Mayor Island waters. The record fish up to the beginning of 1978 was caught by Frederick Parsons, of Tauranga, on Goldie Hitchings' *Luana*. It was a tremendous fight – the fish was hooked at about 10 am and not boated until nearly midnight, a gruelling battle of 13½ hours. The fish tipped the scales at 303.91 kg.

When R. C. Faulkner of Wellington caught his even bigger (307.53 kg) thresher on 60-kg line near Mayor Island on February 23, 1978, he was fishing in the national contest from the *Loxsoma*, skippered by Neill MacDougall. The fish rapidly ran off 800 metres of his 900-metre line and settled down to a fight which lasted for six hours. When boated, the 4.57 m shark was found to have a bite mark on its side which was thought to have been due either to an attack by another shark or an attempt by its mate to help to free it.

The club is known almost as much for its fishing facilities as well as its fishing; its clubhouse in South East Bay continues to build up its reputation for good company and good hospitality. It caters for fishing people and the vagaries of their sport, as the crew of one boat has cause to remember. They fought a large blue marlin well out to sea and into the night but lost it about 11 pm, when it got away, still jumping fit. They got back to Mayor Island at 4 am to find the hostel staff still up waiting to give them a meal.

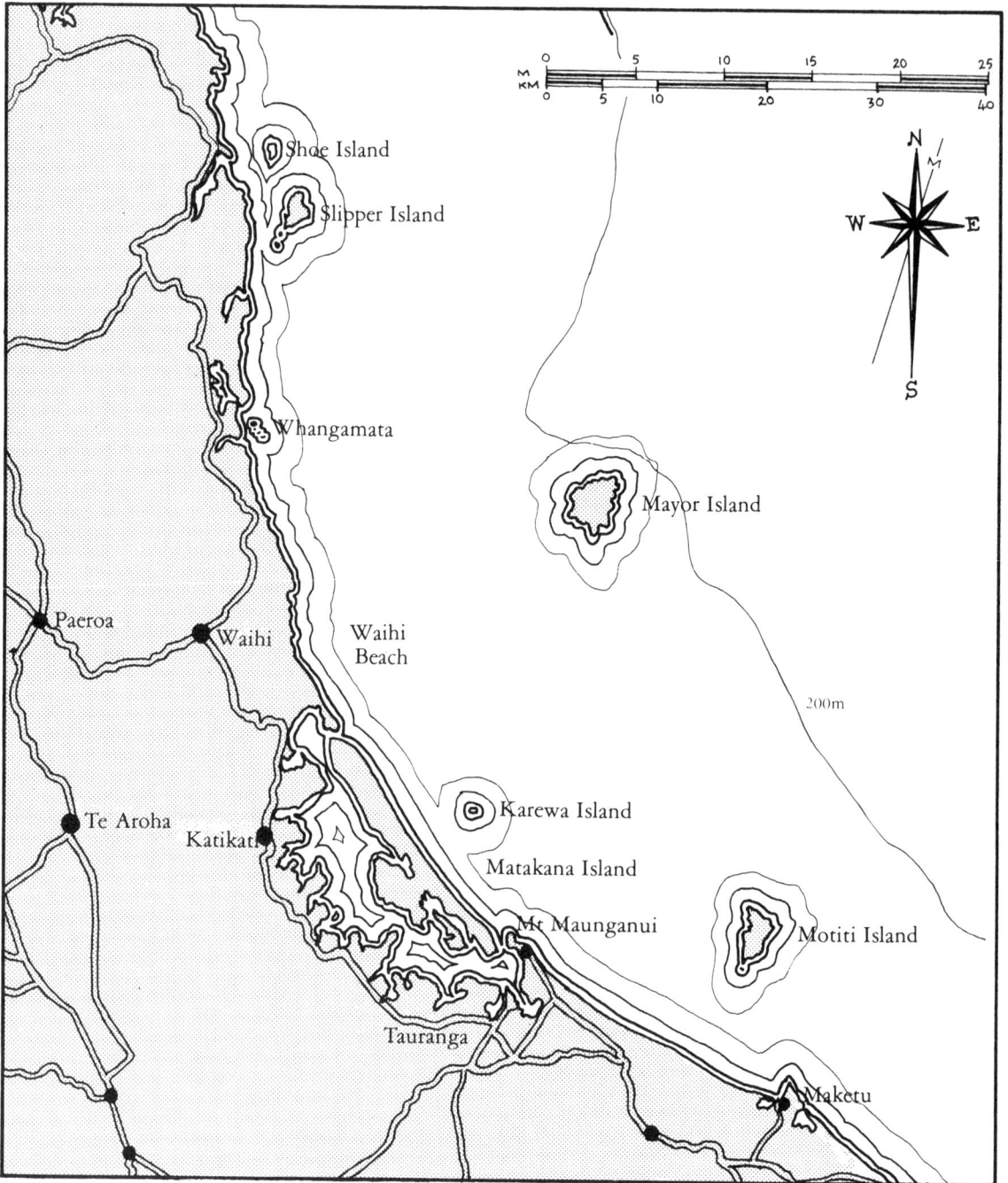

Map 6   *The fishing waters of the Tauranga Big Gamefishing Club.*

East Auckland
Current

200m

Two Fathoms

Flat Top Is

Queen Victoria
The Pinnacles

The Maori Chief

Cathedral Bay

Turtle Bay

The Bait Pond

Herbie's Hole

Island Bay

The Stone Wall

Crater Bay

North-West Bay

Hole in the Wall

Crayfish Cave

Honeymoon
Bay

Tuhua Reef

South-East Bay

Western Bay

The Garden
Patch

MAYOR ISLAND

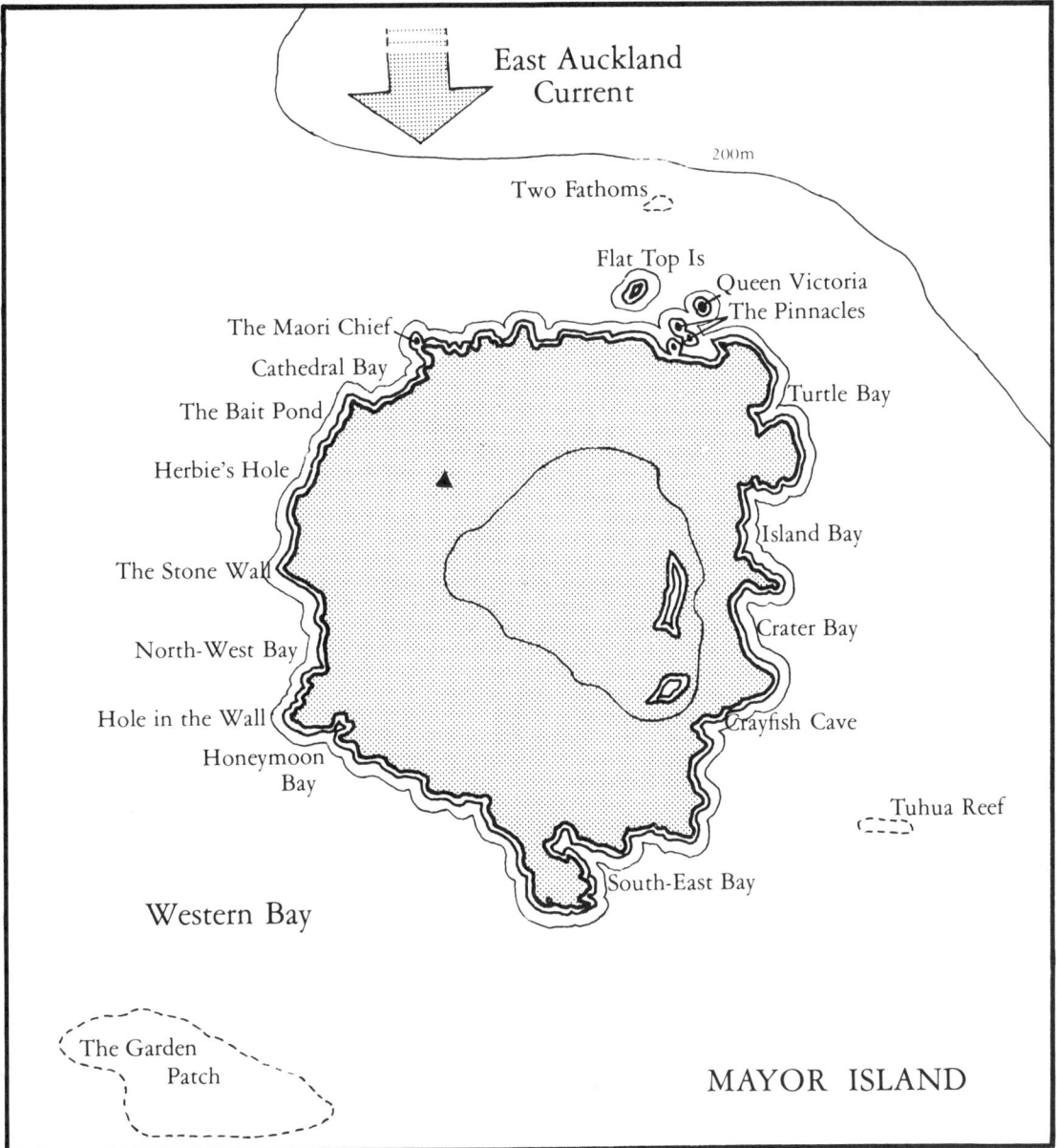

Map 7 *More than sixty years of fishing tradition are recorded in the names bestowed around Mayor Island.*

CHAPTER TWELVE

Eastern Bay of Plenty

Early in the 1960s, two regular weekend fishermen from Whakatane, Stan McMillan and Evan Middlemas, were trolling as usual for yellowtail off Whale Island, about 8 km from port, when they caught three strange and exciting-looking fish. No-one seemed to know what the fish were, and they were displayed in Cutler's sports shop for identification. They turned out to be yellowfin tuna, and the two anglers were able to confirm the reputation that came with the identification, that they were tremendous fighting fish.

And now they seemed to be everywhere. An enlarged and enthusiastic group of fishermen, now including Ron Rowson, Alec Gaul, Ray Moore and Ken Tebbutt went out on regular expeditions in a hired launch, the *Rata*, seeking the big tuna with lures made of unravelled rope and bits of plastic. On one of their best days they caught 11 tuna each weighing more than 45 kg – using the one rod and reel.

And on an evermore significant occasion in 1965, Ken Tebbutt went out with his friends on a different launch, Bruce McIntyre's *Takapu*. The group's fishing equipment had by now stretched to two rods, and on one of these, a snapper bottom fishing rod with a light reel, with a

harness made from light rope and a couple of snap hooks, and a lure made from a peg and a piece of frayed rope, Ken fished for more tuna. Instead, he hooked a striped marlin. Boated after about 2½ hours amid excitement that can only be imagined, the marlin was taken ashore to attract the newsmen, half the children and most of the adults in the district. The marlin was never weighed but has gone into history as weighing about 136 kg, a figure defended as a good guess.

The small town was now agog with fishing possibilities. Jim Rivett and Willy Arends, who were president and secretary of the local branch of the New Zealand Travel and Holiday Association, sensed a new attraction. They convened a public meeting on August 13, 1966, to organise a deep sea fishing contest for the town's jubilee celebrations the following year. Sixty enthusiastic boat owners from Whakatane, Opotiki, Kawerau and Rotorua came along and took the idea a step further by proposing to set up a new big game fishing club. They appointed Stewart Reidpath of Kawerau to chair a steering committee, with the job of making the club fully operational by the end of the year.

Well before the deadline, in November, a public meeting of enthusiasts now grown in

Close to the centre of the thriving township of Whakatane and protected from the open sea by a narrow coastal strip, the headquarters of the Whakatane Big Gamefishing Club front on to the calm waters of the Whakatane River, centre left. Whites Aviation.

numbers to more than 100, endorsed the club plans put forward by the steering committee, adopted a constitution and elected a committee. Sir William Sullivan was first patron, later succeeded after Sir William's death by Mr Rex Morpeth. The first president was S. Reidpath, with Bon Morpeth, as secretary.

The new club was accepted on incorporation as the seventh member of the New Zealand Big Game Fishing Council and straight away began to justify its status. Its first year membership of 328 had risen to 740 by the third year. The do-it-yourself small boat tradition on which it was founded was also promptly successful. On February 25, 1967, 119 game fish were weighed

in – a tremendous single day's catch. In 1967 also, Rod Bellerby caught a 190.51-kg mako on 24-kg gear, Vern Timbs the club's first striped marlin, of 101.60 kg, Jim Bayliss a 75.75-kg yellowfin tuna, and J. Bloomfield a 117.03-kg hammerhead.

While Whakatane club members know that almost anything may be caught in what they call the magic triangle – between Maketu and Te Kaha, each more than 40 km from town on the mainland, and White Island a similar distance out to sea – they do not object to having their area called the tuna capital of New Zealand and the yellowtail capital of the world. It also came as little surprise when Ken Schultz, associate fishing editor of the American magazine *Field and Stream* visited their Bay of Plenty waters and dubbed them also the grouper (hapuku) capital of the world.

The yellowtail fishing out of Whakatane is so consistently outstanding that it brings regular parties of American fishermen there on packaged fishing tours which take them on two eight-passenger launches the *Toa Tai* and the *Ariki Tai* out to the waters around White Island for two and sometimes three days at a time. There the big yellowtail are so strong that the capacity of gear used has usually to be greater than the weight of the fish, not considerably less as in most other angling.

Coming from an area where their yellowtail (a slightly different fish – *Seriola lalandi dorsalis* instead of *Seriola lalandi lalandi*) grow little bigger than 14 kg, the American anglers have been known to be disturbed when unweighable New Zealand fish, below 13.6 kg, are unhooked and thrown back, but recover when they are promised a good chance of catching one of 35 kg to 40 kg to make up for it.

The bigger charter boats – The *Toa Tai, Ariki Tai* and Colin Warrington's more recently added *Cara Mira* – not only go out to White Island but more regularly up to 40 km further out looking for, among other fish, the even bigger blue-fin tuna. Most of the Whakatane fishing, however, is still done from privately owned runabouts, or "deep sea dinghies". On good days these boats also have White Island within range, but they concentrate on the excellent fishing around Whale Island, with its good prospects of yellowtail and yellowfin tuna, and chances of a shark or a marlin.

Whakatane thinks of itself as predominantly a tuna club, and holds the New Zealand women's records in the two heaviest line classes. Yellowfin tuna can be caught almost anywhere in the magic triangle, although they seem to be more prolific to the east, toward Te Kaha and beyond.

Few marlin are caught out of Whakatane and most of those hooked in the area tend not to be boated, because they are picked up on small lures and light tackle rather than on bait. One keen and expert fisherman not long ago hooked six striped marlin in a day and lost them all. Another

W. A. Cawthorn's New Zealand record yellowfin tuna (75.50 kg) caught off Pearly Shells *out from Whakatane on 28 March 1980.* Whakatane Beacon.

This winning fish in the Whakatane Big Gamefishing Club's open tuna tournament in 1979 was a 45.79 kg yellowfin, caught by Colin Warrington from Restless. Whakatane Beacon.

calculated that not more than three in every ten hooked in this area were brought aboard. However, in the 1972 international big game fishing contest, when club members were urged to try for marlin by trailing baits and appropriate lures, six marlin were taken off Whakatane in one day.

Some of the failure stories suggest that the fish lost were too big for the small craft from which they were tackled. Jack Ludwig, of Kawerau, lost a big blue marlin, hooked on a blue lure and a 24-kg line out beyond Whale Island, largely for this reason. The fish was struck from John Baker's launch *Aquarius* at 1.15 pm. It took off a lot of quick line, and was at first variously judged to be a small mako or a large albacore. However it soon settled all doubts by broaching 300 metres from the boat and putting on a marathon display, leaping from the water about 20 times,

dragging the small boat around in circles and along the coast – almost to Te Kaha at one stage – and dashing off five times when about to be boated. It finally got away at 11.25 pm when the knot on the clip broke as the trace was being seized again. "It was a massive fish," recalls John Baker.

"We were inexperienced with such a catch, and there we were in a little boat (it was a 4.8-m runabout) with a fish almost as long, out in the middle of the night. It was not a good prospect at all."

Enough big fish were boated soon, however, to establish the club's reputation, and among them have been the two biggest black marlin caught in New Zealand waters since 1926, when Captain Laurie Mitchell set a New Zealand, and then a world, record of 442.71 kg, with a monster fighting fish caught off the Cavalli Islands.

The first of these Bay of Plenty blacks was taken by John Bloomfield, of Gisborne, fishing out of Whakatane in the launch *Arawana* in the national contest of 1972.

The fish took the bait about a kilometre east of Whale Island at about 1.15 pm and took six hours to boat. When brought into Whakatane, the biggest fish ever to be brought across the bar, it proved so heavy that it almost defied attempts to weigh it. The club's scales swayed and groaned as they took the strain at 413.68 kg – still 29 kg lighter than Captain Mitchell's record. John Bloomfield afterward expressed the feelings of many anglers when the fight is over. "It is one of those things that you dream about . . . . Only one thing makes me unhappy. It was such a beautiful fish and I am a little bit sad at having to kill it." A cast of the fish dominates the trophy-hung walls of the clubhouse.

When Denis Hodson finally got a large mako tied to the back of the 5.8 m *Rhan* (skipped by Stan McMillan) one March day in 1979, he felt that he might well be looking at a record catch. The huge shark had fought on the surface in a demonstration of tremendous power in the $3\frac{1}{2}$ hours it took to bring to the boat. It was by no means completely done even after all its aerobatics when, with two gaffs driven home, it was secured with strong lashings and a brand new stainless steel strop.

The mako, however, proved too heavy to pull right up on to the boat and was left half hanging over the stern while the boat set off carefully back to port. It heaved away at its bonds there, recovering its vigour minute by minute until with a final violent shake, it tore itself free. The new stainless steel strop with its 2,086-kg breakingstrain, unlaid by twisting, was just pulled apart.

In the early days of European settlement, when small coastal ports were regularly worked around the coast, a few larger vessels came to grief at the Whakatane entrance, but today the main effect of the bar is to make fishermen wary of weather and tide for their exits and entrances, and to encourage the continued use of smaller boats. Apart from the three larger charter craft, almost all the fishing launches are runabouts 5 m to 6 m

long. To cater for these, the club has a good launching ramp and trailer park almost at the harbour mouth, and close to the roomy club headquarters in former port buildings. Nearby is also the site of a planned marina.

Once out to sea, the Whakatane fishermen are soon into a rich game fishing area from which it is declared to be almost impossible to return in the afternoon empty-handed. The fishing starts a mile or two off the harbour and is into its best within 20 minutes' run around Whale Island.

John Bloomfield's big black was hooked not far off the island in 25 metres of water. Whale Island offers the best offshore shelter in several bays, although one may need to move around the island if the wind changes. There is good fishing also but less shelter around the Rurima Islands, a cluster of rocky islets about six kilometres to the west of Whale Island.

From Whale Island out – 90 per cent of bigger fish are caught in this area – trolling prospects are good until the 200-metre line is reached about two thirds of the way to White Island. Here, in a region known as the Mad Mile, the East Auckland Current produces strong up-wellings from a deep trench.

This special environment for bait and bigger fish exists all the way down the 200-metre line as it runs south-east from Mayor Island in a sweep inside White Island and around close to East Cape.

Those boats proceeding on out to White Island normally pull in their heavy trolling lines once past the 200-metre line and put out light gear for bait fish (kahawai and skipjack) until the area of the island is reached. White Island creates its own marine environment standing on a small shelf with 400 metres of water close in around it. The steaming volcano offers little welcome shelter but also no danger to the fisherman off its shores.

It is around White Island, and even further out, where the American anglers seek their yellowtail – often winning the yellowtail section of the national big game championships for their

Two mighty record tuna. Early in 1980 anglers fishing out of Whakatane got a quadruple strike off Lottin Point from Sea Lee, skippered by Colin Lee, of Te Puke. One fish was soon lost, and a second got away after being played for 20 minutes, but the battle was on for the other two. After two hours Graham Potter, of Te Puke, brought in a 107 kg northern bluefin tuna on a 24 kg test line for a New Zealand record. Just over two hours later – after a struggle of 4 hours 10 minutes – Rex Wood of Tauranga boated a 158 kg northern bluefin for a new record. In the photograph above Rex Wood and his fish are in the foreground and Graham Potter stands with his prize.

Whakatane Beacon.

adopted club – and where one of their number, Matt Maxwell, caught a world record fish of 34.01 kg on a 10-kg line in February, 1976. The average angler needs tackle a good deal heavier than this to stand any chance of catching one of these big fighting fish. A minimum of 24-kg line is used, usually 36 kg and sometimes 60 kg for fish which have an initial explosive run, usually in the direction of the bottom, where in the rocks the line is soon broken. The world record catch on 60-kg line was also made at White Island, by J. V. Bayliss in 1975.

The Americans have brought some of their own methods of catching yellowtail, introducing Bay of Plenty fishermen to the art of using jigs dropped into deep water. Bottom fishing in more than 200 metres – the bottom is largely mud with rock pinnacles rising from it – is a special sort of sport. Yellowtail are also caught trolling, by casting and retrieving, and with lures or bait. Another popular method is to catch skipjack or albacore on the way out to the island and use either the whole fish, a fillet from it, or the fish stripped on one side, as bait for deep drifting.

For the yellowfin tuna off Whakatane it is usual to troll with lures at 5 to 10 or 12 knots – 9 knots seems a successful speed. When hooked, these fish set off in a blazing run, taking up to 600 metres of line straight off. Smoking reels are no figment of imagination with these fish, which go commonly to more than 40 kg, all packed with streamlined lively muscle. The ultimate situation for catching them is to run into a school of anchovies or small mackerel in the same area as a school of tuna; and use the one as live bait for the other.

Whakatane's tuna numbers have had their thin years, but they are returning. Rather more than the effects of the large fleet of Japanese longliners which fish about 100 kilometres off the coast each late winter, the on-off seasons are thought to be due to variations in water temperatures. Local opinion is that the tuna do not appear in numbers until the surface water temperature is about 19°C, and when the temperature rises to

His 200 kg mako pleases Phil Lynds of the Whakatane Big Gamefishing Club. The fish was caught in a New Zealand Open Tournament. Whakatane Beacon.

22° they dive deeper to find a thermocline that suits them.

The yellowfin off Whakatane (as indeed they are everywhere) are very good to eat. Locals usually smoke, bake or bottle them. Skipjack taste good, too, and perhaps best of all are albacore, which in these waters reach New Zealand record weights of about 18 kg. Many of them do not get to a weighing station. They are wrapped in tinfoil and baked out on the boat for splendid meals.

The sports fishing club at Waihau Bay, 100 kilometres from Opotiki along the curve of the Bay of Plenty towards East Cape, and 240 kilometres from Rotorua where the club's president – now J. R. (Jack) Honey – and secretary tend to live, is the centre of perhaps the smallest, but not the least proud, of the game fishing clubs of the coast. The bay, with a stretch of about two kilometres of safe beach, has long been a family holiday area for those who liked a quiet place and were prepared to tackle a long rough road to get to it. The bay did not get an electricity supply from the grid until about 10 years ago. The road to it was not tar-sealed until about three years later (and it is thus not so hard to get to it today).

Among those who took refuge on holidays there was Pat Burstall, later Conservator of Wildlife in the Department of Internal Affairs, Rotorua. He thought long about the merits of a local fishing club, as an alternative to Whakatane and its troublesome bar, and to reach new waters beyond the normal reach of the Whakatane launches. In 1966, with Jack Edlin donating material for a boat ramp and helping to build it, the handful of permanent and periodic residents of Waihau Bay set up their club. Harry Dutton, then manager of the boarding house, and his wife Mary helped to get the fishing going and produced a newsletter on what was being caught. In the course of the following years the boat ramp – situated in a small natural bay in the rocks, difficult to use only with the wind from the north-east and then only at high tide – was

doubled in size.

Scales were set up, able to weigh up to 226.8 kg. Nothing prestigious here but the sort of fishing club that holidaying New Zealanders wanted. And they swore by the fishing they got.

They still do. The Waihau Bay Sports Fishing Club is now affiliated to the New Zealand Big Game Fishing Council and takes part in its national tournaments. Then maybe 15 runabouts will assemble and go out to show the world how good the fishing is. The club membership is about 150. But the fishing grounds matter more than number of anglers or numbers of boats to a fishing club, and the grounds off Waihau Bay are something special.

On this stretch of exposed coast the continental shelf is at least as close to land as in any other club area in the north. And off Cape Runaway, which the club regards as its eastern boundary, the 200-metre line comes in closer to land – within about three kilometres – than anywhere else on the North Island coast. The deep blue water of the oceanic environment, borne down here in the East Auckland Current, has been seen right up to the shore at Cape Runaway.

Through all this good water, rocks and reefs encourage passing fish to pause and feed long enough for fishermen to go out and meet them. This is a consistently good area for commercial crayfishing, and for gathering hapuku, tarakihi and moki. It is prolific, too, in flying fish, which are said to be harbingers of marlin. A few striped marlin have been caught, usually about three km from the shore and about 90 kg in weight. The biggest fish so far is a black marlin of 286.67 kg.

The local Maoris told the pakeha holiday-makers that there were tuna in the area, and so it proved when the fishermen went looking for them. The yellowfin off Waihau Bay – they usually come in November and go in May, with the best months from January to March – average about 30 kg to 35 kg, with the biggest caught so far going to 66.67 kg. They seem to travel in uniform-sized schools so that the first

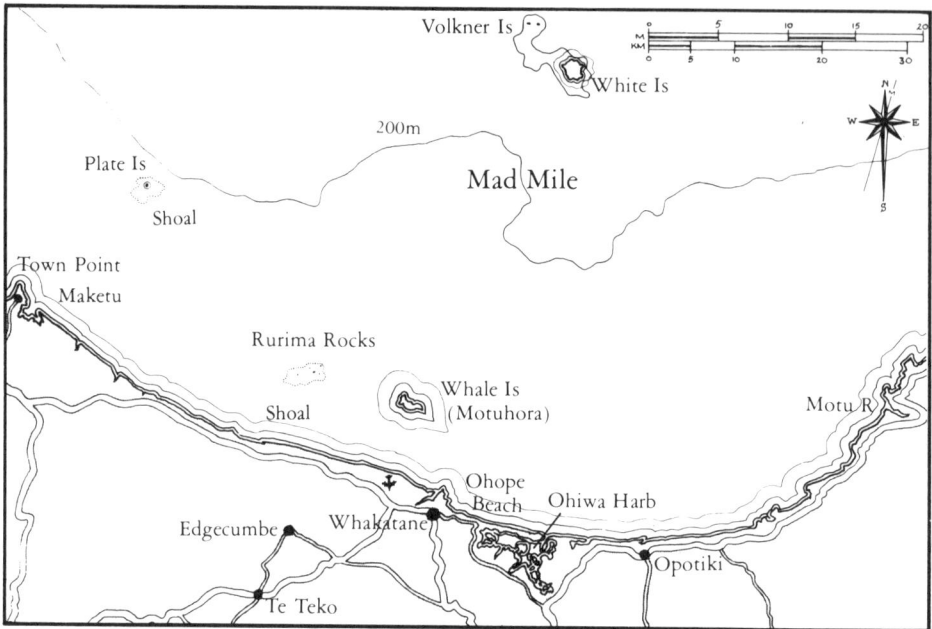

Map 8 *The "magic triangle" waters of the Whakatane Big Gamefishing Club.*

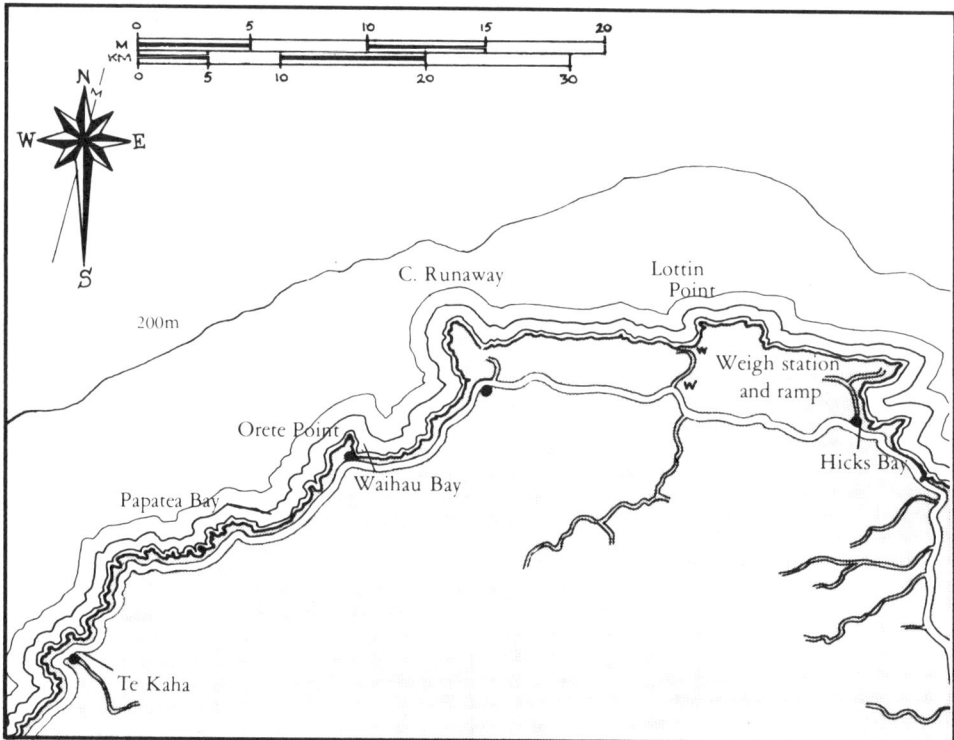

Map 9 *The fishing waters of the Waihau Bay Sports Fishing Club — from Te Kaha to Cape Runaway — meet in the coastal strip off Lottin Point, the northern waters of the Gisborne-Tatapouri Sports Fishing Club.*

The first marlin caught from Whakatane, leading to the foundation of the Whakatane Big Gamefishing Club in 1966. From left: S. McMillan, Ken Tebbutt, Ron Rowson, Bruce McIntyre, Alec Gaul. Ken Tebbutt holds the snapper rod on which the reputedly 136 kg marlin was caught.

one caught sets the weight for those to follow. There are occasional blue-fin tuna, too, and albacore. November and December usually sees a run of yellowtail, numerous and large: they weighed from 26 kg to 32 kg in the summer of 1979–80. Then they usually disappear about Christmas, and smaller schools come back later, fish of 3 kg to 4½ kg.

When the dolphin fish (mahimahi in Hawaii and dorado in Mexico) came to the New Zealand shores in 1978 they came to Waihau Bay first of all the grounds, and in the greatest numbers, C. A. Flinkenberg, fishing out of Waihau Bay on

February 19 of that year, caught a dolphin fish of 11.25 kg which was not only the New Zealand record on 15-kg line but the heaviest of these fish caught in New Zealand waters on any tackle.

The only other New Zealand record fish caught from Waihau Bay has been a 134.93-kg hammerhead caught on 15-kg line by P. Batchelor on February 23, 1978, a record since shared by M. A. Armstrong at Tutukaka. But records are not everything. The fishing from Waihau Bay is not just good, it is consistently good. Not even the activities of long liners off the coast nor the presence for several years, under strong local protest, of a box net installed by the Department of Agriculture and Fisheries in conjunction with a Japanese company, have been able to spoil it.

CHAPTER THIRTEEN

East Cape to Fiordland

Formed in 1967, the Gisborne-Tatapouri Sports Fishing Club was not originally zeroed on big game fish and still cheerfully mixes snapper with its sharks. However, what began as an organisation of keen family fishermen, getting together for safety in company on an exposed coast with no offshore shelter at all, has worked in much solid game fishing, with a couple of world records to its credit.

Trevor Charles and Tony Eastgate, two of the foundation members of the club, were its first and second presidents. The others who started it off were John K. Aitken, Syd Parkes, R. G. (Ray) Webb and M. R. (Mick) Sheridan. The club's presidents since 1969 have been J. R. (Jack) Honey, P. D. (Paddy) Wanklyn, J. E. (John) Hough, Gordon Hobcroft and W. B. (Bill) Cooper.

Wide open waters – the club-house and ramp of the Gisborne-Tatapouri Sports Fishing Club. Whites Aviation.

The club's world records are for the heaviest hammerhead shark caught by a woman on a 60-kg line – a fish of 184.16 kg caught off Lottin Point on February 26, 1974, by Mrs H. M. Wood, a member of the family whose generosity, in making it possible to build a boat launching ramp and weighing station on private land at the point, has opened up to the club one of the most exciting areas for big game fishing on the New Zealand coast.

On the day Mrs Wood caught her record fish the sea conditions were "difficult but not dangerous for small craft". It was late February on the third day of the New Zealand open championship of 1974. Mrs Wood, who had some game fishing experience, was the only crew with her son Brian in a new 5-m runabout. Two miles out from Lottin Point they drifted east with the strong current into the wind and sea with freshly caught skipjack out as three baits. When the strike came after a few minutes, Mrs Wood realised that she had a big fish.

The tussle itself was tremendous but it was obvious that the hardest part was going to be for just the two of them to boat the fish in the difficult sea conditions. However, when she got the fish alongside after a 53-minute battle Mrs Wood – sore in the neck, back, arms and legs and shaking with fatigue – secured the hammerhead by the tail while her son held it by the gaff in the head. The shark was longer than the cockpit by nearly a metre and it took several minutes at full stretch over the side of the rocking boat to get the fish secured for the hour and a quarter trip back, to weigh in at 184.16 kg – which is still the world 60-kg record for women.

The other world record fish caught by a club member A. G. (Tony) Eastgate, was a 198-kg thresher shark caught on a 24-kg line during a national tournament, on February 22, 1978. It took him 3¾ hours to bring to his 6-m runabout. He had made a tougher catch the day before when a 165.56-kg hammerhead took 6¾ hours to boat.

Lottin Point is an outpost with a difference of the Gisborne-Tatapouri Club. The 200 kilometres by road that separates Lottin Point from base means a change from a coast that faces south-east to one that lies to the north, with different sea conditions, and from an area where the 200-metre depth lies well offshore to one where the edge of the continental shelf and the tail end of the East Auckland Current run very close to the coast. A prime zone – with the upwellings and extra thermoclines and resulting rich fish populations which on many other parts of the coast have to be sought well offshore – lies within three or four kilometres out from the 16 kilometres of coast between Cape Runaway and Matakoa Point which can be fished from Lottin Point. Little wonder that the still small band of anglers who regularly fish from Lottin Point claim that in terms of fish it has just about everything.

Ashore, the weighing station is capable of weighing 453.6 kg (1,000 lb) ready for the big ones but no more than half taxed in the eight years it has been there. There is reason for the relatively few catches apart from the isolation. Lottin Point is on a spectacular area of open coastline and the rocky cove where the ramp is situated is completely sheltered only from winds from the south. Any wind with a touch of north in it puts paid to fishing from there. Yet when the weather is good the water is crystal clear, and many sorts of fish – marlin, makos, albacore, yellowfin tuna and a lot of hammerheads – can be caught.

In 1972, when Gisborne-Tatapouri's *Blue Spray* team won the shark section of the international contest, the winning catch came from the Lottin Point area.

Once out to sea the area is free of rocks and reefs. A mud bottom forms at a depth of about 120 metres and slopes steeply away. Bonito (or skipjack) is the main bait used, caught on the troll, with some albacore. Those who prefer kahawai usually catch it off the rocks, although some troll for it.

The heart of the club is at Tatapouri, a resort a

few kilometres north of Gisborne, on a pleasant coast looking south-east into the open sea. The club house is there and a ramp and a weighing station (the club's third set of scales is at Gisborne). The club has no charter boats and most of the club's 350-odd members fish from trailer craft. The seas off Tatapouri are open to big ocean swells which come up from storms around the Chatham Islands area. As the 200-metre line is about 25 kilometres off Tatapouri, most of the club's fishing is concentrated on the area of the Ariel Bank, about 14 kilometres out and at an average depth of about 15 m, and on the other foul ground a mile or two to the south-east.

It is also always worth investigating several smaller areas inshore where the seabed rises to 40 m, and an area of deeper water off the lighthouse at Gable End Foreland, about 12 miles up the coast. The main game fish in this area now are makos (yellowfin tuna were more plentiful when the club was formed), but they are mainly small so much of the fishing in this area is with 6-kg and 10-kg line.

A few striped marlin had been seen before and even a few hooked, but the first one was not brought in to be weighed until 1972. Then the present club president Bill (W. B.) Cooper, who was also an early prime-mover in the club was out in his 5.5-metre launch *Star Hunter* with his 12-year-old son Ian. As he drifted with live bonito outside the Ariel Bank, the line suddenly screamed out, and a striped marlin leaped from the water. In now roughening seas, and soon about 12 miles from land, Bill fought the fish without benefit of a chair, while his son manoeuvred the boat in the three hours that it took, after several attempts, to bring the marlin to gaff. It was still too heavy for the two of them to haul aboard, so was tied behind while the boat made a slow slog of more than 19 miles back to base.

Normally the club's season for big fish starts in November, but the first fish, as in other areas, have of recent years tended to come along later.

And the fishing has gone up and down. In the 1979–80 year the club recorded 45 makos, one black marlin of 289.2 kg, two hammerheads, a thresher and five yellowfin tuna. Obviously more and bigger fish are around to be caught, particularly off Lottin Point.

Between Lottin Point and Gisborne there are a number of other accessible areas of lovely coast, and at Tolaga Bay, Tokomaru Bay and Hicks Bay (where there was a weighing station before Lottin Point was established) fishing clubs have been formed or are forming.

It was in 1963 that a small group of keen amateur boat fishermen in Napier called together by E. S. Wiig (father of E. K. Wiig 1981 president of the N.Z. Big Game Fishing Council) decided it was high time Hawkes Bay had a fishing club. From that decision has grown a lively go-ahead Hawkes Bay Game Fishing Club, with its own marina for moored boats, four-lane concrete launching ramp, launching basin, and well-appointed new club house with all required facilities for the club's current 634 membership.

During the summer period in particular, mako sharks range all over the bay, even into the shallower water, in large numbers. An indication of this was the 27 tagged and released during the 1980 national contest. Double that number would have been tagged had the weather not taken a hand during the contest. And many of that 27 were lured up to the boat with a bait and tagged without even being hooked.

Tuna, albacore and sizeable yellowtail all appear on the club's game fish record board in addition to mako, hammerhead and thresher sharks.

With the dredging of the silted-up Iron Pot inlet in 1967, the club built a floating finger-type marina facility for moored boats in the inlet. In 1974 this was replaced by a permanent facility. An intensive works programme over the last four years has seen a modern clubhouse erected, mostly funded by debentures from members, and complete permanent re-construction, with

E. Wiig, of Hawkes Bay, now the president of the New Zealand Big Game Fishing Council, with a mako. Herald-Tribune.

expansion of the launching basin, ramps, sealed car and trailer park and other facilities.

With increasing numbers of billfish sightings, and a couple of short-lived hook-ups in the last few seasons and more members gearing themselves up for game fishing, the Hawkes Bay Game Fishing Club, already with a New Zealand tournament title and four women's and two men's New Zealand records for light tackle catches on its belt, is each year making its presence felt more strongly on the New Zealand game fishing scene which it entered back in May 1971, when it affiliated with the New Zealand Game Fishing Council.

I went to Napier Technical College with Ernie Wiig's father. My father always had motor launches and was a very keen fisherman. One of his closest friends was Stanley Adamson of Hastings who moved to Russell in about 1919 and became well known in swordfishing circles as skipper to Alma Baker who fished from his launch *Reliance*. His stories about "swordfish", the Bay of Islands and his big launch with electric lights and a 100 h.p. engine made an indelible impression on me, a 10-year-old kid with a "flattie", a 3-m rowboat on the river.

High adventure to me was to be taken on Cape Kidnappers fishing trips by Sam Hawkins on his 9-m Bailey-built *Airina* with a two-cylinder Frisco Standard engine and forward

149

Not big but numerous: sharks caught by members of the Hawkes Bay Big Gamefishing Club during a day of the New Zealand national game fish tournament. Herald-Tribune.

cockpit. What I liked most was running the bar at the Ngararora river mouth – it scared the hell out of me. What he taught me about counting the waves to get the groups and sequences in order to know which particular wave would be followed by a calm period long enough to let us in, or out, has served me well at sea, in the surf, and in many entrances all my life.

The latest club to be affiliated to the New Zealand Big Game Fishing Council is based on Dunedin, where the Tautuku Fishing Club takes its name from a peninsula in the Catlins district which was for hundreds of years the site of a seasonal Maori fishing camp and in more recent years has drawn a faithful band of holiday anglers. A group of the fishermen, meeting informally at first in the bars of various hotels, and then as a club, finally settled on a permanent headquarters in the old two-storey Smaill homestead on the outskirts of Dunedin, beside Smaills Beach, a frequently used launching site.

The progress made ashore in 10 years – the club was formed in 1970 and admitted to membership of the New Zealand Big Game Fishing Council in 1979 – has been matched by a broadening of interest offshore. The 70-odd club members own 25 boats ranging from 5 m to 7.5 m and, using various launching sites, regard the 200 miles of sea from Moeraki to Stewart Island as home waters. There is a club bach at Tautuku, down the coast from Dunedin.

Compared with the warmer northern coasts, the range of game fish is restricted. Most of the earlier and much of the present interest centres in the groper and blue cod which abound in the area. The recent recognition of blue sharks as gamefish has widened the club's horizons, as has a growth in interest in fly-fishing for kahawai. A group of members is determined that the first marlin or broadbill to be landed in the South Island will come from their ranks.

The 1980–81 club president is K. Wilson, with F. Morgan vice-president, secretary T. Corbett and treasurer A. Falconer. The club captain is A. Miller, with V. Hughes as assistant secretary and a six-man committee consisting of M. Eckhold, S. Hughes, K. McCullough, M. Mattingly, K. Cunningham and R. Magee.

Early one morning in 1972 Brent Vincent, assistant fisheries officer in the southern lakes district of the South Island, was aboard the fishing boat *Victor Hugo* leaving Milford Sound for the open sea. The surface of the water for hundreds of yards around was alive with leaping tuna. Many, he reported later, could be seen clear of the water at a single glance, "hammering sprats, herring, kahawai and other varieties of bait fish in a manner that had to be seen to be believed".

Brent had already seen albacore in the southern sounds, and what he believed to be southern bluefin tuna. A crayfisherman had told him of a sighting of marlin. Such fishing potential in an area of unsurpassed scenic beauty presented an opportunity which could not be allowed to go unresolved any longer. The Fiordland Game Fishing Club was formed in 1972. Brent was elected its first president, with Kevin Crosbie of Dunedin as secretary, J. McFarlane as vice-president and Dave Lamming as club captain. By the time the club held its first annual meeting in September, 1973, it was able to report the first landing on game fishing gear anywhere in the world of a butterfly, or scaled tuna, and the catching also of southern bluefin tuna, albacore, yellowtail, and kahawai; and the likely presence, still to be confirmed on the rod, of striped and black marlin — with the marlin sighted being reported as "large".

The club soon extended its original fishing grounds to include trips to Doubtful and Thompson Sounds and other arms of the sea running deep into Fiordland National Park. To get to these areas necessitates journeys as adventurous as the fishing at the other end. At the end of the early journeys lay a camping spot on Pandora Beach surrounded in the summer by thousands of white orchids in the peak of bloom. Only a couple of small albacore were caught on the rod on one such day but bluefin tuna

estimated to weigh nearly 50 kg were seen jumping two metres clear of the water.

The club soon added several blue sharks and a small thresher to the fish caught. Trout fishing in some of the excellent inland waters supplemented the fishing explorations in and outside of the fiords. Then came the first hint of record fish from the sea with a 67.13-kg southern bluefin tuna on 10-kg line — a possible world record fish which could not be claimed because the angler had used — without realising that the rules then forbade it — a lure containing triple hooks to catch it.

The club got its first — and Brent Vincent *his* first — New Zealand record with 23.31-kg southern bluefin on 10-kg gear in 1976.

In 1978, Fiordland with its *Samara* team fishing from its home grounds won the tuna section of the New Zealand Open Game Fishing Tournament with a total of 241.3 points — compared with Whakatane's 83 points.

Since then a Fiordland club member, Murray Hill, has set another New Zealand record for a 54.43-kg southern bluefin tuna caught on a 24-kg line — although this has since been surpassed by a Nelson hotelkeeper, Desmond Benson, first, and later by R. Wood of Whakatane with a fish of 158 kg.

And in February, 1980, Denny Arnott out with Dick Marquand in *Samara*, battled for nine hours and a quarter on 15-kg line with a mako estimated at 3 m long and to weigh more than 225 kg. The mako was hooked at 12.15 pm about a mile out from Transit Beach, south of Milford Sound and broke off, after being twice up to the trace, at 9.30 pm. It took the boat about 16 miles out to sea.

Fiordland's membership of about 120 is one of the smallest among all the clubs affiliated to the New Zealand Big Game Fishing Council, to which it was admitted in November, 1975, but from its base at Te Anau it draws on one of the more lightly populated areas in New Zealand. Its fishing grounds on the West Coast lie between Jackson's Bay in the north and Puysegur Point in the south, encompassing 197 miles of rugged coastline indented with twelve major sound or fiord complexes.

The fiords lead deep water into the heart of the mountains of the Fiordland National Park, with some of the most magnificent scenery in the world. There is road access to Jackson's Bay, south of Haast township, to Milford Sound, where there is a major tourist hotel; and into Thompson Sound by a power station access road over the Wilmot Pass.

The club's favourite access is Deep Cove at the head of the Thompson-Doubtful complex, and which is reached by barging trailer boats and towing vehicles across Lake Manapouri and then travelling them over 19 km of steep road to the sound. From there they motor to a base camp at either Pandora Beach or Deas Cove, where there is a 16-bunk camp.

For most of the fishing waters, a party has to be self-supporting in everything for the period of their stay. Something of a hassle? The scenery is worth it and club members swear the fishing is, too. A lot of the angling is done on lures, mainly on light lines. Fish in these waters include southern bluefin tuna, albacore, butterfly tuna, yellowtail, thresher, mako, blue and white sharks, and broadbill. Several broadbill have been seen by club members and commercial fishermen have found them entangled in their lines, but none have been caught on rod and line around Fiordland yet. The club intends to make up for this and at the time of writing is planning to fish at night for them, using light sticks.

Although the club has made its reputation so far on smaller game fish caught on light tackle – and a member holds a New Zealand record with a 3-kg blue shark on 3-kg line – it is prepared for anything. It has recently bought club scales which will weigh up to 500 kg – big enough for a New Zealand record in any game fish and a world record in most.

There may one day be a big game fishing club centred on one of the harbours of the West Coast of the South Island – there is fishing out there –

but the bar harbours and the strong westerly winds from the south Tasman Sea which can make the bars impassable for weeks at a time, particularly in the summer, do not make it an immediate prospect.

The main target fish off the coast are southern bluefin tuna, which were discovered there by fishing trawlers going further afield in search of new fishing grounds late in the 1970s. The first contact is attributed to Tom Fishburn; he returned to port, grabbed everything that looked like a tuna lure and came back from his following trip with a few bluefin tuna, no lures, rope burns everywhere and a new outlook on the power of these fish.

Commercial fishermen also found there was a specialised technique to be followed in handling the fish when caught if the high price offering on the Japanese market was to be obtained. It took a couple of years for rod and reel fishermen to try the fishing. They were handicapped by the need to fish in mid-winter from trawlers which did not boast any gimballed chairs. And they had to wait for invitations to be forthcoming to go out on the trawlers in any case.

Roy Woolly is one of those who have tried game fishing from trawlers, on an expedition which landed in all 31 bluefin, about one quarter of these by rod and reel.

Another has been Des Benson, of Nelson, invited to try the area from a trawler fishing for hoki. A tuna enthusiast for years, he was winner of the New Zealand open tuna section in 1975 and runner up (from Whakatane) in 1976. Trout-fishing guide Tony Haultain from Whakatane, was also invited along.

Fishing for only one night (4 August 1980) Des Benson took three bluefin tuna weighing 75 kg, 97 kg and 98 kg (the latter, the fish in the photograph, was a New Zealand record, since broken, as well as a world prospect). Tony Haultain, using 37-kg line throughout, caught two fish, of 115 kg and 133 kg, the latter a candidate for a world record but not claimed.

Des Benson went back again by trawler in late

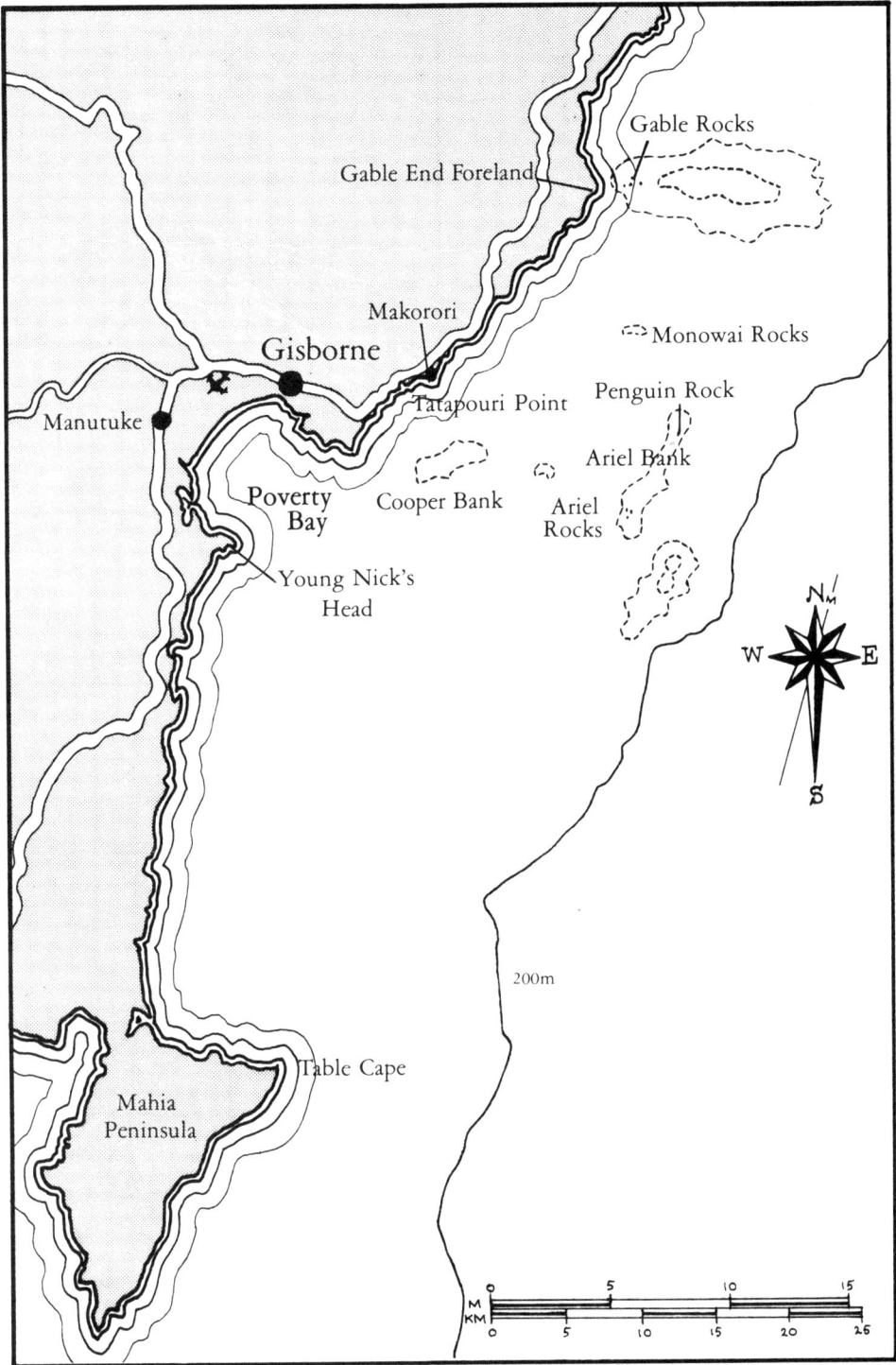

Map 10 *The southern waters of the Gisborne-Tatapouri Sports Fishing Club.*

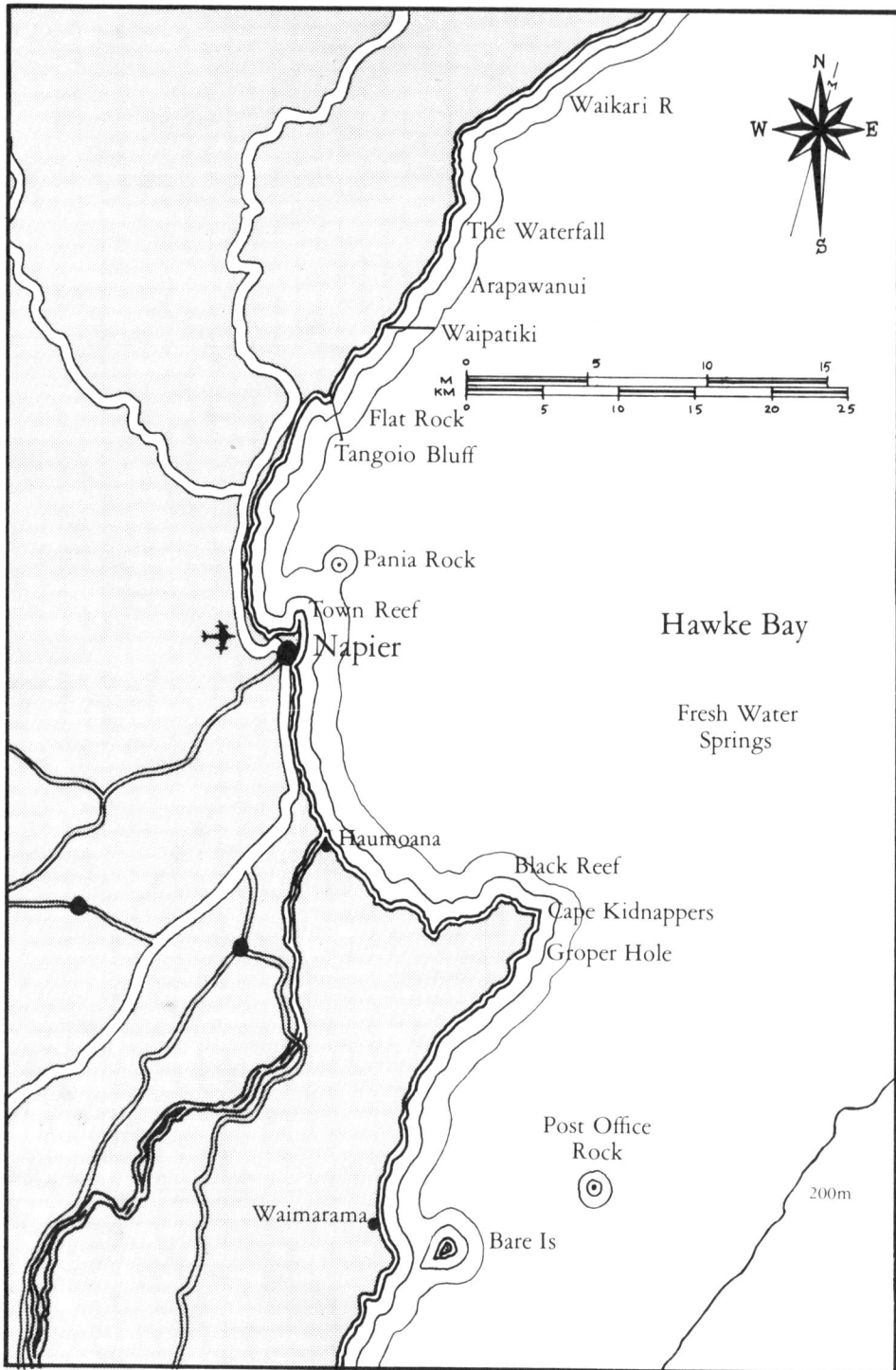

Waikari R

The Waterfall

Arapawanui

Waipatiki

Flat Rock
Tangoio Bluff

Pania Rock

Town Reef
Napier

Hawke Bay

Fresh Water
Springs

Haumoana

Black Reef

Cape Kidnappers

Groper Hole

Post Office
Rock

200m

Waimarama

Bare Is

N
NE
W   E
S

M
KM
0   5   10   15
0   5   10   15   20   25

Map 11 *The Hawkes Bay Gamefishing Club waters.*

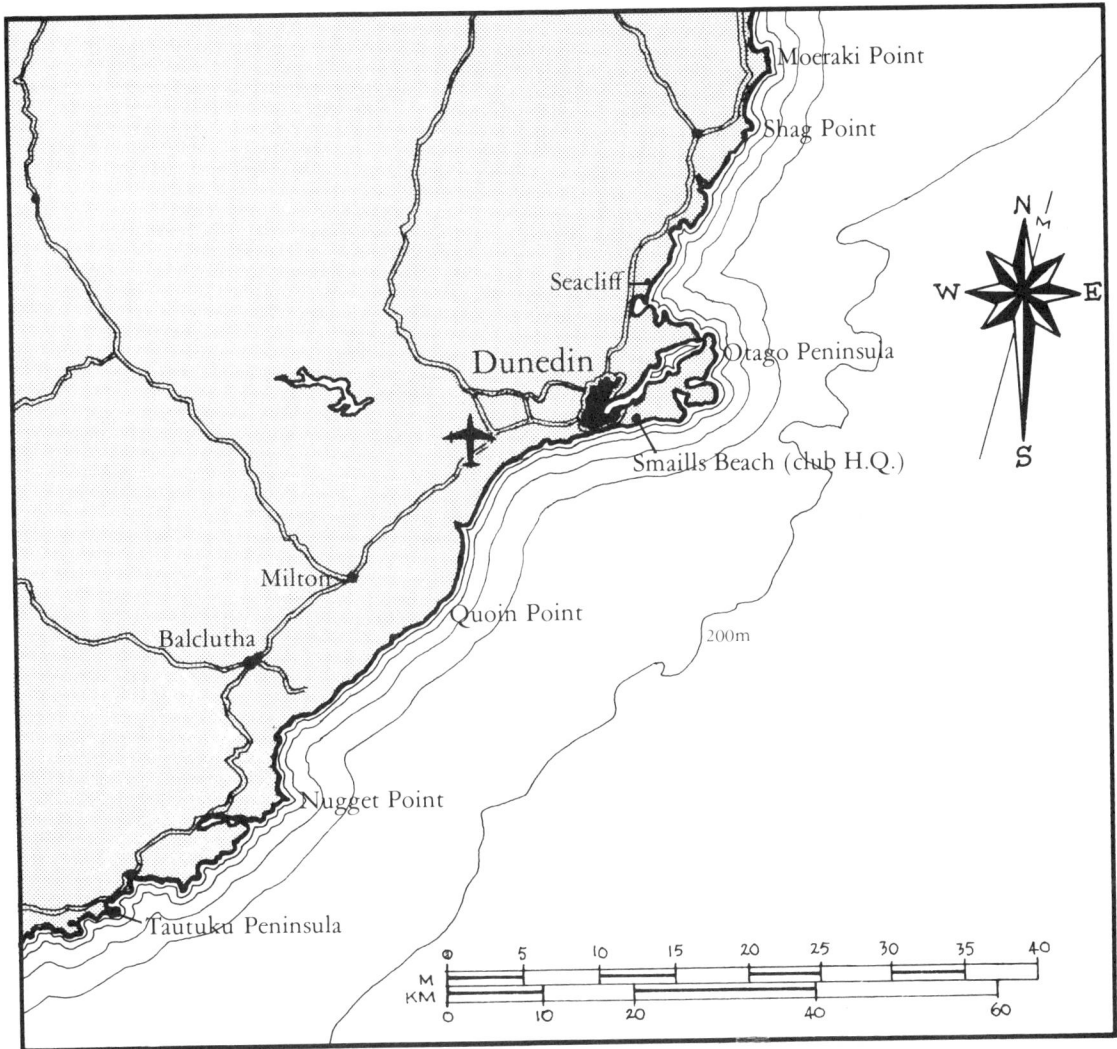

Map 12 *The Tautuku Fishing Club's coast.*

June 1981. The first night out he landed a 104-kg fish on a 37-kg line, a New Zealand record claim. The next night one fish was hooked and lost. Another of about 80 kg with old injuries was caught, and a third estimated to weigh at least 140 kg (against the current world record of 116.5 kg on a 37-kg line) was chopped by a shark close to the boat after a fight of an hour and a half.

As Des says, two New Zealand records and two near world records on only two trips was good going. The extent of the West Coast tuna season after late August is still unknown as the hoki season finishes then and no trawlers fish the area. And it may not start until mid-June; one Greymouth trawlerman laid a long line in late May 1981 and caught no tuna – only three broadbill from 100 kg to 220 kg dressed weight. The same fisherman expressed surprise at Benson's interest in the broadbill, commenting that at times during the summer albacore season off Greymouth they had seen five or six per day.

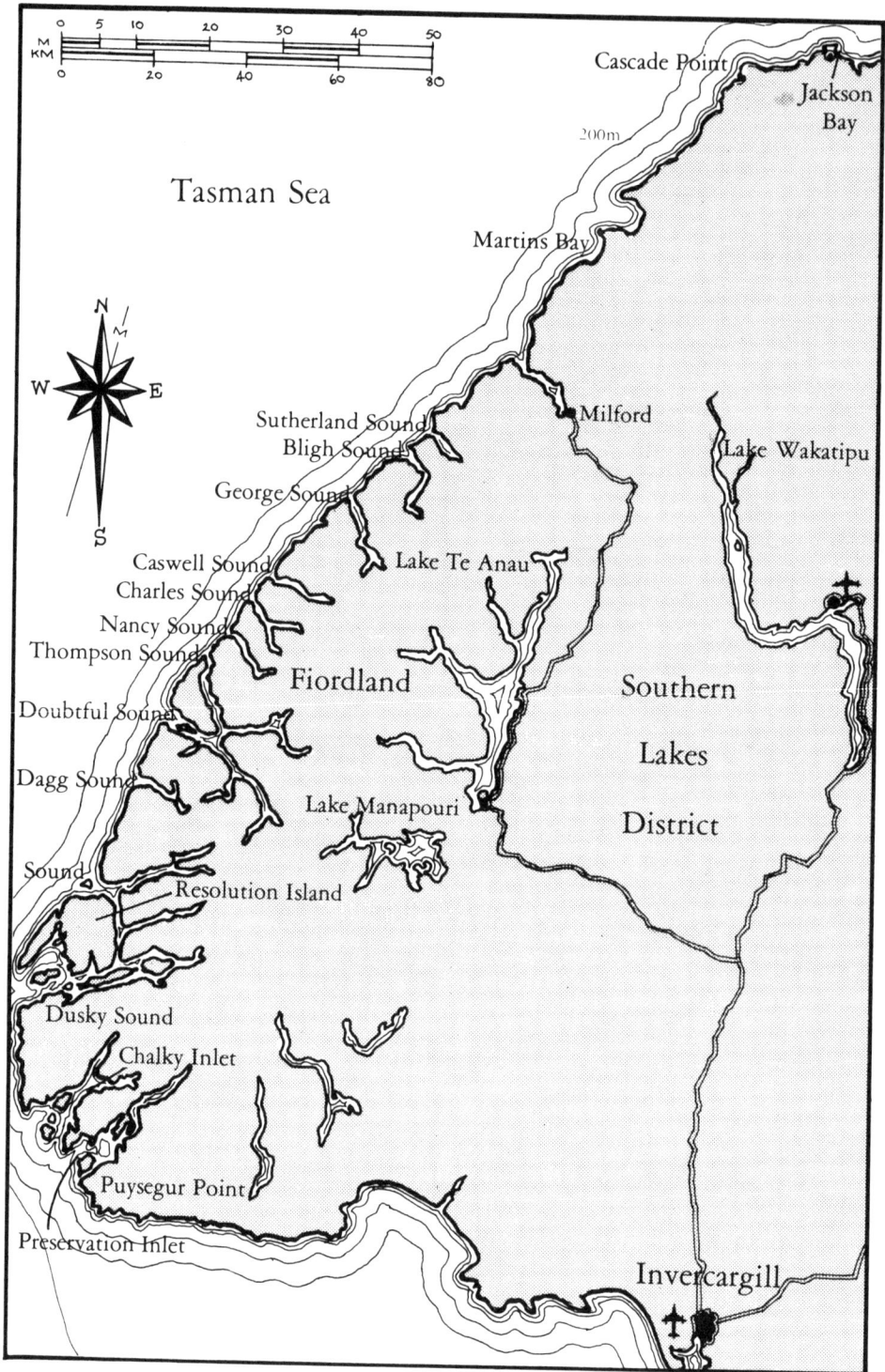

Map 13   *The deeply indented coast of the Fiordland Gamefishing Club.*

156

The broadbill were actually a nuisance, breaking up the albacore trolling gear. Other fishermen report numerous large makos and white sharks, along with billfish tentatively identified as black marlin.

The known tuna area off the West Coast is from Westport south to at least Greymouth, but the bluefin have been reported to follow Nelson-based trawlers as far north as Farewell Spit, the northern extremity of the South Island. The fish appear to be in a water depth of 550 to 650 m, and about 80 to 100 km offshore. The Japanese report a maximum weight of about 185 kg, but this appears open to question. Trawler crews fishing for the Japanese sushami market (fresh chilled fish) land fish averaging 80 to 100 kg with three men on heavy handlines; but the same crews have had some fish outpull five men and break the gear used. And while the maximum weight quoted for *Thunnus maccoyii* by a fishing authority was previously 226 kg, the fish landed by E. Andrews at Mayor Island in 1970 weighed 298 kg.

On their night expeditions off the coast the technique needed to hook bluefin tuna was found by Des Benson and Tony Hauldain to be different from those reported elsewhere. They suspect the fish's behaviour patterns may be different in the daytime. They found that tuna would often follow the last trawl lifted to the surface and feed on chum spilled from the net and scuppers. Once raised they usually remained with the boat all night and could be caught by trailing with chum.

Their fight was not as dramatic as the fast yellowfin surface runs, but the bluefin are a very determined fish, prone to sounding and hard plugging. One fish on the 1980 expedition took at least 500 m of 37 kg line under maximum tension before breaking off.

These are new waters – game fishing in this area of the New Zealand coast was unknown until 1980 and even the hoki have been commercially fished only in the last few years – but it is difficult to see how their gamefishing potential can be easily realised. The areas are 90 km or more offshore, the season appears to be in midwinter when the usually rough seas are even rougher, and all-weather access is lacking to either Westport or Greymouth, the nearest harbours, both of which have bars. The nearest all-weather port, Nelson, is a minimum of 18 hours' travel from the known fishing ground.

Perhaps the area could be game-fished with a heavy displacement hull launch or a largish motor sailer equipped for trips lasting a week or more. West Coast-based trawlers down to about 11 m in length fish the area; but although Des Benson and Tony Haultain caught their tuna while passengers on a couple of the trawlers they cannot recommend them for deep-sea angling. There is no clear deck space on a stern trawler and they found their best platform on stern gallows 8 m above the water. Even there it was difficult to make effective use of medium or heavy gamefishing tackle without a fighting chair and footrest.

CHAPTER FOURTEEN

Organising the sport

The organisation of big game fishing in New Zealand has evolved slowly according to need and opportunity. The formation of local clubs, starting in the mid 1920s, preceded the formation of the New Zealand Big Game Fishing Council, which now co-ordinates the sport in New Zealand, by more than 30 years. On several earlier occasions the need for a central body to regulate the sport was seen, and several times the necessary organisation was nearly achieved.

The first attempt was the formation of the New Zealand Deep Sea Anglers Association, which had a brief existence from 1940, until the Second World War brought an end to organised game fishing for the duration, and even longer in some areas.

Dr Harold Pettit, of Auckland, was the president and Sir Ernest Davis, then Mayor of Auckland, was patron of the association. It did not have the full support of all the clubs, however, and did not last long, nor did an attempt in 1952 to revive the association resolve the differences and sometimes jealousies which were keeping the clubs apart.

The present New Zealand Big Game Fishing Council came into being indirectly in 1957 when the then Governor General of New Zealand Sir Willoughby Norrie, (later Lord Norrie) who was an experienced angler in both fresh and saltwater presented a gold cup for annual competition between the game fishing clubs. There were then

five such clubs – Whangaroa, Bay of Islands, Whangarei, Whitianga and Tauranga – and their representatives met in Auckland in March, 1957 to consider how the trophy should be awarded.

With a unanimous decision that the cup should go to the angler catching the heaviest striped marlin each season, came the realisation that a central organisation of the clubs was necessary to administer this award, and to deal with common problems and aspirations of the sport. Thus the representatives of the five clubs decided to explore the possibility of forming a national association. Rob Dinsdale, of Whangarei, was asked to draw up a draft constitution. The inaugural meeting of the New Zealand Big Game Fishing Council was held in Whangarei in May 1957.

Since then clubs at Auckland, Whakatane, Waihau Bay, Gisborne, Napier, Dunedin and Fiordland have been affiliated with the council, most of them after being in an observer status with the council for a couple of years. The role of the council has been to co-ordinate rather than to govern – the clubs each having autonomy in their local affairs and equal representation on the council itself – but a number of important functions have by consent fallen to it.

Chief among these tasks have been to further the interests of ethical big game angling, to encourage the sport as a recreation, and to promote it as a potential source of scientific data.

A photograph from the early days of the New Zealand Big Game Fishing Council – Jack Crawford of Mercury Bay (left) and Rob Dinsdale, the national secretary. Northern Advocate.

In the interests of ethical fishing the council has the task of overseeing the rules of the International Game Fish Association, to which it is affiliated. It also operates in the same field on its own behalf. It has for instance ruled that, although 60kg line is still recognised for international records (and thus also for New Zealand records) the heaviest line accepted for catches in the national contests in New Zealand is now 37 kg. This move offsets the reputation New Zealand had in the past for the widespread use of extra (and by implication – in some instances unfairly) heavy line.

In the contests the council organises, it has also adopted a progressive policy to reduce the number of fish landed and increase the number tagged and released. It has also discussed such issues as whether the use of stainless steel hooks in combination with stainless steel traces should be barred as likely to inhibit the survival of fish that break loose. Many leading launchmen without waiting for any ruling have already opted for a combination of tackle (especially in the use of galvanised hooks which quickly corrode) which gives escaped fish the best chance.

In the area of encouraging the sport as a recreation, the council was a prime mover in the formation of a New Zealand Marine Recreational Resources Council in 1976. This move met with initial enthusiasm and the wholehearted unanimity of 30 saltwater recreational organisations meeting at Taupo. Mr P. J. Burstall, himself a keen angler and speaking on behalf of a subcommittee of the N.Z.B.G.F.C. gave the opening address, stating that the aim was to ensure the best use of one of the world's finest marine areas, with harmony between the commercial and recreational interests and with a dialogue with government so that sportsmen's views were considered in the use of marine resources.

Later the concept lost momentum but at the time of writing it is being revived; the need for an active and positively thinking body on these lines has grown, not diminished, as the pressure for commercial use of the coastal fishing resources has increased.

However, some advance has been made, particularly in the allied field which sees big game fishing catches as a potential source of scientific data, by the appointment in 1979 of Mr Peter Saul, of the Ministry of Agriculture and Fisheries, as a recreational research officer attached to the council. One field in which progress is being made as a result is in tagging fish, in which game fishermen are well placed to help. A trophy for tagging of fish is now among the awards made annually by the council.

One of the early moves of the council was to promote international contests in New Zealand to promote the sport abroad. Several of these contests were held but the idea was finally abandoned by the council when visiting anglers queried the continuance of a situation where a few of them were required to compete against thousands of local anglers, often fishing in different situations where they had an advantage. There were, however, some very successful contests. The first, between Australia and New Zealand in March 1969, succeeded in spite of being delayed by a hurricane. It was spread over five venues, with representatives from each side fishing at each one.

The Australians won by the very narrow margin of 2,548 points to 2,530 – an exciting finish that encouraged the promotion of a world

contest the following year in which teams came from California, Hawaii, South Australia, Queensland and South Africa – and which ended with the game fishing club of South Australia, first; the Tuna Club of Avalon, California, second; and the Moreton Bay Big Game Club, Queensland, third. New Zealand teams from Whangarei, Mercury Bay and Tauranga clubs filled the next three places, with South Africa, fishing with me on *Sou' East* at Mayor Island, down at seventh after striking four fish in the last half hour of the contest and losing all but the third marlin hooked. We boated this after it had its tail chopped off by a very large mako which was probably also responsible for cutting off the second marlin when it sounded shortly after the third was hooked. We then hooked the mako, but after a very spectacular few minutes it wrapped itself in our line and broke free. So, incredibly, after hooking and fighting four fish in half an hour we were left with only one mutilated – no points – marlin.

These contests were replaced, as council events by annual open championships. The only "international contests" now are run locally in the Bay of Islands – the Bay of Islands International Billfish Tournament held in March each year, and a Bay of Islands light tackle international (for yellowtail) each June. Teams for the international billfish contests have come in recent years from most of the other New Zealand clubs and from overseas clubs in the United States, Canada, the Pacific Islands and Australia, so the original concept has not been lost.

The national contest held by the New Zealand Big Game Fishing Council is normally held for a week in February. Awards are made for heaviest fish for most species, but the prestige events are for team fishing in which anglers vie for their clubs in four sections – billfish, sharks, yellowtail and tuna. Besides providing fairer competition, in that the various game fishes are difficult to cross-relate in terms of merit of catches, this division caters for the specialist nature of the

An early photograph of a striped marlin leaping.

Black marlin greyhounding, an early shot. E. V. Simpson.

A striped marlin leaps off Cathedral Bay, Mayor Island, held by a line from Naomi. E. V. Simpson.

fishing done by various clubs. The council has also instituted a separate award for the first marlin to be landed each season after the starting date of July 1 – an event which recognises a long-standing point of rivalry in which, although the northern clubs are favoured, most clubs have a chance, as the marlin come in with the blue water on a wide front from the north-east.

Other fishing contests around the country are organised by individual clubs – the Whakatane Open Tuna Tournament; the Hawkes Bay Coruba Contest in which sharks are the main target; the Whangaroa One-Base Contest, divided into billfish, shark and tuna/yellowtail sections; the Tutukaka One-base Contest, for individual and team catches and special classes in marlin and sharks; the Tauranga Club Contest for all classes of fish, and in the Bay of Islands, an end-of-the-season South Pacific Contest organised by the local charter skippers. These contests span the period from early January until mid June.

A further function of the council, to collate national records for big game catches and to process applications to the International Game Fish Association for world records, involves the council in standards which are internationally set. It publishes each year a booklet which sets out the existing local and world records in the various species and line classes, the rules which govern their acceptance, details of local contest results and developments in fishing of interest to New Zealand anglers.

It lists also the winners through the years of the three major New Zealand game fish trophies – the Old Man and the Sea Trophy, a handsome silver cup for the most meritorious catch each season which honours outstanding fishing rather than outstanding fish; the Lord Norrie Gold Cup, the trophy around which the council evolved, for the heaviest striped marlin each season, and the Fisherman of the Year trophy, a cup awarded for the heaviest game fish caught each season in New Zealand waters.

The first winner of the Old Man and the Sea Trophy, which was given by Jack L. Warner, the

film maker, to commemorate the making of a film of Ernest Hemingway's story, was a typically worthy one. On March 3, 1959 Jim Price, who was later to become a president of the Whangarei Gamefishing Club, was out line fishing from Tutukaka on his boat the *Stephanie*. It was a day when nothing seemed to be biting, and, while drifting and dangling his line to no purpose, he saw a mako and decided to toss it a bait. In no time the mako hooked on and Jim found himself fighting a very lively fish while alone in his boat, with no harness, no fishing chair and not able to steer or control his boat. The best he could do to make his task easier was to snatch up a pillow to rest the butt of the rod against as he stood and played the fish. When the mako decided to go around the boat after two long runs and two hours later he walked around the outside following it. He had no handrail to steady himself by, and had to pass the rod around two outrigger stays on each circuit.

While he was in the course of one of these circuits, between the Sugarloaf and the Pinnacles, Hugh Going came past in the *Kitty Vane*. Unable even to get to his radio telephone to call up for some assistance in handling the boat during the fight, Jim shouted and waved to Hugh Going as he came up. Hugh did not recognise it as a sign of distress. He waved cheerily back and carried on. When eventually after three and a half hours Jim got the fish to the boat on his own, gaffed and tailroped it and got it home he found it had been worth it – he had a then world record mako of 109.7 kg on a 24-kg line.

The president of the New Zealand Big Game Fishing Council is elected each year, the 1981 president being Mr E. K. Wiig, of the Hawkes Bay Game Fishing Club. The venue of its annual meetings has changed each year from one club centre to another, apart from years two to six of its existence when all the annual meetings were held in Auckland.

The other presidents have been R. G. Chitty (foundation president), Tauranga, 1957–58; L. W. Waldron, Whangarei, 1958–59; R. G.

George Wooller and Sir William Stevenson, noted New Zealand anglers, with the 329 kg black marlin caught by Wooller off Matoy Island in February, 1961. N.Z. Herald.

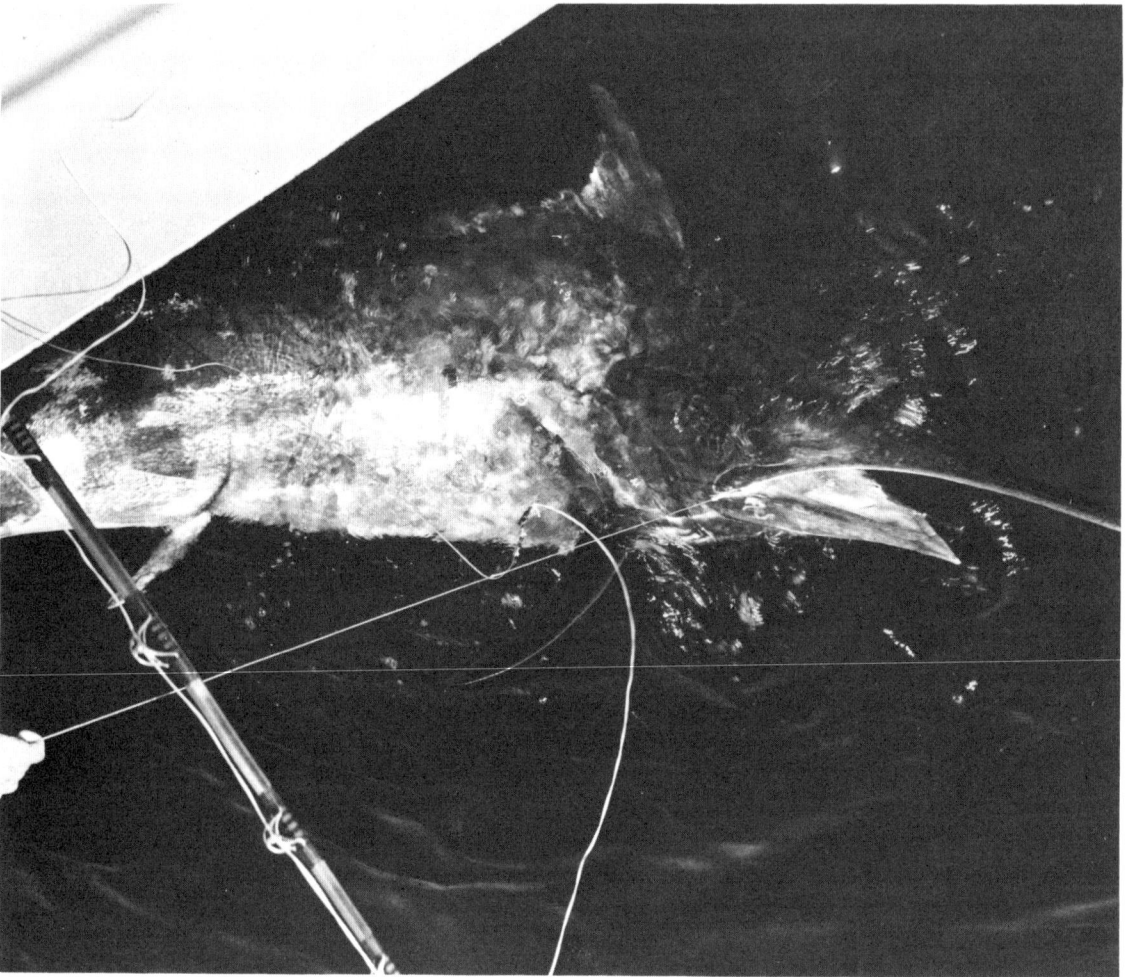

A black marlin beaten at the boat. National Publicity
Studios.

Chitty, Mercury Bay, 1959–60; R. H. Barnsley,
Bay of Islands, 1960–61; A. St. C. Belcher,
Tauranga, 1961–62; C. D. Thomas, Whangarei,
1962–63; F. J. Webber, Whangaroa, 1963–64; J.
P. Crawford, Mercury Bay, 1964–65; N. R.
Brady, Bay of Islands, 1965–66; A. D. Baldwin,
Kawau Island, 1966–67; R. H. Barnsley,
Whangarei, 1967–68; G. S. Traill, Tauranga,
1968–69; J. P. Crawford, Mercury Bay, 1969–70;
F. J. Webber, 1970–71; C. R. Mason, Kawau
Island, 1971–72; A. D. Baldwin, Kawau Island,

1972–73; R. K. Morpeth, Whakatane, 1973–75;
N. C. Hudspith, Bay of Islands, 1975–77; A. G.
Eastgate, Gisborne-Tatapouri, 1977–79; R. C.
Dinsdale, Whangarei, 1980.

The pin system of rewarding successful anglers
was in existence before the New Zealand Game
Fishing Council came into being, but it is part of
the recognised trophy procedures of the New
Zealand scene. It dates back to the earliest years
of the club system in New Zealand when the
Auckland jewellers A. Kohn Ltd, encouraged the
sport by presenting fish miniatures in silver, with
initials and date of catch inscribed. The first fish

landed each season in each class received a pin, and as each weight was eclipsed through the season a new pin would be won. For a world record the pin was in gold and where the angler was a lady the fish had ruby eyes.

Although the principle of the awards remains, the pins are now provided by the clubs. The silver pins are awarded to their members for the first fish of the club season for each major species, and for succeeding heavier fish as the season progresses. The ruby eye now signifies a New Zealand record. Gold still stands for a world record.

The pin with a diamond eye – for two world records set by the same angler in one day – was won for the first time in 1981. Carolyn Thies, of California, qualified for the pin with a record 78.50 kg southern bluefin tuna and a 38.25 kg yellowtail. Both were caught on a 37 kg line from *Toa Tai*, skippered by Rick Pollard, fishing from Whakatane, on 12 February, 1981.

The only angler previously to come close to the diamond pin was Miss Kura Beale, who caught two world record yellowtail on the one day, but in the wrong order. However Miss Beale is one of the honoured few who have been awarded the Old Man and the Sea trophy for her contributions to the traditions of the sport. Miss Beale, in 1979 at the age of 71, caught on four days of fishing between March 19 and March 22 three striped marlin, weighing 129.1 kg, 132.3 kg and 100.7 kg and a mako of 62.14 kg.

The fish were taken off Stephenson Island, Ruahine Reef and Takau Bay from the *Lady Doreen*, skippered by Curly Ellis. However, the award recognised not only some exceptional sustained angling but a fishing career which goes back to 1938, and which has included world records not only for a 36.74-kg yellowtail taken on 36-kg line, but for a yellowtail of 32.66 kg on 24-kg line, and a blue marlin of 195.95 kg on 60-kg line, which was the third of three successive marlin, any one of which would have broken the previous world record.

As one of the early areas to establish a world

reputation for big game fishing, New Zealand has had links with the international game fishing movement since its inception. The first move to establish a world-wide organisation of marine anglers was made before the Second World War by the British Tunny Club. When the threat of war put the plans aside, the idea was taken up by Michael Lerner, a millionaire American businessman and pioneer angler, who thought it over while on a fishing expedition to Australia and New Zealand in conjunction with the American Museum of Natural History in New York. On an Australian suggestion that such an organisation should be centred in the United States, Dr William King Gregory, a member of the expedition further offered that the organisation be affiliated with the American Museum of Natural History – where in June, 1939, the I.G.F.A. was formally launched.

The aims of the organisation were, "To encourage the study of game fishes for the sake of whatever pleasure, information or benefit it may provide: to keep the sport of game fishing ethical, and to make its rules acceptable to the majority of anglers: to encourage this sport both as a recreation and as a potential source of scientific data: to place such data at the disposal of as many human beings as possible: and to keep an attested and up-to-date chart of world record catches."

Michael Lerner not only conceived the idea of the I.G.F.A. – he funded it. He led other expeditions to obtain valuable specimens and to initiate research into marine environments and fish species and founded research projects. This work has been steadily expanded, as has the record keeping into saltwater fly fishing and fresh-water angling. New fields of interest have opened, such as the establishment of an international library of fishes.

This association has an international committee of sport fishermen in all its areas, chosen for their integrity, fishing knowledge and a concern for sportsmanship and conservation. The current New Zealand committee members are Arnold D. Baldwin of Auckland, Robert C. Dinsdale of Whangarei, Norman C. Hudspith of Kaikohe, and Ernie K. Wiig of Napier – the president and three former presidents of the New Zealand Big Game Fishing Council.

The I.G.F.A. each year runs an international contest – with certificates awarded for the first, second and third heaviest fish caught, and details submitted, in accordance with I.G.F.A. angling rules each year. New Zealand placings have been;

1976   Southern bluefin tuna: Second, 21.33 kg, Brent Vincent, Fiordland.
1977   Striped marlin: First, 189.37 kg, Phillip Bryers, Cavalli Islands; Second, 154.22 kg, Mrs Robyn Hall, Bay of Islands.
        Thresher shark: First, 303.90 kg, Frederick Parsons, Mayor Island.
        Southern bluefin tuna: Third 22.22 kg, Schonda Vincent, Fiordland.
1978   Hammerhead shark: First, 180.53 kg, Mrs Marilyn Pearce, Mayor Island.
        Thresher shark: First, 306.62 kg, R. C. Faulkner, Mayor Island; Second, 198.00 kg, A. G. Eastgate, Lottin Point.
1979   Striped marlin: First, 167.83 kg, P. R. Bryers, Bay of Islands; Second, 136.53 kg, Mrs Lola Fuller, Doubtless Bay.
        Southern yellowtail: First, 14.51 kg, Mike Godfrey, Tauranga; Second, 9.52 kg, Mike Godfrey, Tauranga.
        Hammerhead shark: Second, 141.00 kg, Mrs Robyn Hall, Great Exhibition Bay.
1980   Striped marlin: First, 183.47 kg, Klaus Rober, Bay of Islands; second, 163.00 kg, Gillian Batkin, Bay of Islands.
        Swordfish: First, 241.76 kg, Bill Hall, Bay of Islands.
        Mako shark: Second, 174.63 kg, Mrs Lola Fuller, Cavalli Islands.
        Southern bluefin tuna: Third, 98.00 kg Des Benson, Westport.

The I.G.F.A. last year invited applications for fish not already listed as game fish to see if any should be considered for world record and for line classes to be set.

Over the years the number of species recognised as gamefish has been steadily widened. The 1980 edition of World Gamefish Records, published by the International Game Fish Association, lists records of 66 different saltwater species plus a couple of extra for saltwater fly fishing. Three recent additions on the New Zealand sportsfisherman's list have been blue sharks, bronze whalers and white pointer sharks. How far the list may be extended up or down remains to be seen. There must be doubts whether the New Zealand Big Game Fishing Council or the I.G.F.A. will ever descend to recognising snapper in their contests as some of the New Zealand affiliated clubs do but, with game fish rating given to smaller fish overseas with comparable weights, the New Zealand council has recently included kahawai, skipjack tuna, slender tuna and trevally in its fly-fishing rating.

The angling rules of the I.G.F.A. are in general terms set out in the course of this book and can, in their latest and most up-to-date form, be checked with any of the game fish clubs. For a fish to qualify for a world record, the requirements for application are stringent.

Some of the requirements are:

The fish must be weighed by an official weighmaster (if one is available), or by an I.G.F.A. official, or by a recognised local person familiar with the scale. Disinterested witnesses to the weight should be used wherever possible; the scales must be certified, and at the time of weighing the actual tackle used by the angler to catch the fish must be exhibited to the weighmaster and weight witness.

Applications for line-class records must be accompanied by the entire leader, the double line and at least 15.24 m of the single line closest to the double line leader and hook (all in one piece).

Photographs must be submitted with the application showing the full length of the fish,

The biggest fish ever caught in New Zealand waters, this 662 kg white shark could not have counted as a record because it was landed on a balloon cable by fishermen in Kaipara Harbour. Scott Photography.

the rod and reel used to make the catch, the scale used to weigh the fish, and the angler with the fish.

There is much more in detail than this and, in its efforts to ensure that records are valid, the association sets out to confirm all details supplied, sends the line to a laboratory for 10 separate strength tests, checks identification of the fish, if necessary with qualified ichthyologists, and if necessary investigates any suggestions that the claim is not all above board. It has been known to have an expert spend more than a month checking on the way hooks were used on a catch for which a record was claimed.

The standing world 36-kg line and all-tackle record striped marlin, of 189.37 kg, caught by Phillip Bryers, of Auckland, off the Taheke Reef, Cavalli Islands, on January 14, 1977 was notable not only for the size of the fish, but for the subsequent disbelief of The International Game Fish Association.

The fish, caught from the *Lady Doreen*, with Brett Ellis as skipper, took exactly an hour to boat and did not – as happens sometimes with the bigger fish – play much in the process. It took the record from Brian Bain, set in 1963–64, so narrowly – by only 1.13 kg – that Phil is prepared to concede that it may only have been his larger bait ("I had on the biggest kahawai I have ever seen") which tipped the scales in his favour. Once the fish was weighed in at Russell, that seemed the end of it.

Not so. It was six months before the International Game Fish Association would recognise the record. Perhaps in disbelief that striped marlin could be so big in New Zealand waters, the association wrote to say that, from the photograph of the fish submitted with the record application, renowned billfish scientists believed that the fish was not a striped marlin but a blue marlin. The association asked for more photographs and comments or pertinent facts as to why the fish had been identified locally as a striped marlin. In the meantime the record claim would be held in abeyance.

Phil Bryers, in complying with the requests, commented on the "controversy in our far-off little islands" created by the association's doubts. In addition to more photographs of the fish and some of its bill, he sent comparison photos of a striped marlin caught previously, and a blue marlin caught the same season by Kura Beale; letters from officers of the Bay of Islands Swordfish Club; a signed statement of identification from Snooks Fuller ("One glance at the photograph of Mr Bryers' fish is enough to convince me"); affidavits from three famous skippers, Francis and Mervyn Arlidge and Jim Whitelaw and a letter from Brett Ellis, skipper of the *Lady Doreen* – with contributory points of identification supplied by A. B. Stephenson, marine scientist at the Auckland War Memorial Museum. The association was finally convinced that this really was a striped marlin as claimed.

Subsequently Phil Bryers temporarily held the world record for striped marlin on 24 kg class line, so that at one stage he held three world records for striped marlin – the all-tackle, the 37 kg and the 24 kg.

Big game fishing began in New Zealand largely as a sport for the rich and largely for the overseas visitor, for the main fishing grounds of the early days – at the Bay of Islands, Mayor Island and Whitianga – were remote from centres of population and it was something of an expedition even to get to them. Only charter boats with expert skippers – expert not only in boating and game fishing techniques but in making their paying guests feel at home – made the sport possible then. Easier access today to big game fishing centres (and there being more of them) and the development of the modern runabout and outboard motor has encouraged a sport-loving generation of New Zealanders to game fish more with their own resources. The professional boats still serve several leading fishing centres and more are likely to join them if the recent improvement in catches on the northern grounds continues and spreads.

The charter rate per day unfortunately goes up

A world record that was queried: the 189.38 kg striped marlin caught on a 37 kg line by Phillip Bryers of the Bay of Islands Club and claimed as the world all-tackle record. It was at first questioned on the grounds that the fish was a blue marlin. The skipper (right) is Brett Ellis. Graham Townsend.

each year with the cost of fuel but at the time of writing the rate varies between about $200 to $260 for a day charter, taking four or six people. In terms of other holiday costs a day's outing game fishing on a well appointed launch at about $45 to $60 a head is not really high.

An unusual contest associated with New Zealand big game fishing – probably unique because few other countries would provide the combination of bill-fish and shark waters in close proximity to habitats of the other game involved – is the Big Three, which involves the catching against the clock, of a game fish, a trout and a deer, under tightly set sporting rules. The fastest time, from the hooking of the first fish, is now down to well under four hours.

The first to do so was a prominent American baseball star Ted Williams who in 1964 caught a 255 kg thresher shark, a 1.36 kg rainbow trout – taken fly-fishing, all others have been on the troll – and shot a red deer, all in 10½ hours. It was six years before his time was bettered, by Rod Bellerby, then of Rotorua and now proprietor of the Whakatane Hotel. Fishing from his own boat the *Mako*, he boated a 123-kg hammerhead after a fight of one hour 17 minutes, three miles behind Whale Island, near Whakatane; made a rendezvous at Whale Island with a float plane

piloted by Captain Fred Ladd which took him to a launch on Lake Rotoaira, there to catch a 1.36 kg rainbow trout; and finally went by helicopter into the bush for a four-pointer red deer stag. Total time: 4 hours 12 minutes.

It took John Boyle of Tauranga, six years more to become the third sportsman to succeed in the Big Three and also take the record. At 10.10 am on the morning of January 13 he hooked a 118.84-kg striped marlin; 25 minutes later he boated it. Taken by float plane to Lake Taupo he hooked a 1.1 kg rainbow trout. A helicopter took him, in stormy conditions, to a river flat in the Kaimanawa Ranges where, at 1.25 pm he shot a Manchurian Sika deer hind. It all took only 3 hours and 15 minutes.

The first woman to qualify, Mrs Lyndsay James (of Rotorua), started in the Bay of Islands, fishing from the Tauranga-based launch *Lady Luck*. She began well, too, with a 124.74-kg marlin taken on a 36-kg line to give her the best points start to date, but she ran out of daylight. She and her husband motored down the 500-odd kilometres to Rotorua through the night, and at 7 am caught a 2-kg rainbow trout, the best of the contest. Then by helicopter into the hills, where her third shot felled a hind. The time was 18 hours and 5 minutes.

CHAPTER FIFTEEN

Scope for research

Although fishing has long been a way of life as well as a way of making a living in New Zealand, local research of it has been slow to develop and was until recently almost exclusively for commercial rather than recreational purposes, and more for exploitation than for conservation. Such emphasis is of concern to the sports fisherman who seems likely to have a finger pointed at him for any diminution in stocks, despite the fact that the recreational level of billfish catches, for instance, is trivial compared with the much larger numbers taken by overseas commercial fishing fleets operating around the country.

It is typical of this imbalance of research that in a country which is world-renowned for its striped marlin game fishing, so little is known about this fish, and most of what is known comes from overseas. Even the location of the breeding grounds of this fish is only vaguely defined, as is the route the marlin take to New Zealand. Very little is known of the early stages of the life of marlin – no striped marlin less than 30 kg is recorded as having been taken in New Zealand waters.

The area where it is thought the striped marlin of New Zealand are spawned lies in the central South Pacific, somewhere between Tonga and the Tuamotu Archipelago, and it is from this area the adults appear to come to New Zealand each summer, and to there they return each autumn. It is vague, but scientific support is

lacking for the alternative that the large New Zealand striped marlin are the small Hawaiian fish come south for our summer. Most New Zealand catches range from about 70-kg to 135-kg, with a few heavier fish which contribute to record catches. Hawaiian striped marlin are rarely more than 70-kg. The idea that these are the same fish is therefore convenient, but several factors suggest the Hawaiian and Californian marlin swim westward across the Pacific toward Japan, never to return, and do not travel south. Fishing records from long-liners in tropical waters show a very low hook-up of striped marlin for 15 degrees each side of the equator, suggesting that the fish find this area of water too warm to cross.

Most conclusive, however, is the fact that striped marlin caught off New Zealand have a small but significant difference in body characteristic from those caught off Hawaii – in the size and shape of the pectoral fin. The New Zealand marlin is therefore probably a South Pacific fish, following the water of the sub-tropical temperature it likes – or rather, perhaps, the food fish that live in that temperature – moving south or north according to season.

The marlin seem to arrive off New Zealand when the surface temperature of the sea is about 19° to 20° C. This temperature is usually reached off the Northland coast in late December or early January, and persists into March or April. Some striped marlin will move in with water as cool as 17° and some seem to acclimatise to colder temperatures as autumn comes on, so, while the height of the marlin season is from January to April, fish are also caught as early as November and as late as August. A few might even be caught during the rest of the year if the fishing effort was there, but the New Zealand winter produces seas too cold and generally too rough for enjoyable fishing – whatever means are taken to keep out the cold.

Blue marlin are even more sensitive to temperature, usually not showing up around New Zealand until the surface water is at 21 or 22° C. (in about February and March). Other migrant fish follow the East Australian Current down around the Tasman before it comes up the west coast of New Zealand, is joined by warmer waters around North Cape and moves down through the big game waters. However, there is a general feeling that most striped marlin arrive on the New Zealand game fishing grounds in a broad front (perhaps swimming down the Kermadec ridge) directly from the breeding areas to the north-east. The annual visits are probably for recuperation after spawning. None of the hundreds of marlin examined after capture in New Zealand have been found by Peter Saul, fisheries advisory officer to the New Zealand Big Game Fishing Council, to have been in breeding condition.

And if it is difficult to state specifically where our striped marlin come from it also seems a problem biologically to age them. With most of the commercial species of fish it is possible to count the age rings on the scales (rather like the rings on a tree) or to read ages in other cases by the rings on certain vertebrae and otoliths (ear bones). But with the marlin, aging by such means has not been successfully done at the time of writing. Reliance has to be placed on measuring as large a number fish as possible, looking for size classes from which age groups can be deduced. Working from this sort of data, a 70-kg striped marlin is probably four to five

years old, and at that stage of its life is probably putting on 14 kg to 18 kg a year. At a guess, striped marlin probably live for only about 10 years. Further, if this age/weight relationship is accepted, no striped marlin strays from the breeding grounds to New Zealand coastal waters until it is at least two years old.

The factor which brings the marlin here at all is probably not water temperature but food supplies in a period when the female fish are putting on condition between one breeding season and the next. The food the fish eat can be established by examining the fish that are caught – for instance the study made at the Tutukaka One Base contest in March 1975 by Peter Saul. He examined 22 striped marlin of which 13 were female and 9 were undeveloped males. Many of the fish were probably not more than six years old and the younger ones about four years, judging from their size.

Two marlin had thrown their stomach contents, four others had not recently fed. Those that had fed contained, in order of quantity, squid, jack mackerel, anchovies, skipjack (bonito) and pink maomao.

The marlin, being active fish, probably fed on anything which crossed their path when they were hungry, yet not one of the marlin contained a kahawai, the bait fish used by 90 per cent of New Zealand deep sea fishermen. These marlin would not have seen a kahawai until they reached New Zealand coastal waters, and did not seem to have developed a taste for it even after having been here for four months. Peter Saul had at the time of writing opened a total of 259 marlin and not found kahawai in more than half a dozen of them. Some of those which had taken a kahawai as bait were so full already that there would not have been room for it in the stomach. Did they strike from curiosity only?

The food chains preyed on by big fish follow no clear patterns, but they usually involve small fish such as pilchards and anchovy with almost everything preying on those small species and on each other as size and opportunity permit –

Michael Lerner, founder of the International Game Fish Association, with a black marlin at Otehei Bay, in the Bay of Islands, during his fishing research expedition to New Zealand just before the Second World War. Tudor Collins.

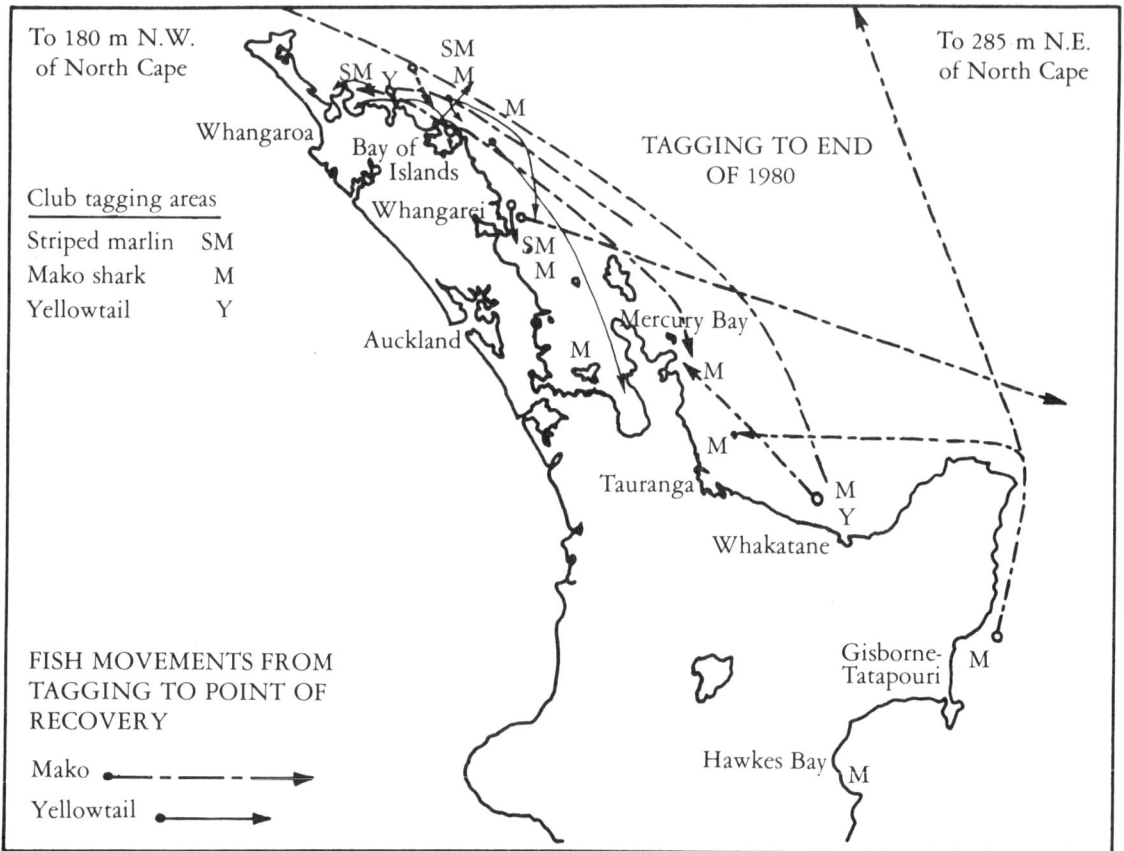

To 180 m N.W.
of North Cape

To 285 m N.E.
of North Cape

TAGGING TO END
OF 1980

Whangaroa

Bay of
Islands

Whangarei

Club tagging areas

Striped marlin   SM
Mako shark   M
Yellowtail   Y

Auckland

Mercury Bay

Tauranga

Whakatane

FISH MOVEMENTS FROM
TAGGING TO POINT OF
RECOVERY

Mako   ● ─ ─ ─ ─ →

Yellowtail ● ─── →

Gisborne-
Tatapouri

Hawkes Bay

Diagram VII
*The tagging results and activity off the North Island
to the end of 1980. Tagging, mainly of blue sharks,*
*was also done by Fiordland (no recoveries to that
date).*

mackerel, kahawai and tuna eating the small fish
and shark or marlin eating everything. Many of
the fish found in marlin and sharks by Peter Saul
were surprisingly small compared with the size of
the marlin. Yet a striped marlin has shown itself
capable of swallowing an 8-kg mako or fish of
that size. Peter Saul once found a marlin with a
2-m frost fish in it and another with a
barracouda. Among fish, everything smaller than
yourself seems fair game.

Marlin are not always caught in the blue water
of the currents reaching New Zealand from the
more tropical seas where they breed. But the
warm water temperature and correspondingly
higher salinity of these waters is a guide to the
likely presence, not only of marlin but of other
migratory fish. One instrument that is useful in
detecting water changes – a salinometer –

measures the salinity, and the usually related
temperature, at any depth up to the range of the
instrument. There is a proven relationship
between the depths which tuna swim and
thermoclines where there can be a rapid change
of temperature of two or three degrees Celsius in
about a metre, and a change in the water density.

If yellowfin tuna tend to swim very close to
thermoclines, so do other fish. Information on
thermoclines is already of great value to
commercial fishermen in setting nets and it
would be useful to the deep-trolling or drift-
fishing game fisherman, too, in setting his baits.
Even to be within four to six metres of a suitable
thermocline would greatly increase his chances of
catching a fish.

Salinometers are not among the usual
equipment of big game fishermen, but water

temperature gauges now are. It is a common sight in a well-equipped launch to see a dial or digital read of the temperature of the surface and immediately sub-surface water in which the launch is travelling.

Fishing researchers have studied the preferred temperature levels of many fish. These temperatures may, of course, be related to the food chains available rather than to the fish's own physical comfort. Levels of preferred temperature have usually been judged on where the greatest catch of fish is made, rather than on the largest fish populations, which are difficult figures to establish – on the basis that large numbers of fish and good catches will usually go together. From these studies it seems to be established that certain fish prefer certain sea temperatures, without it being taken for granted – however good a rule of thumb it may be – that, given the right sea temperatures, a fish will be present.

Ralph Stevenson, of Hastings, then Hawkes Bay representative of the Tauranga Big Game Fishing Club, caught this thresher off Mayor Island. It was not considered heavy enough (about 220 kg) to be worth weighing.

Over the past 100 years or so the sea temperatures around New Zealand have shown a slowly rising trend, no more than about 1°C in that period, but fairly constant since 1910. Yet marlin have become scarcer in the past 50 years, not more numerous, around the New Zealand coast. Nor do season-by-season temperature figures seem yet to show any direct relationship with trends in catches.

Most water temperature studies around New Zealand have concerned commercial species. Research work with skipjack tuna – a commercial catch which has much the same temperature preferences as striped marlin – has confirmed maximum catches in waters with temperatures from 19° to 21° or 22°C. The work has also established the usefulness of the sea surface temperature maps produced from satellites of the National Oceanic and Atmospheric Administration of the United States Department of Commerce through its national environmental satellite service.

The locally available charts show, week by week, the temperature contours of the seas surrounding New Zealand, calculated from

175

measurement of thermal radiation from the ocean surface and atmosphere, as detected by infra-red sensors on the satellites. Primarily intended for meteorological work, the information has been given wider circulation for oceanographers, environmental scientists and fishermen. While commercial fishermen are the most likely to be concerned, sport fishermen have also become interested.

A series of these SST contour maps, as they are called, is shown in this section, marked to reveal the movement of surface temperature gradients in the period preceding and through a recent New Zealand big game fishing season. The satellite service warns that temperature contours close to coastlines are likely to be erroneous, but checks made in New Zealand by fisheries scientists indicate that even close to the shoreline the maps are accurate enough to be used for fish studies. Each contour line on the charts represents a degree Celsius. The temperatures are of surface waters only, and thermoclines down in the water will complicate the marine environment. The charts also do not show the deep-moving Tasman current on the West Coast with its presumably temperate water, but the warmer waters of the East Auckland Current may be revealed in the tongue of higher temperatures which for most of the summer extends on the maps down the East Coast of the North Island to East Cape and beyond. The coastal effects of the East Auckland Current are much more variable, however, than such a chart can show. Hopes that such mapping by satellites might yield forecasts of fishing prospects have yet to be fulfilled.

More immediately useful are the boat water temperature gauges which have, since I first advocated their use in 1948, become standard equipment on most of the bigger game fishing boats these days. Some fishermen get the same results by dipping a bucket over the side and taking the temperature of the water with a hand thermometer in the cockpit. However obtained, the temperature readings are a handy pointer to where the fish are in these days of fewer numbers

and dearer fuel – as an aid additional to the constant scanning of the sea and attention to water colour, current lines, birds, schools, upwellings, radio reports of fish sighted and weather, all of which remain indispensable guides.

Herewith a short guide to water temperatures as they affect game fish in New Zealand waters:

One can hope to find that *striped marlin* have arrived from the time the surface water temperature reaches 18° to 20°C, and they like it up to 22°C. By the time the temperature returns to 17°C in any area they will probably be retreating north.

Blue marlin are partial to warmer water than striped marlin. Their temperature preference of 20° to 22°C or even warmer make them fish of late summer – February or March. These are the preferences, too, of *shortbill spearfish*. The *sailfish* likes it even warmer.

Black marlin have a wider temperature range, being caught in blue marlin temperatures and also in waters below the tolerance of striped marlin.

Broadbill swordfish, also appear to have a wide temperature tolerance. While they usually live deep, where the water is cooler, they are also frequently seen in the warm surface waters. They may, therefore, share with black marlin a greater world wide distribution than any other billfish and, as well, be less affected by thermoclines.

Mako, threshers, bronze whalers, and *blue sharks* are less susceptible to the temperature and are around all the time.

Hammerheads prefer our warm summer waters. *Yellowfin tuna* seem to pass two peaks through the northern New Zealand fishing grounds, one in early summer on their way south and one late in the season coming back. Their temperature range is believed to be about 19° to 22°C.

Skipjack tuna also follow the same sort of waters as striped marlin – from about 19° to 21° or 22°C.

Dolphin fish like the warmer blue marlin waters.

Albacore are caught mainly from 15.5° to 19°C.

Yellowtail (kingfish) are a local population which is there all year round. Most are caught in the winter – probably because they are the main game fish readily accessible to anglers at this time of the year.

So much, or so little, is known or surmised about our game fish. The main stream of future research lies in two areas: first, in a continuing study of fish that are caught – either by examination of those brought in by game fisherman; or by analysing the numbers and location of the catches made and reported by the commercial fishing fleets operating off the coast; and secondly, through the international fish tagging programme now well established overseas and becoming more and more accepted and practised in New Zealand. This programme is of special interest to game fishermen for it can only really succeed if they participate.

Tagging has the merits of being simple and direct, and the information it gives is positive. It involves the placing of stainless steel tags in the backs of fish which are then allowed to roam free until hopefully they and their tags are somewhere met with again. The practice is especially useful when it comes to studying the life histories of fish, their growth rates and migration and distribution patterns. The marlins in particular, are found to be great travellers. A striped marlin tagged off southern California in 1967 was recovered south-west of Hawaii, having travelled a minimum distance of 3,120 nautical miles in three months. A black marlin released off Cairns, Australia, was recovered nearly three years later off Tutukaka, New Zealand.

Such highly migratory lifestyles are found not only in marlin, but in tuna and some sharks. This makes them very difficult and expensive to study effectively. The co-operative tagging programme, which calls for participation by anglers throughout the known range of a species has proved effective and economical, both important points in the area of recreational fisheries and for

which research funds have been traditionally hard to come by.

This type of tagging programme provides a way for each angler to make as big a contribution as he or she wishes to the future of the sport – as well as the continued survival of the fish upon which the sport is based.

The only possible outcome of placing ever-increasing pressures on a living resource is the eventual destruction of that resource. In order to control the pressure – in this case to manage the fishing so that population numbers can be maintained – scientists must be able to provide the managers with certain information. This information includes population numbers, growth rates, spawning rates, mortality from fishing and other causes and geographical distribution by time of year and/or the stage of the fishes' life cycle. Much of this information can be provided by an extensive tagging programme.

The tagging of game fish commenced in New Zealand back in 1952 in the Bay of Islands. On January 30 of that year Alex Arnock of Papatoetoe tagged and released the first striped marlin from the *Alma G*. Within three weeks a Manurewa angler, H. Coxhead, had released three more from *Alma G II*. These examples of tagging came two years before Frank J. Mather III began the first co-operative tagging programme in the Pacific. The programme was later passed to the control of the United States National Marine Fisheries Service, and spread through the Pacific.

The local New Zealand tagging continued for three years in a small way, with the first mako shark being tagged and released from the *Alma G II* by L. Eves of Dargaville on May 16, 1954. When the initial burst of tagging stopped in 1955, 14 marlin and 2 mako sharks had been tagged. None of these fish was ever recaptured and no more were tagged for almost 20 years when, as a result of contact between New Zealand and United States anglers at international fishing contests in the Pacific, the Co-operative Game Fish Programme came to

New Zealand in 1975. Run this time from California by the La Jolla laboratory of the National Marine Fisheries Service, the programme was designed to reach an understanding of the migratory patterns of Pacific billfish, so that some sort of international management plan could be prepared to protect the stocks and ensure the future of the fishery as well.

In New Zealand the programme has been extended to include the other game fish species in addition to billfish and in particular to the mako shark. In its practical application, eight makos were tagged for every marlin in the first six years of the programme in New Zealand, a ratio perhaps to be expected because of the number of small makos available and the relative ease with which these can be tagged compared with striped marlin.

By the end of the 1979–80 season the cumulative totals of fish tagged in New Zealand waters were: 416 mako, 47 striped marlin, 2 blue marlin, 150 yellowtail, 29 blue sharks, 4 tuna, 5 hammerheads, 1 thresher shark – a total of 654 fish. Of these tagged fish 15 mako have been recovered (3.6 per cent of those tagged) and 11 yellowtail (7.3 per cent). No marlin tagged have been recovered. The shortest time a fish has been at liberty before its recovery has been 1 day (for a mako) and the longest time 492 days (for a yellowtail). The makos have averaged 204 days between captures (the longest 452 days) and the average distance they travelled was 130 miles. Most of the young yellowtail tended to stay around home grounds but one older fish travelled 130 miles in 234 days from Cape Brett to Tapu (near Thames in the Hauraki Gulf) where it was caught in a commercial set net. This yellowtail weighed 15 kg.

The recaptures so far have been spread between commercial fishermen (snapper longliners, 7; tuna longliners, 3; set netters, 2; pair trawlers, 1; purse seiner, 1); game fishermen, 6; other recreational fishermen, 6; and with one unknown. But the number of big game anglers

tagging and releasing fish has not yet matched the importance of the task. Of the 49 marlin released up to December 1980 Lola and Snooks Fuller, of *Lucky Strike* in the Bay of Islands and the Going family of Tutukaka in *Hooker* and *Anakiwa* had tagged 38 between them, and of the 150 yellowtail, 100 had been released by Paul Robertson off the Far North coast.

Snooks Fuller is mainly interested these days, after nearly 30 years association with game fishing in the Bay of Islands, in photographing fish from the tuna tower on his boat *Lucky Strike* and shares his wife Lola's interest in tagging. Although among the few fish she has kept, (either because they look like trophy catches or are needed for smoking) have been a couple of world records, they stunned competitors on a recent international tournament by tagging and releasing two blue marlin, one of over 130 kg and one over 190 kg. Another marlin they tried to release after tagging (but would not swim even when they tried to revive it by wagging it by the bill) was big enough when taken reluctantly back to Whangaroa to win the Mavis Rooke Trophy for the heaviest game fish of the national contest at Whangaroa as well as a dozen bottles of beer.

They recognise that most anglers are still unlikely to be enthusiastic about tagging and releasing what may be their first or only fish of a holiday, especially if they know how good it will taste when smoked. Yet they find that tagging presents few problems with the fish alongside the boat – although gentle handling is important (it is better to leave a long piece of trace attached, than to drag the fish up too close to try to cut it off short). They agree that most of the fish released give every indication they will survive. Lola Fuller remembers how lovely some of them look as they swim away.

Of the makos, 27 were tagged and released by the Hawkes Bay Club at the National Tournament in 1980. Fiordland taggings include blue sharks and albacore, and last year recorded the first tagging and release in New Zealand of a bluefin tuna – even though it was Bill Routhan's first.

New Zealand tagging is, however, not something just of local interest. It is part of the long-term international effort which since 1954 under the Co-operative Game Fish Tagging Programme initiated by the Woods Hole Oceanographic Institution has already produced information vital to scientific knowledge of game fish as well as their conservation and management. The programme has as its main objectives the determination of migratory cycles of the fish, and of the geographical extent of their populations; of growth rates of the fish; of the sizes of fish populations and of the mortality of the fish. Important side-results show up the effects of fishing pressures on the populations of certain fish, and which fisheries are affecting them.

One of the successes of the programme has been to pinpoint heavy commercial overfishing of the bluefin tuna of the Northwest Atlantic, which was likened to a gold rush. This discovery resulted in the imposition of strict limits on the fishery and is seen now as probably having averted at the eleventh hour the destruction of the bluefin tuna population of the western Atlantic. Much has been learned also of the migrations and populations of bluefin tuna and their growth rates. From the angler's point of view, one result is the knowledge that the size of the bluefin over the last decade has increased spectacularly, with the I.G.F.A. all-tackle record now being 678 kg compared with 443 kg in 1971.

The Australians at the beginning of 1980 took alarm at what might be happening to the black marlins off the coast of North Queensland where they congregate in large numbers. One New Zealander who was recently with a launch party off Cairns confirmed their numbers. The party hooked 50 black marlin in a fortnight – most of them about 300 kg – but let nearly all of them go after a few minutes, tagging them until they ran out of tags.

Not only game fishermen have been attracted, however, and commercial long-liners began fishing the area so assiduously that the Commonwealth Government in 1980 decided to ban all long-lining in the prime fishing grounds, an area of 48,000 sq miles off Cairns. The decision said it recognised the economic importance of the black marlin sports fishery to Cairns. It said that there was no evidence to show that black marlin stocks had been endangered by long-line fishing but it disclosed that between September and January of 1979 Japanese long-liners had taken 3,700 black marlin in the now prohibited area.

Tags in New Zealand are obtainable through all game fish clubs. The tags have a stainless steel barb to which a short length of nylon monofilament is attached. A yellow polyvinyl sleeve over the monofilament carries a heat-embossed message to the finder of the tag, including a serial number. Each tag is supplied on a card carrying a matching serial number and asking for details of the locality where the tagging was carried out, the species of fish and the date of tagging. The anglers are also asked to estimate the length and weight of the fish, describe how it was hooked and give their own name, address and club together with the name and address of the captain of the boat.

The card should be completed as soon as possible after tagging the fish, and returned without delay to the nearest club secretary or to the address on the back of the card – at the time of writing to the Ministry of Agriculture and Fisheries, Private Bag, Whangarei. The prompt return of the card is most important. A later tag recovery is of no value unless the information requested on the card is on record.

Tagging is done with the use of a pole, preferably of hardwood between 1.5 and 2.5 m long and about 25 mm in diameter but a broomstick will do. Into a hole at the end of the pole a tagging tip of stainless steel rod (one can be made from stainless welding rod) with a slot cut in the tip, should be glued to a depth of about 25 mm, leaving about 50 mm of the tip protruding. The glue secures the tip in the pole and also seals the pole end against moisture, which might otherwise in time tend to loosen the tip. The tag fits into the slot on the rod tip, and a rubber band placed around the vinyl streamer and pole keeps it in place against accidental loss. The tag is then ready for implanting.

Fish should be tagged with as little handling as possible, and only if they appear to be in reasonable condition. A fish that is bleeding badly, is exhausted or badly injured in any way is unlikely to survive and represents a waste of a tag. A fish that is not too lively can usually be brought into a good position for tagging by taking the leader as far forward as possible in the cockpit while the boat is kept moving slowly ahead. At this time the length of the fish can also be estimated fairly accurately, particularly if there are marks or known distances on the coaming or side deck to assist. The tagging angler should remember to estimate the weight if possible as well as the length, and always to include the condition of the fish on the tag card.

The tag should be placed a full 50 mm into the fish, below or just behind the first dorsal fin, and high up on the body to avoid damage to internal organs. The head, gills and lower part of the body must be avoided. The tag should be preferably inclined into the fish, so that it streams easily with the fish's movements through the water. If you feel the fish warrants it and you have the opportunity, strike a second tag into it as well. Research has shown that a high percentage of tags are shed, anything up to 25 per cent of those placed annually. Before placing a tag on any fish it is most important to bring the fish alongside and make sure that it does not already carry one. The first priority with a tagged fish is to recover the tag, only retagging it before release as a second consideration; and if it is necessary to land a fish to get the tag, in the interests of research and conservation, do so.

The mystery why striped marlin are so much bigger in New Zealand waters than in other parts of the world may be related to as simple a factor as less intensive fishing of this area compared with most Northern Hemisphere waters. However, because the striped marlin is the most heavily caught by local anglers of our major sport fishes, it is vital that more of the species are tagged so that more can be learnt of their life history. Unfortunately it seems only low recovery rates can be expected. Of 9,849 striped marlin tagged under the co-operation programme in the Pacific between 1957 and 1971 only 85 or 0.88 per cent were recovered, so it is imperative to tag and release as many as possible. The nil recovery rate of striped marlin during the first six years of the co-operative programme in New Zealand was disappointing but not unexpected, as on the Pacific-wide average less than one recovery could be counted on from the 49 released. Scientists are almost completely dependent on anglers for the tagging of these fish. If the anglers need any incentive, the inclusive goal of ensuring the future of the species should provide it.

The small percentage of tagged fish recovered in New Zealand waters has caused some questioning of how many of the fish tagged do survive to be recaptured. Until much more information is obtained several questions which might provide an answer remain unanswered: Are fish being recovered which have lost their tags? Is the marlin population so high that the tagged fish are only a minute proportion of them? Compared with injuries which they might suffer in hooking, reeling in and tagging, what are the natural risks of a marlin in the harsh environment of the sea? A marlin is a vigorous and large enough fish in adulthood but there are records of their being attacked by sharks, and many are caught with bills broken off, up to one in five fish in some years. Some of these injuries presumably occurred in fights.

A contribution to such a discussion is the experience of Herbie James of Rotorua, who was the first member of the Tauranga Gamefishing Club to tag and release a striped marlin. Fishing in northern waters, off the Mokohinau Islands, he hooked the fish through the bill with one of his own lures. The marlin did not come in to the boat without a struggle but when it came up to the boat, to be tagged and released it was still fit. Reporting that the marlin weighed about 120 kg Herbie said: "We watched him go in two flips and a flap – very much alive."

One lesson from this might be that lures by only lightly hooking a fish in the mouth tend to harm a fish less than ordinary rigs, particularly if taken down deep: another is that tagging is too much in its infancy in New Zealand to pass judgement against it. Above all it is not as easy successfully to tag a fish as it may sound. The angler usually has to fish specially for tagging, or at least handle a fish with special care if he has thoughts of tagging it.

A different aspect of overseas tagging for information is the experimental tagging of broadbill swordfish with a sonic tag – a procedure regarded as too expensive for New Zealand yet. The first sonic tag was attached to a 68-kg swordfish (*Xiphias gladius*) in 100 metres of water off Palmilla Point, South California. The fish was tracked for five days and nights and showed a consistent pattern of behaviour over each 24-hour period. Apart from the occasion when the tag was inserted it reappeared only once

– and that was briefly on the following day. Otherwise during daylight hours it stayed close to the bottom in a consistent territory about five miles long at a depth of 80 to 120 m and 3 to 6 miles offshore. Every evening the swordfish headed straight out to sea for 4 or 5 miles at about the same depth, or occasionally deeper, and then came up quickly as darkness fell, working the surface waters from 2 m to 12 m. At daylight it would travel at depth back to patrol its shore territory all day.

A second fish tagged close to shore behaved in much the same way, but a larger fish of 136 kg tagged about 16 miles offshore spent the nights travelling fast near the surface and did not go near shore at all. All the broadbill stayed deep during the day and close to the surface at night.

Such discoveries have resulted in a stirring of interest for it confirms the reason why offshore longliners catch so many broadbill and anglers so few. Anglers have been fishing in the wrong places and at the wrong times – a conclusion confirmed by some successful fishing in overseas waters at night with chemical light sticks on baits and with floodlights. A few skippers have subsequently tried night fishing here without success. Don Ross of Whitianga has been one, using floodlights on his launch. When our new boat is fitted out I shall be another.

CHAPTER SIXTEEN

Fishing for recreation

The policies of successive governments toward New Zealand coastal fishing waters have consistently leaned to their economic exploitation, with too little thought given toward promoting and protecting their recreational use. Even a benevolent eye on big game fishing as a source of tourist dollars has not fully recognised that it, like other aspects of recreational fishing, is dependent for its future wellbeing on that of the coastal fishery as a whole. Nor have policies toward recreational fishing taken into account that, apart from its social role as perhaps the largest independent amateur sport sector of the community, it is of considerable national economic significance.

No official survey is on record which assesses, as has been done officially in other countries, how this economic value adds up. One study shows that 18,000 boat owners in the Hauraki Gulf area are dedicated to pleasure fishing, and half as many again mix fishing with cruising. Another suggests that game fishing is worth $1 million a year in direct and indirect benefits to the Bay of Islands in a year.

Another estimate in the 1979 Northland Regional Development Resources Survey placed the recreational value of fishing in Northland –

where it is nearly all sea fishing – at about $1.5 million a year. This compared with the then figure of about $3 million a year for commercial fishing around the coasts. The survey said that it was reasonable to suppose that recreational fishing activities could in future match the commercial activities in dollar value, and it was reasonable also therefore to suppose that the amateur must receive a substantial share of research and planning for the future use of marine resources. It might well have said that the amateur deserved a better share of the present use of a resource belonging to the nation.

In contrast to the incomplete and largely unofficial approach to determining the value of recreational fishing in New Zealand and even the number of New Zealanders participating – a figure of 400,000 local anglers suggested four years ago by the New Zealand Marine Recreational Resources Council was a conservative estimate – other countries have gone to great trouble to find out exactly the value of their recreational fishing.

A preliminary survey done two years ago in Queensland, with a population similar to New Zealand's, showed that 54 per cent of the Queensland population went fishing and that there were fishermen or women in 76.6 per cent of households there. More than 12 per cent of the population fished for more than 10 days a year and 41.8 per cent fished 10 days or less, with beach and small boat angling the most popular. State-wide, 395,000 households had invested $919 million in fishing equipment and they spent $244.5 million in recurring fishing expenses each year – $36.8 million of this in baits, hooks and sinkers; $38.7 million in refreshments; $13.4 million in boat registration, insurance and maintenance; $69.9 million in vehicle and boat fuel: $64.8 million in travelling expenses; and $20.9 million in accommodation.

In 1977 a survey in New South Wales showed that 30 per cent of the population had fished during the previous 12 months and that most of these (1 million people) had fished in salt water. A total of 20 million days a year were spent fishing in the state with 57 per cent of all males over 13 and 40 per cent of all females going fishing. The Minister of Conservation and the

The modern face of New Zealand big game fishing. A group of the new generation of fast runabouts with a mixture of inboard, inboard-outboard and outboard motors, which in most fishing venues today outnumber the heavier charter boats on which the sport was built. These boats are on the launching ramp near the clubhouse of the Whakatane Big Gamefishing Club. Whakatane Beacon.

Minister in charge of Fisheries, Mr Gordon, said that this initial survey confirmed what the New South Wales government and amateur fishing bodies had already assumed: that the amateur fishermen were an extraordinarily significant social group and the basis of a big leisure industry.

How big? In the United States in 1976 researchers found that the retail sale of goods and services related solely to marine recreational fishing in the previous year, totalled more than $1,800 million, provided 50,580 person years of direct employment and yielded more than $343 million in associated wages and salaries. A later survey in America showed that along a sea coastline which (excluding that of Alaska) is not as long as that of New Zealand, 16.4 million people spent annually a total of 207.2 million fishing days and $3,450 million on their sport. Almost 6 million of those saltwater anglers were deep-sea fishermen.

It is difficult to interpret those figures in New Zealand terms; but it would not, without a complete survey here showing to the contrary, seem possible to write off recreational sea fishing in New Zealand, a nation which has access to more coastline per capita than any comparable country in the world, as involving fewer than

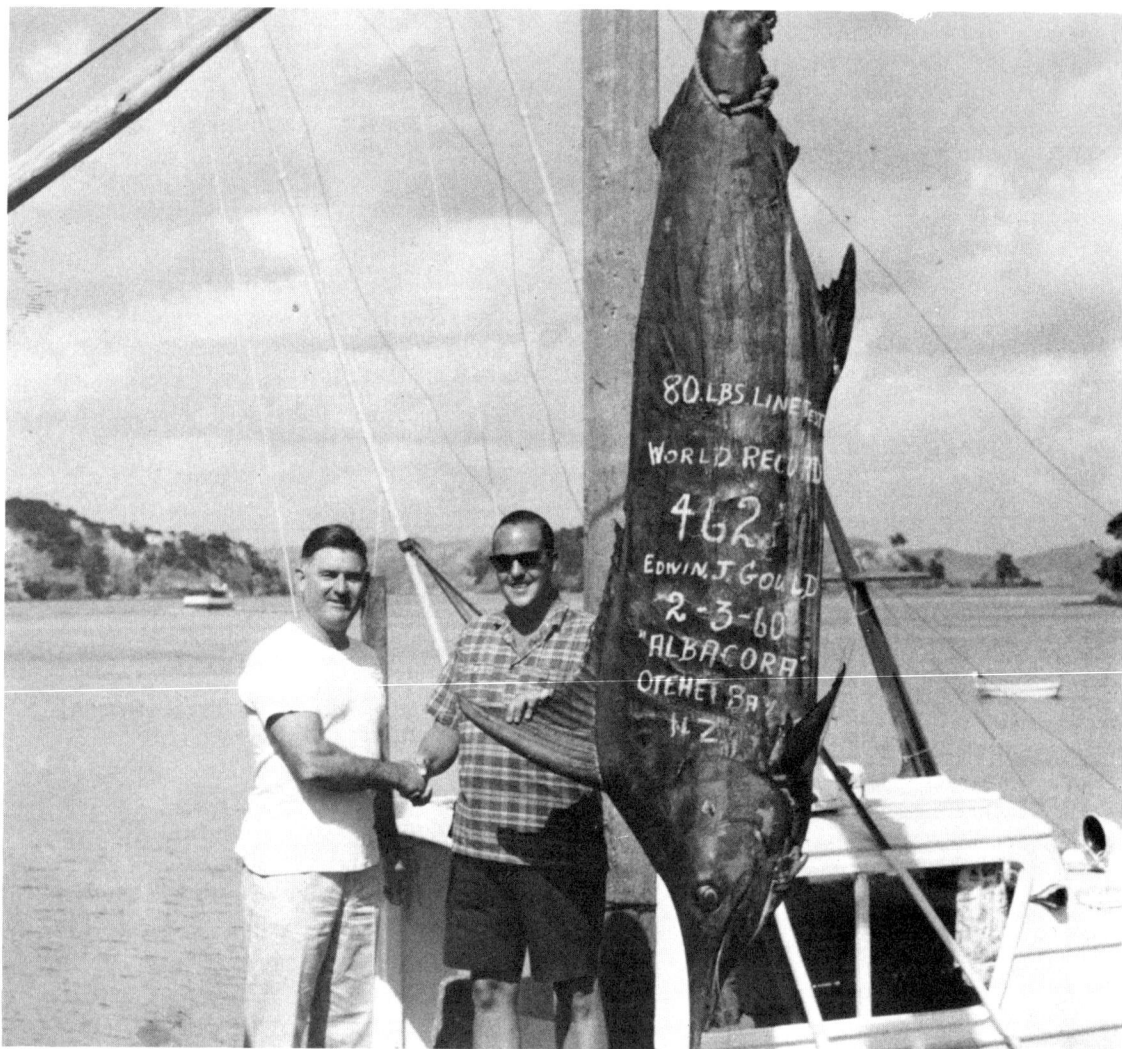

Edwin J. Gould (checked shirt) with a 209 kg marlin caught on 37 kg line in 1960. Congratulating him is George Wooller, of Auckland, himself a successful angler in New Zealand waters and abroad. Ian H. Hanlon.

500,000 New Zealanders, being worth in capital outlay terms less than $500 million, or involving an expenditure of less than $50 million a year. The figures are probably much higher. The importance of such figures, of course, is not to tell fishermen how many of them there are or what they spend on it, but to convince governments that if commercial use of the coastal waters is to continue a priority, on that ground alone recreational fishing, and the protection of present and future stocks for continued recreational fishing have a share in that priority.

A policy of marine exploitation which appeared at the time of writing to be to allow commercial fishing to continue of any stock, or in any areas until the catches became uneconomic – when the fishermen would presumably voluntarily move elsewhere and the depleted

Fishermen of all ages ... Glenn Haddock with a 20 kg albacore, Dave Haddock with a 92 kg striped marlin, with Rick Pollock (right) skipper of the Toa Tai. Whakatane Beacon.

stocks would hopefully in time recover – is no policy at all. It is reminiscent of the days before agricultural husbandry was learned, when tribes moved from area to area as they depleted the soil – a practice which in some areas produced deserts which did not recover. There can be deserts on coasts, too. P. J. Burstall, one of the prime early movers in the formation of the New Zealand Marine Recreational Resources Council has pointed to the lesson of the waters about Hong Kong, where on the coast north and south for 100 miles gill netting so swept the seas that it left no fish longer than a finger.

The point is, of course, that even if money talks, recreational fishing is worth more than money. The New Zealand Marine Recreational Resources Council was established to press this point. It was founded by representatives of the New Zealand Big Game Fishing Council, the New Zealand Underwater Fishing Association and the New Zealand Angling and Casting Association. But it spoke for "shellfish gatherers, the small and large boys on a wharf, divers, surfcasters, rock fishermen, amateur crayfishermen, boaties, beachcombers, buggy enthusiasts, big game fishermen and when applicable the associated commercial boat owners and finally all those individuals who number thousands throughout New Zealand who go down to the sea for what it offers".

Most of these groups have little in conflict with one another but all are affected if the natural fruits of the sea are barred from them or so depleted that directly or indirectly their sort of sport fishing or sea coast enjoyment is adversely affected. They are all (or deserve to be rebuked if they are not) concerned with enjoying the sea or helping with its productiveness, not in depleting it or damaging it, environmentally or biologically.

The way toward this common approach on behalf of sports fisher-people for a better deal was led in 1976 by a sub-committee of the New Zealand Big Game Fishing Council consisting of P. J. Burstall, N. C. Hudspith and J. Chibnall,

which as a first step met the Minister of Agriculture and Fisheries, Mr McIntyre, and the Minister of Tourism, Mr Lapwood. It told the Ministers that saltwater sports fishing existed "despite lack of government support in the past and this lack of support (in the past) is understandable when related to the magnitude of this apparently self-supporting resource".

But, the committee told the Ministers, the present situation was now vastly different from the past, with the greater number of New Zealanders now able to enjoy sport fishing, and with the extensions to commercial fishing, including the declaration of the 200-mile zone then still in prospect. It urged that "the recreational interests of our supporters come under some form of controlled investigation and management to ensure that in future they may be able to participate in their particular pursuits, confident that their interests are being safeguarded".

Some of the commercial fishing activities which the deputation saw as being detrimental to the interests of fishermen, including big game fishermen, were box nets, the detrimental effect of pair trawling on marine ecology, and the apparent lack of restricted inshore limits to commercial fishing, particularly in some popular recreational areas.

Game fishermen were also involved in protests against gill netting which they saw as depleting bait and fish feeding stock; they associated the work of purse seiners and other modern commercial fishing techniques with a dramatic fall off in the number of schools of kahawai and trevally, which in previous years had held the game fish close to the coast. They were also seeking some sort of recreational fishing zone for Mayor Island from which the small fish and the big fish had almost vanished. Fortunately a dramatic recovery is occurring which is perhaps related to reduced pressure from gill netting.

It was accepted then, and some of the prime movers at least still think, that the required controls and body to fix and enforce them could

A good haul of yellowtail being toasted on the wharf at Whakatane by a party of American anglers. The fish were caught from the Toa Tai *(background).* Whakatane Beacon.

187

not be achieved without the recreational fishing community in some way paying for it or toward it. The work of the Marine Recreational Resources Council was originally funded by a 10 cents levy on all members. Experience with freshwater fishing in New Zealand and knowledge of places overseas such as California where a saltwater fishing licence cost $1, suggested that some such financing scheme might need to come in here.

It is a concept which clubs might endorse for their members but which might not go down well with the large number of individual fishermen, women and children who have always regarded fishing in the sea as their right. However, the alternative might be that the poor fishing about which they almost universally now complain may become worse, and that the first sign of regulatory control of a fishery – in the Hauraki Gulf – may not be the forerunner of the controls which would seem necessary in the interest of commercial as well as recreational fishing. The danger lies in the fact that until a great deal more research is done it may not be possible to detect overfishing other than by the past practice of allowing resource to run down, with the time scale of recovery either not known or unacceptable.

The tourist value of big game fishing, in which the State can be expected to be directly interested, is not specifically known. It could only be conjectured how long it might take to recover, and at what cost, if there should be a temporary recession in catches through the whole big game fishing area.

Over recent years there has been a resurgence of marlin fishing in the northern grounds but catches remained poor in the northern and mid Bay of Plenty until last season. The good fishing may spread everywhere again or it may not; it cannot be forecast while the reasons for the lower catches and the better catches are insufficiently known – whether, for instance, the better Far North catches are due to changes in commercial fishing patterns. The overseas fishing fleets which

used to work longlining off the northern part of New Zealand with many billfish and sharks taken incidentally – and not ungratefully – on their millions of hooks, now spend most of their time in a quest for bluefin tuna off the southern parts of New Zealand.

However, the tourist value cannot be small. Nearly a quarter of the anglers who catch fish out of the Bay of Islands are from overseas and many tourists see deep sea fishing only as part, although perhaps a prime part, of the attractions of this country. Most of the tourists come from Australia and the United States. Their welcome presence is noted in the ministerial messages in the official programme of the International Bay of Islands tournaments and the participation in the form of awards and trophies for game fishing of Air New Zealand.

An argument in favour of some sort of fee system is that it would in theory give the fee-paying fisherman a right to demand action to protect and preserve his interests. But such protection would have to be assured in legislation which gave a new authority power to act, regulate and enforce in consultation with, but preferably independent of, commercial fishing controls. A tax on all fishing equipment might provide the money needed – if those advocates of action are right who see little hope of positive action unless fishermen contribute toward it – but such taxes get lost in government funds, and the opportunity to demand accounting for them is lost.

Perhaps the only way in practice to safeguard recreational fishing is in fact to have a statutory body charged with the task – kept in balance by organisations representing commercial fishing and recreational fishing working on each side of it, and perhaps recreational interests should be ready to help in establishing the process. But the balanced use of a national resource would seem a matter of principle which people can expect to happen, and not withheld unless and until they pay.

CHAPTER SEVENTEEN

The game fish

There are many things common to all sports game fishing areas and sometimes fish which are highly regarded in some areas are not so favoured in others. It is a matter of what is best in local conditions – and largely determined by the competition, which for instance reduces the value placed on a food fish if more tasty varieties happen to be plentiful.

The largely temperate waters around New Zealand, tapering to cool toward the south of the country, which although narrow extends over 1,200 kilometres from a latitude of about 34° south to nearly 48° south attract a different combination of game fish from most other areas, in species and sizes, and offers some smaller game fish which are not matched elsewhere.

The big game species recognised by the New Zealand Big Game Fishing Council which controls the sport in New Zealand are:

Billfish: broadbill, blue, black and striped marlin, shortbill spearfish.

Sharks: mako, thresher, hammerhead, tiger, white, blue and bronze whaler.

Tuna: yellowfin, bluefin, big-eye, butterfly and albacore.

Other varieties: yellowtail, dolphin fish.

All these species are also recognised for saltwater fly fishing by the New Zealand Council – plus kahawai, skipjack tuna, slender tuna and trevally, although kahawai and slender tuna were not recognised by the International Game Fish Association at the time of writing.

Enough is known of the game fish described on the subsequent pages to allow anglers to identify them, but much more about them, particularly the breeding places of the marlin remains to be learned. And there are great open gaps for anglers to speculate on when they are out fishing – how fast the various species can go, for instance and which is the fastest. Most of the figures bandied about are fairly subjective – coloured by the excitement of hectic movement aboard as well of the fish, with the screaming of the rod helping to distort judgement.

In the calm of their offices – away even from the yarn-spinning of the clubhouse – experienced anglers agree that there is nothing that they have seen even tailing across the water that exceeded 25 to even 30, 40 to even 50 kilometres an hour. The fastest of all the marlin is probably the blue, but estimates of it doing more than 80 kilometres an hour sound too high; and striped marlin, if they sometimes greyhound at 35 kilometres an hour, do not do it for long. Fish do often swim faster than a launch can follow them and either run out a line or force an angler to put on such drag that they can snap it where it joins the double – the usual place of breakage – but then few of the launches from which this has happened would go more than 10 to 12 knots in open sea conditions. And then mako attack broadbill, and billfish can run down the swift tuna . . .

Diagram VIII

Dorsal fin height

body depth

body depth

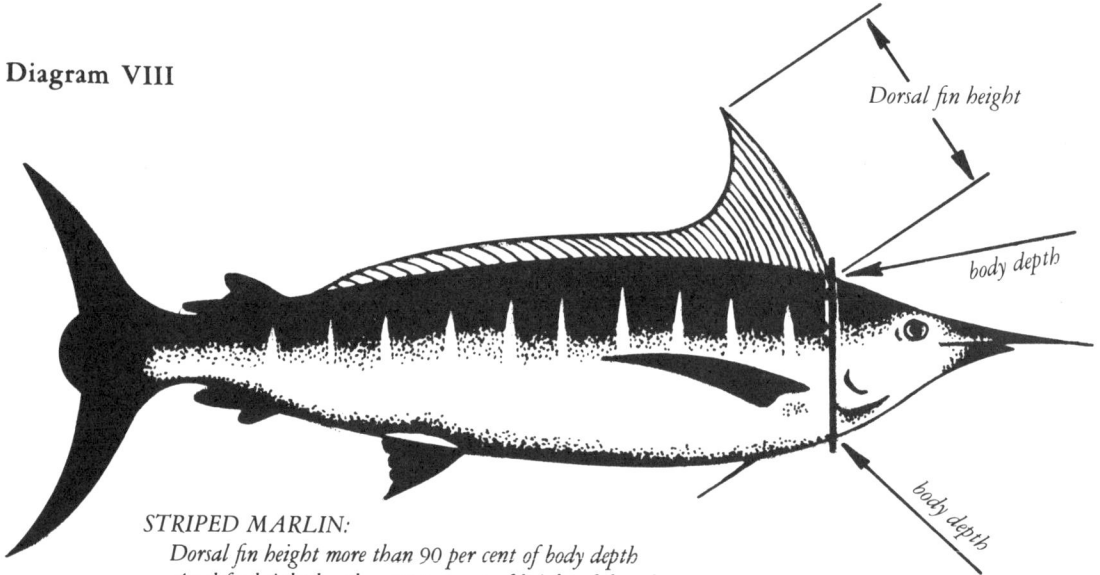

STRIPED MARLIN:
    Dorsal fin height more than 90 per cent of body depth
    Anal fin height less than 76 per cent of height of dorsal
        fin (average 66 per cent)

BLUE MARLIN:
    Dorsal fin height less than 90 per cent of body depth
        (usually much less)
    Anal fin height more than 76 per cent of height of dorsal
        fin (average 86 per cent) anal fin height

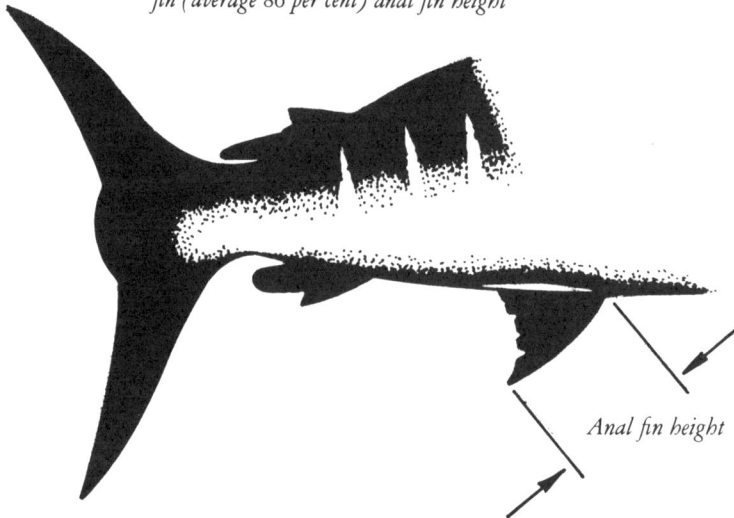

Anal fin height

190

STRIPED MARLIN
Tetrapturus audax

Description

The most common of the larger game fish in New Zealand waters, the striped marlin is a brilliantly coloured billfish with vertical pale blue stripes across a body which is dark metallic blue on the back fading through silver to white underneath, with blue spots on the high fin. The stripes show up especially brightly when the marlin is feeding or playing (then known as "lit-up").

The striped marlin is distinguishable from other marlin in New Zealand waters by (1) having a single lateral line that curves over the pectoral fin and then goes straight to the tail – and which can best be seen immediately after capture; (2) a dorsal fin that always exceeds 90 per cent of the body depth at the origin of the first dorsal fin; (3) the height of the anal fin: always less than 76 per cent of the height of the first dorsal fin and averaging 66 per cent; (4) pinkish-orange flesh; (5) the stripes remain prominent after death; (6) the body form is more slender and tapered than blue marlin.

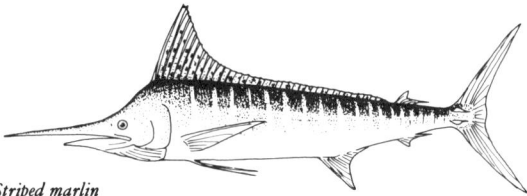

Striped marlin

Where found

A fish of the temperate latitudes, the striped marlin appears to be of a Southern Hemisphere sub-species, migrating to New Zealand after spawning well to the north of the country. It is most common on the east coast of the North Island from North Cape to East Cape, although it has been sighted elsewhere off the coast. It has been more numerous in recent years in the northern parts of that coastal range. The striped marlin prefers the water temperatures of late summer and autumn and is found in both blue (oceanic) and green (coastal) waters.

How caught

It is caught on both troll and drifting lines, on baits live or dead, and on lures. Although it is a wide-ranging feeder usually of oceanic fish, it will take baits of New Zealand coastal species such as kahawai and trevally. It is notable for its leaping and tail-walking displays when being fought.

Size

The New Zealand striped marlin are large compared with other world communities of the species, ranging usually from 70 kg to 160 kg, with a minimum in New Zealand waters of about 35 kg, and the maximum being the world record of about 189 kg. Length: To about 4 m.

Food qualities

Excellent for eating, the striped marlin smokes well and can also be fried in thin steaks (which should not be overcooked) or may be marinated and eaten raw (sashimi style).

BLACK MARLIN
Makaira indica

Description

A more heavily built fish than the striped marlin, and a good deal bigger, the black marlin is dark blue above, changing to white quite distinctly halfway down the body. It sometimes shows faint stripes and may have a light haze over the body which has led to suggestions that there is also a "silver" marlin. The black marlin's main distinguishing features are the jutting pectoral fins, which cannot be folded back against the body, its comparatively small dorsal fin (smaller than striped or blue marlin) and its white flesh. It is heavy in the shoulder and deep in the body and has a lateral line which shows more clearly when the fish is dead.

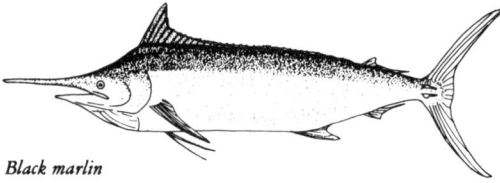

Black marlin

Where found

The black marlin is a wide-ranging fish, those in New Zealand waters being linked by tagging recoveries with those on the black marlin grounds off Cairns, Australia. It is the only marlin species to be so linked from New Zealand with another sports fishing area. Off New Zealand it is a largely coastal fish often caught off reefs, usually travelling in ones or twos only. The black marlin is found from the Northland coast to the Bay of Plenty. Season: About December to May/June, and can appear at any time in this period.

How caught

May be caught trolling with live or dead bait – kahawai and trevally again being accepted; or by deep drifting, black marlin being a bottom – as well as a surface – feeding fish. While caught in the same areas as striped marlin, it is usually found around shallow reef and other foul bottom areas even quite close inshore. It is one of the most highly-rated game fish, with exceptional stamina and size. It broaches frequently and its airborne size is unforgettable.

Size

The black marlin is a much bigger fish than the striped marlin – averaging about 200 kg, with a maximum size caught of 444 kg. Length: To about 4.5 m.

Food qualities

A good eating fish, and may be smoked, grilled or baked.

PACIFIC BLUE MARLIN
Makaira nigricans

Description

Has many of the characteristics of both striped and black marlin, being dark blue on the upper part of the body and changing, fairly abruptly, to silver below. Blue marlin can be distinguished by: (1) no lateral line usually visible: if it is, consists of a reticulate pattern of loops, not a single line; (2) the height of the dorsal fin: always less than the depth of the body at the origin of the first dorsal fin, and normally less than 90 per cent of that depth; (3) the anal fin: always more than 76 per cent of the height of the first dorsal fin (the actual average being 86 per cent); (4) the white flesh; (5) stripes which tend to fade within two to three hours of death; (6) a body that is stouter and less cylindrical than that of a striped marlin.

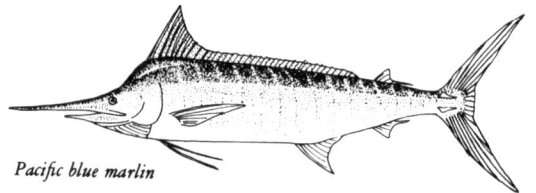

Pacific blue marlin

Where found

A fairly common fish in warm semi-tropical waters, the blue marlin occurs as a deep-water fish off the New Zealand coast. It is usually found in 200 metres of water or more, and not often outside the hottest months, February and March. It is most commonly caught off the north-east coast of New Zealand, although a couple have been taken in a purse seine net off the west coast of the South Island. They appear to be about in ones and twos only and those caught here are almost all females.

How caught

Caught mainly by trolling in deep water and

192

only since this practice became widely adopted in the 1950s. A more aggressive fish in attacking the bait than the striped and black marlin.

Often lost when they tangle with the line at the strike.

Size

Average weight much the same as for black marlin – about 200 kg – with few lighter than 115 kg caught and the largest, of 461.31 kg the heaviest billfish caught in New Zealand waters. Length: To about 4.5 m.

Food qualities

Although it does not smoke well – being inclined to dry out – it is excellent eating, grilled or with sauces (sashimi), or in fish sausages.

SAILFISH

Istiophorus platypterus

Description

The Pacific sailfish is very like a small marlin in body, colour and shape, but is clearly distinguished by its very large dorsal which may reach twice the body depth when fully raised and extends along much of the back. The sailfish has a longer bill than the spearfish. Perhaps liking tropical water temperatures too much to be seen often in New Zealand waters, it is not on record as having been caught by rod and line here but an 18.5-kg specimen (the world record is 100.24 kg, caught off Ecuador) was driven ashore near Whangarei in 1948.

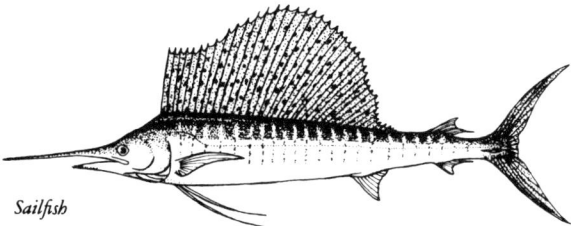

Sailfish

BROADBILL SWORDFISH

Xiphias gladius

Description

The broadbill is the only true swordfish (although the name is often given to marlin also) and is distinguished by a broad, flattened sword longer and wider than that of any other billfish. The sword is about one-third the length of the fish, which has a rounded, evenly tapering body with a large keel each side near the tail. It is dark-coloured on the back – deep blue, brown or black – and has a light coloured lower half, sometimes with a bronze overlay. It can be distinguished on the surface by its high dorsal fin, which is not retractable, which means that, with its tail, it has two fins showing, not one like other billfish which retract their dorsal when on the surface.

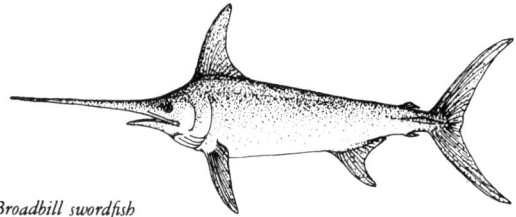

Broadbill swordfish

Where found

The broadbill is distributed widely over the world's oceans and probably about New Zealand waters for although few are caught by anglers, they are a major catch by longliners. This probably occurs because broadbill appear to live deep during the day and come near to the surface mainly by night.

How caught

Sometimes by troll, sometimes on the drift with bait. Some attempts have been made to catch them while drifting at night with overhead lights or light sticks above baits, but not seriously in New Zealand waters up to the time of writing. This seems the best approach, although a return to deep drifting, especially if practised further off the coast could produce more catches. A determined rather than spectacular fighter; rarely broaches.

Size

The largest swordfish caught in New Zealand was of 305.27 kg, and that was in 1928. Most of those caught since have been between 120 kg and 200 kg. Length: To about 5 m.

Food qualities

A very highly esteemed food fish, especially baked, fried or grilled.

PACIFIC SHORTBILL SPEARFISH

Tetrapturus angustirostris

Description

The Pacific shortbill spearfish resembles a marlin but is smaller and has a very short bill which is hardly any longer than the bottom jaw. It is coloured deep blue on the back and on the membrane of the prominent dorsal fin (which runs at almost an even height from the head well back toward the tail), is brownish blue on the sides and silver white below. It has no stripes but may have a green tinge along the lateral line. It has shorter pectoral fins than any other billfish.

Where found

The shortbill spearfish is found scattered in the Indian and Pacific Oceans and in the Atlantic west of the Cape of Good Hope. To judge from

small but regular catches of this fish by longliners working between East Cape and Kermadec Islands it is around in larger numbers than the small number of catches by anglers – only three – so far reported would seem to indicate. All of these catches have been in the Bay of Plenty, the first in 1973 and the others in 1979, although a report of "a small slender marlin with short pectorals" well outside the Poor Knights Islands in 1978 was probably also of a shortbill spearfish. These appear to be deep water fish, and the Bay of Plenty catches probably reflect the extra distance that anglers tend to go out to sea there because of the draw of White Island, and its nearby trench.

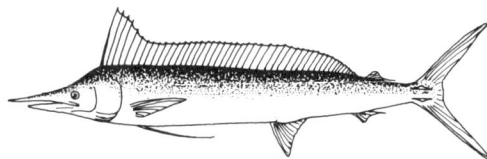

Pacific shortbill spearfish

How caught

Both the more recent catches were made on lures but they can be caught also on trolled baits – which need to be smaller and can be on lighter lines than other billfish.

Size

The 16.75-kg New Zealand record fish, caught by P. Bouley off the Whakatane charter vessel *Toa Tai* south-east of the Volkner Rocks, near White Island on February 22, 1979, is of good average size for the species. The largest ever caught was one of 36 kg off Hawaii, but catches above 20 kg are considered rare. Length: To about 2 m.

Food qualities

Fairly good. The flesh is dark.

MAKO SHARK

Isurus oxyrhinchus

Description

The mako is a strong-swimming fish streamlined from its pointed nose to its crescent tail, the top lobe of which is notched. It is a brilliant dark blue on the back (a colour which quickly fades after the fish is caught) changing abruptly on the lower part of the body to white. It has five long gill slits just in front of the pectoral fins, behind the line of which rises the large triangular main dorsal fin. The shark is noted for its rows of long smooth razor sharp teeth which curve inward. It is a wide-ranging and ferocious predator. The International Game Fish Association yearbook reports an instance where a 331-kg mako was found to have swallowed a 54-kg swordfish whole.

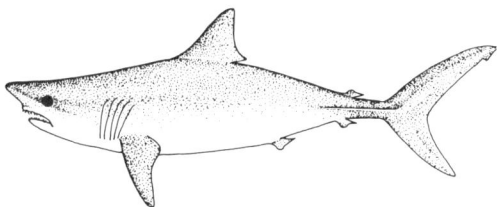

Mako shark

Where found

The mako shark is found all over the world in tropical and temperate seas, and in New Zealand waters off most of the coast, while tending to be larger in size further north. The record catches range from Whangaroa in the north to Gisborne in the south. The mako is not as seasonal in its presence as the marlin although some are believed to move north away from New Zealand in the winter.

How caught

Similar methods to those used in catching marlin will produce mako — trolling with kahawai or trevally bait for instance, and with lures. The large mako can be a dangerous fish and should not be boated "green", especially in smaller boats, as they have been known to leap aboard and attack both the boat and occupants.

Size

The average New Zealand mako weighs from 70 kg to 140 kg — but fish are frequently caught above this level to the New Zealand all-tackle record of 481.26 kg. Length: to about 3.5 m.

Food qualities

Small makos are very good smoked, cooked or marinated. Large makos tend to taint.

BRONZE-WHALER SHARK

Carcharinus brachyurus

Description

Bronze-whalers get their name from their golden brown backs, which merge into white undersides. They are slender fish with nose slightly blunted, and flattened above and below, and have an upper tail lobe much longer than the lower. Their triangular teeth are slightly saw-edged. Reasonably good fighters, they have been ranked with hammerheads.

Bronze-whaler shark

Where found

Although only recently added to the list of recognised game fish, they have been long known in North Island waters. They are also well known off the Australian coast where they are regarded as dangerous. They have been caught here both off the coast and in harbours, and usually close to reefs, where they feed mostly off school fish.

How caught

Usually by deep trolling or drifting with baits.

Size

Grows to about 3 m and to more than 200 kg.

Food qualities

Not usually eaten.

THRESHER SHARK

Alopias vulpinus

Description

The thresher is clearly identifiable by the lengthy upper lobe to its tail, which is as long as the rest of its body and with which it lashes the bait as it comes up behind a troll, and by which it is therefore often hooked. Its slender body, somewhat flattened at the sides, is dark in colour, varying from dark rust grey or green to undersides white or mottled.

Where found

A world-wide species, the thresher is usually oceanic but in New Zealand waters often enters bays and harbours and has been caught over offshore reefs. Specimens have been caught all through the older established fishing waters on the east coast of the North Island, and off the South Island, notably Fiordland.

How caught

Threshers are caught both drifting and trolling, usually with bait in New Zealand waters. Many launchmen believe that the launch should be thrown into neutral as soon as a thresher hits a trolled bait with its tail, allowing the bait to sink in simulation of a stunned fish. While it does not attack people or boats as the mako does its thrashing tail is a daunting weapon when a shark is alongside the cockpit being boated.

Thresher shark

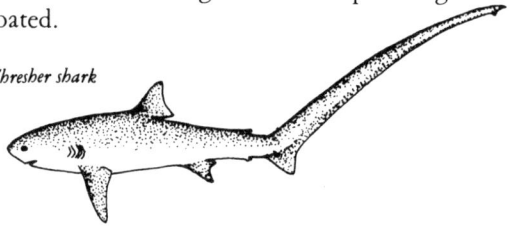

Size

New Zealand threshers are large by world standards. The all-tackle world record is held out from Tutukaka, and other line class world records are also held from 15 kg to 60-kg line in areas from Northland to East Cape. Length: Up to about 6 m.

Food qualities

Excellent smoked or fried thin as for striped marlin. Commands a high price in some overseas fish markets.

TIGER SHARK

Galeocerdo cuvieri

Description

A large fish, the tiger shark is identifiable by its broad flat snout and its wicked array of notched teeth which curve in and to the side. It is grey brown on the back with marked tiger-stripes especially when the fish is young. The underside is white. The first dorsal fin is well forward toward the five gill slits, the rear two of which are above the pectoral fins.

196

Where found

Known the world over and feared in some regions as a man-eater (it will apparently eat anything from animals and fish, big and small, to driftwood and a coil of wire) the tiger shark has been mainly known in New Zealand in the Bay of Plenty. Not a great many have been caught, but enough to confirm its reputation as a hard-fighting game fish.

How caught

Drifting with live or dead bait.

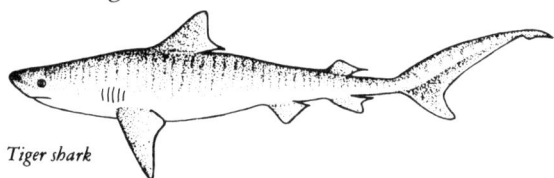

Tiger shark

Size

Overseas this fish often goes over 453.6 kg (1,000 lb) and the world record is of 807.40 kg; but in New Zealand catches have been somewhat smaller, the biggest ever caught being of 499 kg, and the official record being 429.55 kg – still a very big fish. Length: Up to about 6 m locally.

Food qualities

Not eaten here but elsewhere pronounced edible.

HAMMERHEAD SHARK

Sphyrna zygaena

Description

There is no mistaking this fish with its wide hammer-shaped snout, with the eyes at the end of the two protrusions. Its colour is grey-green or grey-brown above, shading down to white below. It has a high front dorsal fin and a long upper lobe to the tail.

Where found

Different species of hammerhead shark are found world-wide. In New Zealand waters their range is normally about as far south as Cook Strait and they are more plentiful the further north and the warmer the water. Most catches are made from January and February, when they can be seen finning on the surface, distinguishable by their high fin and long tail, travelling downwind like marlin but not as fast nor as straight. It has always been known in New Zealand waters but was recognised as a game fish by the New Zealand Big Game Fishing Council only since 1959.

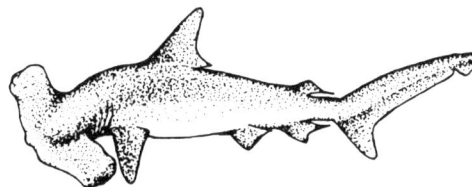

Hammerhead shark

How caught

The hammerhead eats a variety of fish including stingrays (the I.G.F.A. quotes a report of a hammerhead found with 96 stingray barbs imbedded in its jaw, mouth and head) and is best caught drifting, usually ignoring fast-trolled baits. When hooked on light to medium tackle they are strong, almost tireless fighters, difficult to boat.

Size

The average hammerhead in New Zealand waters runs at about 130 kg, but down to about 30 kg and often near 200 kg. The heaviest caught so far is 211.83 kg; and the world record for women on 60-kg line is held by Mrs H. M. Wood of Lottin Point. Length: To about 4 m locally.

Food qualities

Not liked in New Zealand, although a very small hammerhead smoked tasted well enough to one of the authors. Overseas it is classed as good if fresh and properly prepared, with the fins used in soup.

BLUE SHARK
Prionace glauca

Description
A shark similar in appearance to a mako, with brilliant blue colouring above and white below, with slender pectoral fins, long pointed nose but somewhat longer and more slender than a mako. The larger serrated teeth in the upper jaw differ from those in all other sharks by the way they are curved. They gained an alternative name of blue whalers by following whaling ships to feed on the offal. One of the previous non-game sharks not sought by New Zealand fishermen, they have recently been recognised by the New Zealand Big Game Fishing Council, and are listed by the I.G.F.A.

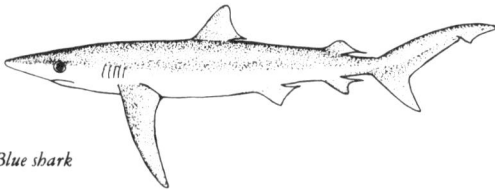

Blue shark

Where found
They range widely, alone or in groups, in cool to temperate seas and are one of the most common sharks in New Zealand waters, in all latitudes.

How caught
They are voracious feeders and can be caught by trolling with baits or lures, although in New Zealand are regarded as suitable only for light-line fishing because of their poor fighting qualities when hooked. Those caught by the Fiordland Club, for instance, where they seem to shadow summer tuna schools are almost always tagged and released, unless of potential light-tackle record size.

Size
They commonly weigh about 50 kg but can grow to more than 180 kg. Length to 2.4 m.

Eating qualities
Not normally eaten but edible if prepared promptly.

WHITE SHARK
Carcharodon carcharias

Description
Sometimes known as the great white shark, it is greyish on top fading to white, with a streamlined body and pronounced keels each side in front of the tail, like those of the mako.

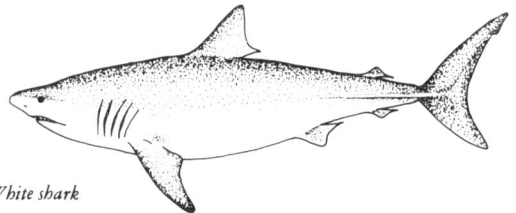

White shark

Where found
Considered a cool-water shark, it is not familiar to Northland fishermen but about a dozen a year become entangled in commercial lines or nets off the Fiordland coast. None have at the time of writing been caught here by anglers, although some may have been hooked and lost, and they were well known about the whaling station at Whangaruru. Another was recently caught by commercial fishermen at the Three Kings Islands. It weighed 771 kg (1,700 lb).

How caught
Well known in Australia, they are caught drifting or trolling using a wide variety of large baits. They are caught in shallow water as well as deep, and are surface fighters. The Fiordland

Club recommends anyone fishing for them to use chum to attract them, a 16/0 hook to carry a large bait, and a trace consisting of chain or heavy aircraft cable. And to play out any hooked fish before attempting to boat them.

Size

No figures are available of New Zealand specimens, where the fish has only recently been classed as game fish by the New Zealand Big Game Fishing Council. Overseas, particularly in Australia where most of the world records are held, they go over 1,000 kg. Length: A one-tonner is about 4.5 m long.

Food qualities

Edible but not often eaten.

PORBEAGLE SHARK

Lamna nasus

Description

Not yet hooked in New Zealand waters and not recognised here by the New Zealand Big Game Fishing Council although reported from Fiordland, this is a well-known game shark overseas, resembling the mako and white sharks. Distinguished by its smooth teeth, which have small cusps on each side at the base, a small secondary keel fin, a white patch on the rear and base of the first dorsal fin and a blue-grey colouring on the back.

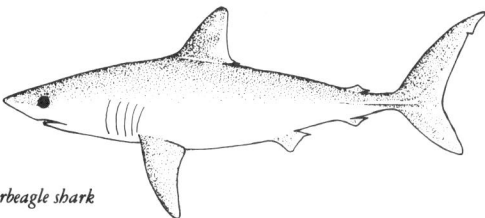

Porbeagle shark

SOUTHERN BLUEFIN TUNA

Thunnus maccoyii

Description

This beautifully proportioned fish is equally beautifully coloured, being dark blue on the back, changing to white below. It has a yellow or grey first dorsal fin, a reddish brown second dorsal fin and a silver-grey anal fin – with other fins being usually dark yellow edged with black. None of its fins are elongated like those of the yellowfin.

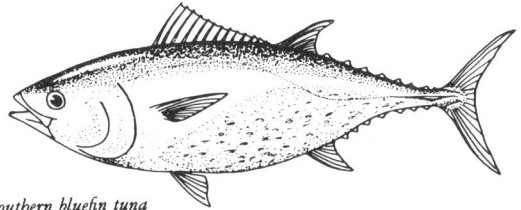

Southern bluefin tuna

Where found

The Southern bluefin is a Pacific species, pelagic and migratory according to season. Although only isolated specimens have been caught on rod and line in New Zealand waters they are believed to travel in schools of equal age. They are caught over the whole range of the New Zealand big game fishing waters, with new areas off the West Coast of the South Island potentially the most rewarding. They are the prime target of the Japanese fishing fleets in the New Zealand fishing zone.

How caught

The biggest bluefin tuna caught in New Zealand waters so far have been on trolled bait, and this may well be the best way to catch the larger specimens, but lures are the most likely to attract them. Commercial fishing for them is done on jigs. They are very hard fighting fish.

Size

The bluefin is the largest of the tunas. The New Zealand record catch is 298.46 kg and bigger fish are considered likely up to 350 kg, with the possibility of world record giants beyond that. The fish are believed to live for at least 20 years. Length: Grown specimens reach 2 m long but they grow bigger.

Food qualities

Excellent eating, hence the interest of the Japanese commercial fleet about New Zealand. The red meat can be eaten raw or cooked (smoked, baked or poached) and, like other tunas, canned or bottled.

YELLOWFIN TUNA
Thunnus albacares

Description

A colourful fish, blue-black on the back fading to white underneath and sometimes with a yellow or blue stripe running from eye to tail. It is distinguishable because all its fins are yellow; except that in very large specimens the elongated dorsal and anal fins (another distinguishing mark) may be silver edged with yellow. The smaller fins have black edges.

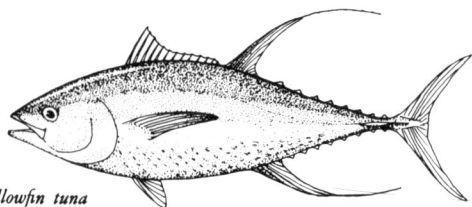

Yellowfin tuna

Where found

The yellowfin tuna, a migratory fish following temperate waters, is found all around the New Zealand north-east coast in summer. It is normally caught in deeper waters, a fact reflected in the larger catches made out in the Bay of Plenty, although the New Zealand records have been spread right down the coast from Northland to Whakatane.

How caught

Usually trolling with bait or lures but can also be caught on the drift using bait – especially live bait. A very good fighting fish. Fished for commercially on long set lines. Often found in company with dolphins.

Size

The yellowfin tuna in New Zealand waters average about 25 kg to 30 kg with larger fish over 60 kg and a few record class fish – by New Zealand standards – over 70 kg. Most of the fish caught are probably fairly young, as the species grows very quickly, reaching 60 kg within four or five years. Average length: 80 cm to 195 cm.

Food qualities

Excellent, the flesh being very light and especially favoured when deep fried.

PACIFIC BIG-EYE TUNA
Thunnus obesus

Description

This fish, which is only rarely caught in New Zealand waters – and then by means similar to the other tuna – is distinguished from the yellowfin tuna, with which it was formerly confused, by its much larger eye, its longer pectoral fin and shorter dorsal and anal fins, and its variation in colour. The dark blue back changes through a band of lighter iridescent blue to bluish white underneath. The main fins are yellow and the finlets edged with black. All other qualities are as for yellowfin tuna, except that big-eye tuna are on the average larger and may exceed 2 m in length.

Pacific big-eye tuna

SKIPJACK (Striped bonito)

Katsuwonus pelamis

Description
A colourful small tuna, with blue-black colouration above and silver below, with five lateral blue stripes on each side.

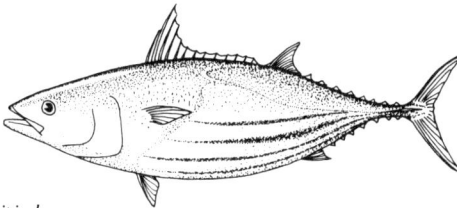

Skipjack

Where found
A cosmopolitan inhabitant of tropical and sub-tropical seas. The skipjack migrates to New Zealand waters in early summer, leaving in autumn. It is found on most of the fishing grounds on the edge of the continental shelf – 150 m to 250 m, as well as inshore. Apart from its own fighting qualities, it makes good, if not very durable, bait for larger fish.

How caught
Usually on fast-trolled lures.

Size
The skipjack normally ranges in size from 1 kg to 2 kg and from half a metre to a metre in length.

Food qualities
A heavy soft red flesh which is best baked.

BUTTERFLY TUNA

Gasterochisma melamphus

Description
This tuna is distinct from all other Scombridae in that it has no caudal keel and also that the body is covered in large cycloid scales. The top of the head and back is a metallic blue in colour, the rest of the body is an intense silver. The pectoral fins are silvery, the ventrals and caudal fins are black or almost transparent. The ventral fins lie directly beneath the pectorals and fit into a deep slot along the underside of the belly when not in use.

Where found
The butterfly tuna is widely distributed throughout the southern oceans of the world between 2°C and 10°C. Each year from December until May, schools of butterfly tuna can be found off the Fiordland coast where they prey on anchovies and other small schooling fish. They appear to prefer water ranging from 12°C to 20°C.

How caught
Schooling butterfly tuna will readily take trolled plugs, lures and flies. However very little is known about the fishing methods for larger specimens. Fish up to 5 kg provide excellent sport if taken on fly fishing or light spinning gear.

Size
Most of the Fiordland specimens caught in

recent years have weighed up to 5 kg. However a few years ago one specimen weighing 36 kg was shot by a commercial fisherman in Doubtful Sound. In Graham's book *Treasury of N.Z. Fishes* he records this species as weighing up to 90 kg. They grow to a length of at least two metres.

Food qualities

This is by far the best eating of all the tuna species, being comparable to snapper. The flesh can be eaten raw as sashimi or cooked.

ALBACORE

Thunnus alalunga

Description

A chunky tuna, with the usual dark blue back shading through yellowing blue on the sides to a white underbelly, the albacore can be distinguished by its very long pectoral fins, the lack of stripes or spots on its under surface and a thin white trailing edge to its tail fin.

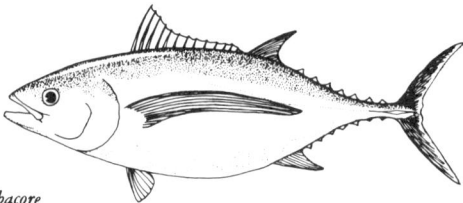

Albacore

Where found

A world-wide migratory fish, the albacore has been caught mainly in the warm summer waters of the Bay of Plenty but has a water temperature tolerance which makes it a likely candidate for any New Zealand fishing waters.

How caught

Usually on lures, but also with trolled, preferably live bait. An excellent fighting fish on light tackle.

Size

From .5 m to 1.3 m long and up to 18 kg in weight.

Food qualities

First-class eating, with fine white flesh.

SOUTHERN YELLOWTAIL (Kingfish)

Seriola grandis

Description

A streamlined fish distinguished by the yellow colouration in its tail fin (mainly), in other fins and usually associated with the dark lateral band which runs through the eye all the way back to the tail. A dark upper body (blue-black, blue-grey or grey-green) gives way to silvery sides and underparts. There is a low spiked forward dorsal fin but the main dorsal fin is well back on the body running through to the tail and matched by a shorter anal fin. The scales are very small for the size of the fish and, with the yellow tail, easily distinguish it from the kahawai. Smaller yellowtail are sometimes used as bait for bigger game.

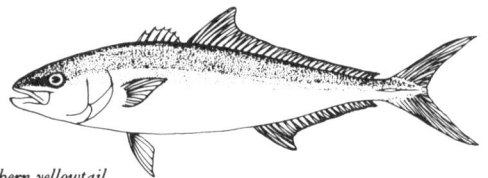

Southern yellowtail

Where found

The yellowtail is a local population of a world-wide species which differs little from area to area except in size. Those around New Zealand are among the biggest. They are found around the

North Island and northern parts of the South Island. Tagging results show that yellowtail move moderate distances up and down the coasts. They are encountered feeding on shallow schooling fish and also frequent deeper reefs, as well as harbour entrances and open bays.

How caught

Usually caught on the troll with lures, but bigger specimens are fished for in deeper waters with live baits or jigs. They are a good fighting fish, with an especially powerful first run. Heavy gear is necessary for big fish because of their disposition to use this first run to dive for foul grounds, where they are usually lost. Present in the fishing grounds thoughout the year. Best fishing time: dawn.

Size

Average length less than a metre but range from half a metre to more than 2 m when they reach more than 40 kg.

Food qualities

A little dry but very acceptable eating, either fried as steaks with sauces or baked.

DOLPHIN FISH

Coryphaena hippurus

Description

A brilliantly coloured fish: blue-green above, silvery below, with a bright yellowish band along greenish gold sides. The fins are also brightly coloured in blue (dorsal), gold and silver (anal), with the others gold, edged with blue. The dolphin fish has a blunt head and a long body compressed at the sides. The long dorsal fin runs from the top of the head to the tail. Very fast fish, they will broach or tailwalk when hooked. Not to be confused with the mammalian

dolphins and porpoises, to which they are not related.

Where found

A fish of tropical and warm subtropical surface waters, the dolphin fish is usually encountered only in northern New Zealand waters, down to, and especially in, the Bay of Islands in the deeper waters regularly fished there. It is not encountered in any numbers, however, and only in full summer.

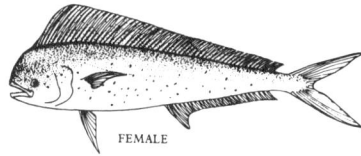

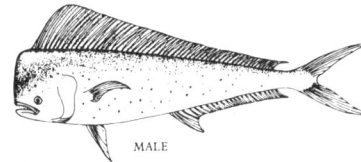

Dolphin fish

How caught

The dolphin fish is a surface feeder and is caught by trolling lures, or bait as for marlin. A very good fighting fish. Tends to school under floating debris.

Size

Specimens caught off New Zealand have averaged about a metre to a metre and a half in length, with the heaviest weighing 11.25 kg — well down, so far, on the world record range of about three times this size.

Food qualities

A delicious food fish — certainly, from experience, when smoked.

KAHAWAI

Arripis trutta

Description

A slender fish very like a yellowtail in shape but without its distinctive yellow markings – it is usually blue-green above and silver below – and also has relatively large scales. It may be spotted or blotched on the back. The dorsal fin is in two parts, the forward spined, with the longest spines forward, and the rear part softer, as is the shorter anal fin. These fins both end in points near the tail.

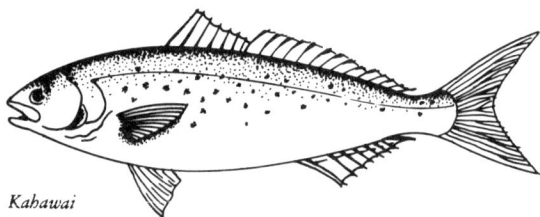

Kahawai

Where found

Common in northern New Zealand coastal waters and river mouths (hence its widespread use as bait by big game fishermen). Less common around the South Island. Usually found close to the surface and often schooling.

How caught

Readily takes lures trolled at fairly low speeds, or by casting and fast retrieval. While it has a wide acceptance of lures it can be fussy on occasion, when different varieties need to be tried. A good fighting fish on light tackle, and the only small sea fish which will leap on the line.

Size

Catches usually range from 40 mm to 80 mm long, but they are found all the way up from a few centimetres in length, in sandy shallows, to a maximum of nearly a metre and a weight of about 8 kg.

Food qualities

Kahawai smoke well and can be baked or canned. Best if bled when caught.

SNAPPER

Chrysphyrs auratus

Description

Although not a recognised game fish, the snapper is a noted food fish indigenous to New Zealand waters and is included in the targets of some New Zealand fishing clubs. It is a deep-bodied fish, with a steep forehead, reddish-gold coloured on the top of the body and lighter below, usually with some blue-green spots. It is fully scaled, with sharply spined dorsal and anal fins.

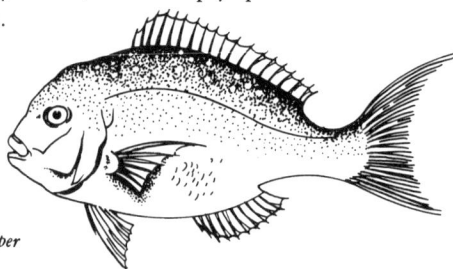

Snapper

Where found

The snapper is most common around the North Island coast, although it travels as far south as the Banks Peninsula, South Island, in summer. It is a bottom-feeder, travelling usually in schools, although some large loners live in rocky areas.

How caught

Normally caught on the baited hook, with sinker or on floating line, but it can also be caught on lures which are jigged, or slowly retrieved.

Size

Snapper of 10 kg are prizes these days although they used to be common enough, and fish of half that size are now better than average.

Food qualities

An excellent eating fish, prepared by any means including smoking.

TREVALLY

Caranx georgianas

Description

A well shaped fish compressed at the side, bluish green above, silver-green on the sides, and with a gold tint to flanks and fins. The trevally has a separate front dorsal fin with high spines. The rear dorsal fin is softer and is matched by an anal fin. A smaller fish than the giant tropical trevally.

Where found

In North Island coastal waters and around the South Island down to Banks Peninsula. Schools of the fish were a distinctive feature of the reefy areas associated with early big game fishing, but less so now as a result of extensive purse seining.

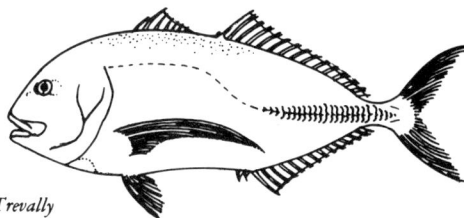

Trevally

How caught

Usually will not take lures when schooling, when jagging is usually the only way of capture. Isolated specimens will take a hook or can be attracted in deeper water by jigging.

Size

Average fish about half a metre in length; largest ones still less than a metre.

Food qualities

Good, for all methods of cooking, especially for smoking.

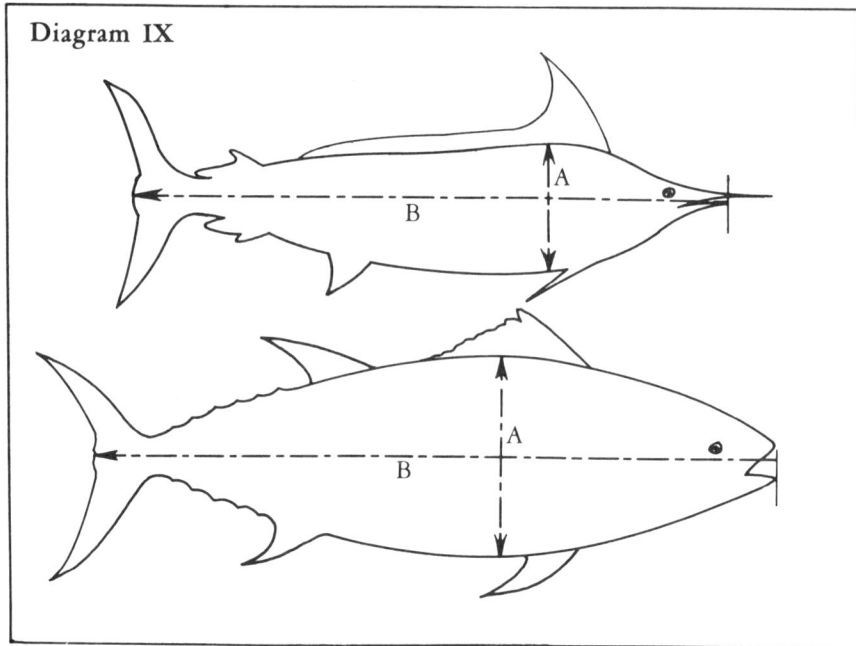

Diagram IX

To estimate the weight of a fish: measure the girth in cm at the thickest part, and the length in cm from the point of the lower jaw to the crotch of the tail. Multiply the square of the girth by the length and divide by 29,000 to get the approximate weight in kg. This method of estimating works for "average" shaped fish. (Note: I.G.F.A. measurements require total length.)

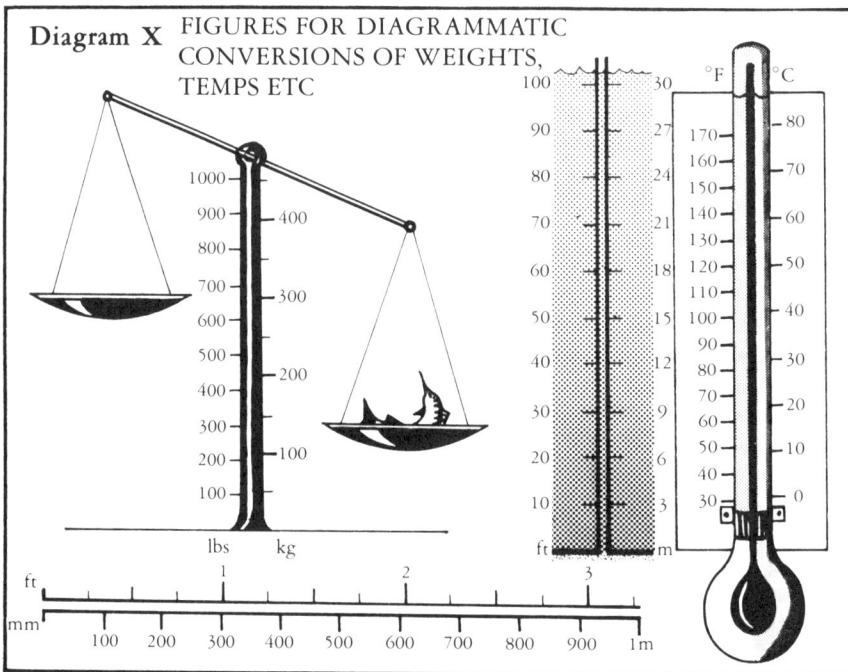

Diagram X FIGURES FOR DIAGRAMMATIC CONVERSIONS OF WEIGHTS, TEMPS ETC

SALTWATER GAME FISH RECORDS

The following list gives the world (I.G.F.A.)
saltwater game fish records set in New Zealand waters
and the New Zealand records – ratified as at September 1981.

ALL-TACKLE WORLD RECORDS

Species	Weight kg.	Angler	Place	Date
Striped marlin	189.37	Phillip Bryers	Cavalli Islands	14.1.77
Thresher shark	383.80	Mrs D. North	Tutukaka	8.2.81
Sth Yellowtail	50.34	A. F. Plim	Bay of Islands	11.6.61

LINE CLASS WORLD RECORDS

Line		Weight	Angler	Place	Date
STRIPED MARLIN					
6 kg	M	123.00 kg	B. Hill	Bay of Islands	26.4.81
10 kg	W	154.22 kg	Robyn Hall	Bay of Islands	21.1.77
15 kg	W	136.53 kg	Mrs Lola Fuller	Doubtless Bay	27.4.79
24 kg	M	183.47 kg	Klaus Rober	Bay of Islands	12.3.80
24 kg	W	181.89 kg	Mrs Margaret Williams	Cavalli Islands	24.2.70
37 kg	M	189.37 kg	Phillip Bryers	Cavalli Islands	14.1.77
37 kg	W	188.00 kg	Mrs J. J. Main	Whangarei	1.5.81
60 kg	M	180.53 kg	J. K. Boyle	Mayor Island	30.12.74
HAMMERHEAD SHARK					
60 kg	W	184.16 kg	Mrs H. M. Wood	Lottin Point	26.2.74

Line		Weight	Angler	Place	Date
MAKO SHARK					
15 kg	W	174.63 kg	Mrs Lola Fuller	Cavalli Islands	27.3.80
24 kg	W	224.50 kg	Miss J. Going	Whangarei	22.12.79
60 kg	M	481.26 kg	J. B. Penwarden	Mayor Island	17.2.70
THRESHER SHARK					
15 kg	W	136.07 kg	Mrs Anne Clark	Bay of Islands	23.6.72
24 kg	W	166.01 kg	Mrs Avril Semmens	Bay of Islands	6.5.72
37 kg	M	335.20 kg	Brian Galvin	Tutukaka	17.2.75
37 kg	W	363.80 kg	Mrs D. North	Whangarei	8.2.81
60 kg	M	306.62 kg	R. C. Faulkner	Mayor Island	23.2.78
60 kg	W	330.67 kg	Mrs V. Brown	Mayor Island	3.6.59
SOUTHERN BLUE-FIN TUNA					
10 kg	W	22.22 kg	Miss Schonda Vincent	Fiordland	17.4.77
24 kg	M	158.00 kg	R. Wood	Whakatane	16.1.81
37 kg	W	78.50 kg	Carolyn Thies	Whakatane	12.2.81
SOUTHERN YELLOWTAIL					
3 kg	M	17.23 kg	Dr G. D. Tetro	Rangitoto Channel	17.12.72
6 kg	M	29.71 kg	J. Farrell	Cavalli Islands	13.7.72
6 kg	W	27.66 kg	Mrs Barbara Brittain	Cavalli Islands	14.6.76
10 kg	M	34.01 kg	M. Maxwell	Whakatane	23.2.76
10 kg	W	30.16 kg	Mrs Margaret Niven	Cape Brett	12.7.70
24 kg	M	50.34 kg	A. F. Plim	Bay of Islands	11.6.61
24 kg	W	37.19 kg	Mrs Francine Swales	Three Kings Is	1.10.75
37 kg	M	48.98 kg	Robin O'Connor	Cape Brett	15.1.62
37 kg	W	38.25 kg	Carolyn Thies	Whakatane	12.2.81
60 kg	M	43.09 kg	J. V. Bayliss	White Island	11.4.75
60 kg	W	36.74 kg	Mrs Patricia E. Jack	Mayor Island	8.4.66

NEW ZEALAND RECORDS

Line		Weight	Angler	Place	Date
Line		*Weight*	*Angler*	*Place*	*Date*
ALBACORE					
3 kg	M	6.80 kg	C. D. Murray	Hawkes Bay	30.12.78
6 kg	M	10.88 kg	P. J. Christensen	Gisborne-Tatapouri	26.2.74
6 kg	W	4.50 kg	Mrs J. A. Ball	Gisborne-Tatapouri	1.2.81
10 kg	M	16.78 kg	M. Cooney	Whakatane	3.2.79
10 kg	W	9.52 kg	Mrs D. Titter	Hawkes Bay	29.12.78
15 kg	M	23.25 kg	D. D. Dunn	Whakatane	21.2.81
15 kg	W	11.50 kg	Mrs M. E. Easton	Gisborne-Tatapouri	31.1.81
24 kg	M	22.25 kg	B. J. Tanner	Whakatane	5.3.81
24 kg	W	11.50 kg	Mrs C. D. Atwood	Whakatane	25.3.81
37 kg	M	20.00 kg	G. Haddock	Whakatane	3.2.80
37 kg	W	9.00 kg	Mrs M. Pollock	Whakatane	25.4.81
DOLPHIN FISH (Mahimahi)					
10 kg	M	7.90 kg	J. Callanan	Whangaroa	15.2.81
15 kg	M	11.25 kg	C. A. Flinkenberg	Waihau Bay	19.2.78
24 kg	M	5.50 kg	R. N. Sato	Whakatane	17.1.79
24 kg	W	5.50 kg	Mrs V. E. Going	Whangaroa	17.2.81
60 kg	M	10.50 kg	S. D. Haddock	Whakatane	3.4.81
BLACK MARLIN					
15 kg	M	153.77 kg	B. E. Irvine	Bay of Islands	22.2.69
24 kg	M	287.58 kg	G. Young	Bay of Islands	12.3.76
24 kg	W	159.66 kg	Mrs L. Fuller	Bay of Islands	18.1.78
37 kg	M	350.63 kg	G. A. Wooller	Bay of Islands	5.1.65
37 kg	W	322.50 kg	Mrs L. J. Tremewan	Bay of Islands	26.1.73
60 kg	M	444.00 kg	D. Hague	Whakatane	23.4.78
60 kg	W	383.74 kg	Mrs E. Brownson	Bay of Islands	14.2.50

Line		Weight	Angler	Place	Date
PACIFIC BLUE MARLIN					
15 kg	M	198.67 kg	W. W. Hall	Bay of Islands	2.12.72
24 kg	M	236.55 kg	G. Baxendale	Tutukaka	13.3.78
24 kg	W	160.11 kg	Mrs L. Fuller	Bay of Islands	30.3.78
37 kg	M	373.31 kg	A. G. Nicol	Mayor Island	27.2.72
37 kg	W	260.40 kg	Mrs C. Pedersen	Tutukaka	22.2.79
60 kg	M	461.31 kg	R. Greig	Bay of Islands	13.3.68
60 kg	W	252.65 kg	Mrs M. Jones	Whangaroa	25.2.66
STRIPED MARLIN					
6 kg	M	123.00 kg	B. Hill	Bay of Islands	26.4.81
10 kg	M	150.14 kg	C. H. Hopkins	Bay of Islands	16.3.54
10 kg	W	154.22 kg	Mrs R. Hall	Bay of Islands	21.1.77
15 kg	M	147.87 kg	C. Shields	Bay of Islands	25.2.76
15 kg	W	136.53 kg	Mrs L. Fuller	Bay of Islands	27.4.79
24 kg	M	183.47 kg	K. Rober	Bay of Islands	12.3.80
24 kg	W	181.89 kg	Mrs M. Williams	Bay of Islands	24.2.70
37 kg	M	189.37 kg	P. Bryers	Bay of Islands	14.1.77
37 kg	W	188.00 kg	Mrs J. J. Main	Whangarei	1.5.81
60 kg	M	180.53 kg	J. K. Boyle	Mayor Island	30.12.74
60 kg	W	170.55 kg	Mrs J. Collie	Bay of Islands	23.3.64
BLUE SHARK					
3 kg	M	35.65 kg	B. J. Walker	Hawkes Bay	25.1.81
6 kg	M	48.00 kg	P. J. Easton	Gisborne-Tatapouri	24.1.81
6 kg	W	34.50 kg	Mrs K. Bayliss	Whakatane	15.12.79
10 kg	M	35.00 kg	S. Sheard	Whangaroa	26.1.81
10 kg	W	112.50 kg	Mrs S. M. Richardson	Mercury Bay	23.2.81
15 kg	M	146.00 kg	P. M. Searle	Gisborne-Tatapouri	21.2.81
15 kg	W	104.00 kg	Miss B. Head	Whakatane	15.11.80
24 kg	M	149.50 kg	M. Cruse	Whakatane	4.1.81
24 kg	W	102.20 kg	Mrs P. Raxworthy	Whangarei	10.3.81
37 kg	M	140.00 kg	L. R. Campbell	Auckland	25.4.80
60 kg	M	87.00 kg	D. Holland	Whangaroa	13.1.80
BRONZE WHALER SHARK					
10 kg	M	90.26 kg	N. M. Pawson	Tauranga	22.2.81
24 kg	M	164.00 kg	K. McKee	Whakatane	4.1.81
24 kg	W	118.00 kg	Mrs D. Preston	Whakatane	26.1.81
37 kg	M	163.00 kg	E. C. Bryenton	Whakatane	1.2.81

Line	Weight		Angler	Place	Date
HAMMERHEAD SHARK					
6 kg	M	16.00 kg	B. J. Rhodes	Kawau Island	21.2.77
10 kg	M	111.58 kg	W. W. Kehely	Mercury Bay	11.1.75
10 kg	W	86.18 kg	Mrs R. Hall	Bay of Islands	13.4.74
15 kg	M	134.93 kg	M. A. Armstrong	Tutukaka	14.3.78
15 kg	M	135.00 kg	P. Batchelor	Waihau Bay	23.2.78
15 kg	W	160.12 kg	Mrs R. Hall	Bay of Islands	6.1.74
24 kg	M	182.80 kg	T. Darby	Bay of Islands	11.2.78
24 kg	W	168.74 kg	Miss V. Johnson	Bay of Islands	28.1.80
37 kg	M	211.83 kg	A. W. Paul, Jnr	Bay of Islands	18.12.77
37 kg	W	184.00 kg	Mrs K. I. Bayliss	Whakatane	22.1.77
60 kg	M	203.21 kg	A. Brown	Bay of Islands	14.1.76
60 kg	W	184.16 kg	Mrs H. M. Wood	Gisborne-Tatapouri	24.5.74
MAKO SHARK					
3 kg	M	30.84 kg	J. K. Butters	Mercury Bay	7.1.79
3 kg	W	14.20 kg	Mrs M. Nilsson	Hawkes Bay	26.1.80
6 kg	M	70.00 kg	A. L. Wood	Gisborne-Tatapouri	12.2.78
6 kg	W	59.70 kg	Mrs R. Going	Whangaroa	29.1.79
10 kg	M	157.40 kg	D. K. Butters	Mercury Bay	3.1.73
10 kg	W	90.72 kg	Mrs R. Hall	Bay of Islands	29.3.75
15 kg	M	145.15 kg	J. R. Chibnall	Bay of Islands	5.2.72
15 kg	W	174.63 kg	Mrs L. Fuller	Bay of Islands	27.3.80
24 kg	M	317.00 kg	K. Gilbert	Whangaroa	9.4.78
24 kg	W	224.50 kg	Miss J. Going	Tutukaka	22.12.79
37 kg	M	371.95 kg	T. Culshaw	Whangaroa	28.3.64
37 kg	W	261.27 kg	Miss J. Fuller	Whangaroa	6.11.70
60 kg	M	481.26 kg	J. Penwarden	Mayor Island	17.2.70
60 kg	W	389.18 kg	Mrs R. Beaver	Whangaroa	14.4.51
THRESHER SHARK					
10 kg	M	30.16 kg	P. J. Farry	Fiordland	10.3.78
15 kg	M	139.25 kg	G. Pierce	Tutukaka	18.4.74
15 kg	W	136.07 kg	Mrs A. Clark	Bay of Islands	23.6.72
24 kg	M	198.00 kg	A. G. Eastgate	Gisborne-Tatapouri	22.2.78
24 kg	W	166.01 kg	Mrs A. Semmens	Bay of Islands	6.5.72
37 kg	M	335.20 kg	B. Galvin	Tutukaka	17.2.75
37 kg	W	363.80 kg	Mrs D. North	Whangarei	8.2.81
60 kg	M	306.63 kg	R. C. Faulkner	Mayor Island	23.2.78
60 kg	W	330.67 kg	Mrs V. Brown	Mayor Island	6.3.59

Line		Weight	Angler	Place	Date
TIGER SHARK					
37 kg	M	353.80 kg	H. Gilbert	Mayor Island	24.4.62
60 kg	M	429.55 kg	D. J. Brophy	Mayor Island	21.2.63
SPEARFISH					
24 kg	M	16.75 kg	P. Bouley	Whakatane	22.1.79
SWORDFISH (Broadbill)					
37 kg	M	241.77 kg	W. W. Hall	Bay of Islands	10.2.80
60 kg	M	305.27 kg	H. White-Wickham	Bay of Islands	9.1.28
PACIFIC BIG-EYE TUNA					
6 kg	M	12.24 kg	L. E. Dyer	Tutukaka	17.3.78
24 kg	W	20.41 kg	Mrs A. Coburn	Tutukaka	13.1.77
SOUTHERN BLUEFIN TUNA					
10 kg	M	31.07 kg	B. Vincent	Fiordland	18.4.78
10 kg	M	31.07 kg	R. G. Marquand	Fiordland	19.2.78
10 kg	W	22.22 kg	Miss S. Vincent	Fiordland	17.4.77
15 kg	M	29.93 kg	M. Williams	Tutukaka	31.1.77
24 kg	M	158.00 kg	R. Wood	Whakatane	16.1.81
37 kg	M	104.00 kg	D. G. Benson	Whakatane	21.6.81
37 kg	W	78.50 kg	Carolyn Thies	Whakatane	21.6.81
60 kg	M	298.46 kg	E. Andrews	Mayor Island	3.2.70
60 kg	W	113.40 kg	Mrs H. M. Conyngham	Mayor Island	22.2.61
YELLOWFIN TUNA					
6 kg	M	31.25 kg	V. A. Mountier	Tauranga	13.3.81
10 kg	M	50.35 kg	D. K. Butters	Mercury Bay	20.1.67
10 kg	W	31.75 kg	Mrs S. Pierce	Tutukaka	9.3.77
15 kg	M	66.00 kg	L. R. Campbell	Whangaroa	7.4.81
15 kg	W	56.24 kg	Mrs B. Buchanan	Mayor Island	15.1.66
24 kg	M	80.00 kg	G. Smith	Bay of Islands	27.3.81
24 kg	W	64.41 kg	Miss G. M. Fleming	Bay of Islands	6.2.66
37 kg	M	76.43 kg	W. E. Brazendale	Bay of Islands	25.1.66
37 kg	W	68.00 kg	Mrs K. I. Bayliss	Whakatane	31.1.78
60 kg	M	69.85 kg	L. R. Nilsen	Bay of Islands	17.3.67
60 kg	W	48.99 kg	Mrs G. J. Grace	Whakatane	28.12.70

Line		Weight	Angler	Place	Date
YELLOWTAIL					
3 kg	M	17.23 kg	G. B. Tetro	Auckland	17.12.72
6 kg	M	29.71 kg	J. R. Farrell	Bay of Islands	13.7.72
6 kg	W	27.66 kg	Mrs B. Brittain	Bay of Islands	14.6.76
10 kg	M	34.01 kg	M. Maxwell	Whakatane	23.2.76
10 kg	W	30.16 kg	Mrs M. Niven	Bay of Islands	12.7.70
15 kg	M	39.91 kg	J. R. Chibnall	Bay of Islands	25.6.63
15 kg	W	33.23 kg	Mrs J. O'Loughlin	Bay of Islands	19.6.77
24 kg	M	50.34 kg	A. F. Plim	Bay of Islands	11.6.61
24 kg	W	37.19 kg	Mrs F. Swales	Whangaroa	1.10.75
37 kg	M	48.98 kg	R. O'Connor	Bay of Islands	15.1.62
37 kg	W	38.25 kg	Carolyn Thies	Whakatane	12.2.81
60 kg	M	43.09 kg	J. V. Bayliss	Whakatane	11.4.75
60 kg	W	36.74 kg	Mrs P. E. Jack	Mayor Island	18.5.60

SALTWATER FLY-FISHING

BLUE SHARK					
7 kg		1.93 kg	G. J. Simcock	Hawkes Bay	25.2.81
KAHAWAI					
3 kg		2.72 kg	G. Kemsley	Mercury Bay	17.12.80
5 kg		2.00 kg	R. J. Whitehouse	Whakatane	28.1.80
SOUTHERN YELLOWTAIL					
5 kg	M	14.51 kg	M. Godfrey	Tauranga	12.5.79

LATE RECORDS

Gamefish records have continued to be broken in the 1981–82 fishing season, but not all of those claimed have been ratified at the time the book has gone to print. Those new New Zealand records ratified up to April 1982, have been:

Line		Weight	Angler	Place	Date
DOLPHIN FISH (Mahimahi)					
6 kg	M	8.5 kg	P. Johansen	Whangaroa	14.1.82
37 kg	W	10.00 kg	Miss K. Walters	Whangaroa	14.1.82
BLUE SHARK					
10 kg	M	95.25 kg	M. Lindsay	Gisborne-Tatapouri	22.2.82
MAKO SHARK					
6 kg	M	93.00 kg	S. Sheard	Whangaroa	24.1.82
SPEARFISH					
24 kg	M	22.60 kg	L. Jones	Whangaroa	28.1.82

MAJOR AWARD WINNERS

OLD MAN AND THE SEA TROPHY
(Most Meritorious Catch Each Season)

1958–59	J. R. Price	Whangarei	1970–71	No Award	–
1959–60	D. Martin (Mrs)	Whangarei	1971–72	A. Clark (Mrs)	Bay of Islands
1960–61	W. E. Wagener	Bay of Islands	1972–73	N. Massey (Mrs)	Tauranga
1961–62	C. D. Moloney	Whangarei	1973–74	L. Blomfield	Bay of Islands
1962–63	B. Williams	Whangaroa	1974–75	L. R. Going	Whangarei
1963–64	F. Cotterill	Whangarei	1975–76	Sir William Stevenson	–
1964–65	W. Pocklington	Bay of Islands			
1965–66	M. R. Jones	Bay of Islands	1976–77	A. Stevenson	Whangarei
1966–67	No Award	–	1977–78	R. W. Campbell	Bay of Islands
1967–68	W. Bannister	Whangaroa	1978–79	Miss K. Beale	Bay of Islands
1968–69	No Award	–	1979–80	Miss J. Going	Whangarei
1969–70	J. T. Hannah	Whangarei	1980–81	B. Hill	Bay of Islands

214

LORD NORRIE GOLD CUP
(Heaviest striped marlin each season)

1957–58	(C. G. Wilson	Tauranga	177.35 kg	1968–69	B. J. Moody	Tauranga	175.54 kg
	(J. F. Frew	Tauranga		1969–70	R. E. Thompson	Tauranga	183.70 kg
1958–59	(R. S. Carter	Tauranga	188.24 kg	1970–71	T. M. Hume	Tauranga	156.49 kg
	(B. Livingstone	Bay of Islands		1971–72	E. H. Cox	Whangaroa	178.71 kg
1959–60	G. Maunsell	Whangarei	189.14 kg	1972–73	D. M. Walker	Bay of Islands	161.48 kg
1960–61	J. Livingston	Tauranga	181.43 kg	1973–74	B. Brittain	Tauranga	182.79 kg
1961–62	H. S. Newman	Tauranga	175.99 kg		(Mrs)		
1962–63	J. F. Clarke	Whangarei	171.45 kg	1974–75	J. K. Boyle	Tauranga	180.53 kg
1963–64	B. C. Bain	Bay of Islands	188.24 kg	1975–76	C. Carabott	Bay of Islands	181.89 kg
1964–65	R. M. A. Pearson	Bay of Islands	207.74 kg	1976–77	P. Bryers	Bay of Islands	189.37 kg
				1977–78	D. P. Evans	Bay of Islands	180.95 kg
1965–66	W. W. Boyed	Whangaroa	199.58 kg	1978–79	G. Munro	Whangarei	168.40 kg
1966–67	G. Parlour	Whangaroa	184.61 kg	1979–80	K. Rober	Bay of Islands	183.47 kg
1967–68	G. Cunningham	Tauranga	182.79 kg	1980–81	J. Main (Mrs)	Whangarei	188.00 kg

FISHERMAN OF THE YEAR
(Heaviest game fish caught each season)

1963–64	D. S. Lane	Tauranga	Black Marlin	425.02 kg
1964–65	M. F. Lornie	Tauranga	Black Marlin	406.87 kg
1965–66	B. Evans	Tauranga	Mako Shark	359.24 kg
1966–67	W. Gasquoine	Tauranga	Tiger Shark	357.08 kg
1967–68	R. W. Greig	Bay of Islands	Pacific Blue Marlin	461.30 kg
1968–69	M. L. Larsen	Tauranga	Mako Shark	425.02 kg
1969–70	J. Penwarden	Tauranga	Mako Shark	481.26 kg
1970–71	N. R. Brady	Bay of Islands	Mako Shark	312.98 kg
1971–72	J. Bloomfield	Whakatane	Black Marlin	413.68 kg
1972–73	N. Russ	Whangaroa	Mako Shark	346.09 kg
1973–74	J. Gerulaitis	Whangarei	Black Marlin	287.12 kg
1974–75	B. J. Galvin	Whangarei	Thresher Shark	335.20 kg
1975–76	B. W. Anson	Tauranga	Pacific Blue Marlin	340.19 kg
1976–77	A. Barclay	Bay of Islands	Black Marlin	342.46 kg
1977–78	D. Hague	Whakatane	Black Marlin	444.00 kg
1978–79	F. Wright	Whangaroa	Mako Shark	305.00 kg
1979–80	J. Mildenhall	Whakatane	Mako Shark	302.50 kg
1980–81	D. North (Mrs)	Whangarei	Thresher Shark	363.80 kg

CLUBS AND LAUNCHES

WHANGAROA BIG GAMEFISH CLUB
P.O. Box 155, Kaeo

President: Laurie Ross   *Secretary*: J. de Groot
Clubhouse: Whangaroa   Membership: 640

Charter Boats and Skippers
Carousel (Sid Gammon – from Tauranga)
Maraqueta (Laurie Ross – also Bay of Islands)

BAY OF ISLANDS SWORDFISH CLUB
P.O. Box 31, Russell

President: J. R. Chibnall   *Secretary*: B. W. Lovett
Clubhouse: Russell   Membership: 548

Game Fishing Charter Association
Paihia. Phone 27-311

Charter Boats and Skippers
Ali Baba (Gary Coles)
Balsona (Lindsay Hill)
Double Strike (Curly Ellis)
Eldonna (John Belcher)
Karina (Alan Limmer)
Lady Doreen (Bruce Smith)
Lady Lynn (Eldon Jepson)
Leilani (Don MacKenzie)
Margaret Anne (Claude Conning)
Maraqueta (Laurie Ross)
Sapphire (Kevin Jordan)
Taravana (Doug Sinclair)

Tuatea (Hilton Polkinghorne)
Waima Star (Mick Savage)
Willie-0 (Robin Cutfield)
**Lady Lola* (Jack Brittain)
**Triton* (Chris Brittain)
* Not member of association at time of listing.

WHANGAREI DEEP SEA ANGLERS CLUB
P.O. Box 401, Whangarei

President: L. E. Dyer   *Secretary*: Mrs B. M. Brown
Clubhouse: Tutukaka   Membership: 1621

Charter Boats and Skippers
Kitty Vane (John Going)
Lady Jess (Trevor Williams)
Lady Margaret (Harvey Franks)
Marco Polo (Ross Cotterill)
Norseman (V. F. Belcher)
Sou'-East (Eric Wellington)
Waimana (Kyn Franks)

MERCURY BAY GAMEFISHING CLUB
P.O. Box 76, Whitianga

President: R. S. Cutfield   *Secretary*: A. C. Taylor
Clubhouse: Whitianga   Membership: 418

Charter Boat and Skipper
Lady Lidgard (Don Ross)

AUCKLAND GAMEFISHING CLUB
P.O. Box 6115, Auckland 1

President: J. McMahon   *Secretary*: Mrs J. Groves
Membership: 275

TAURANGA BIG GAMEFISHING CLUB
P.O. Box 501, Tauranga

President: G. Cranston   *Secretary*: N. D. Fletcher
Clubhouse: Mayor Island   Membership: 990

Charter Boats and Skippers
Carousel (Sid Gamman)
Intrepid I (Ross Worthington)
Judith Aimee (Walter Matthews)
Leeway (Graham Crisford)
Luana (Goldie Hitchings)
Masquerade (Russell Gamman)
Ma Cherie (Ces Jack)
Marline (Nigel Brazen)
Ruth (Russell Wright)
Sabra (Jill Gray)
Taiho (Bill Ebdale)
Taimarino (Mervyn Sowerby)
Waimarie II (Max Carruthers)

WHAKATANE BIG GAMEFISHING CLUB
P.O. Box 105, Whakatane

President: B. G. Guy   *Secretary*: Mrs B. Burt
Clubhouse: Whakatane   Membership: 767

Charter Boats and Skippers
Caramia (Colin Warrington)
Toa Tai (Rick Pollock)
Ariki Tai (Frank Price)

WAIHAU BAY SPORTS FISHING CLUB
Post Office, Waihau Bay

President: J. R. Honey   *Secretary*: L. Mills
Clubhouse: Waihau Bay   Membership: 100

GISBORNE-TATAPOURI SPORTS FISHING CLUB
P.O. Box 258, Gisborne

President: D. H. Ball   *Secretary*: Mrs P. Fairlie
Clubhouse: Tatapouri   Membership: 323

HAWKES BAY GAMEFISHING CLUB
P.O. Box 758, Napier

President: D. G. Foreman *Secretary*: Mrs J. L. Wiig
Clubhouse: Napier   Membership: 634

FIORDLAND GAMEFISHING CLUB
P.O. Box 37, Invercargill

President: R. G. Marquand *Secretary*: Dr G. Orbell
Membership: 114

TAUTUKU FISHING CLUB
P.O. Box 1488, Dunedin

President: K. Wilson   *Secretary*: T. P. Corbett
Clubhouse: Smaills Beach   Membership: 60

217

GLOSSARY

Backing — Line that is wound on to the hub of a wheel spool for the dual purpose of cushioning tightly wound monofilament lines, and increasing hub diameter to effect faster retrieve rates.

Billfish — Marlin, spearfish, sailfish and swordfish.

Broach — The leap of a fish into the air.

Burley (or chum) — Minced, pulverised or fine-cut baiting material thrown overboard to attract fish (or the act of doing this). Under I.G.F.A. regulations, the flesh, blood or skin of mammals may not be used as burley (nor for bait), except hair or pork rind used in lures.

Butt — The lower end of a fishing rod, whether of the same or differing material, one piece or detachable.

Charter boat — Game fishing launch available for hire – usually from one day (sometimes a half day) to an extended period. Carries all necessary fishing gear and usually has sleeping accommodation.

Chum — (see Burley)

Continental shelf — The gradually sloping offshore sea bottom to the point of the ocean drop-off.

Double — An optional doubled length of the ordinary line being used, to give extra strength near the hook and give protection against chafe. The length of the double is limited to 9.14 m and

Double ctnd. — the combined length of double and leader is limited to 12.19 m. (See Leader)

Downrigger — A heavily weighted device for towing a trolled line down deep. The actual fishing line must be attached directly to a lightly loaded release device.

Drifting (Drift fishing) — Trailing baited lines behind a drifting boat, with lightly attached breakaway floats for near surface fishing, and weighted with lightly attached breakaway sinkers for deep fishing.

Dropback — The practice of allowing the line to run completely free when the bait is first taken.

Fathom — The customary measure of depth now replaced under metrics by the metre. One metre equals 0.5468 fathoms.

Fighting (fishing) chair — A strong swivelling chair for fighting big game fish. It is fitted with gimballed or dipping rod butt socket cups for use when fishing heavy gear, but may not have any mechanically propelled devices to aid the angler.

Finning — Swimming with the upper lobe of the tail and/or the dorsal fin exposed.

Fly — A light artificial lure designed for casting.

Flying gaff — A large gaff with a detachable head or hook which is attached to the boat by a strong rope on which large fish are handled after the handle is discarded.

Fly rod	A special light casting rod designed for unweighted flies.
Foul-hooked	Hooked other than internally.
Foul ground	Rocky or otherwise broken sea bottom.
Free spool	Allowing the line to run without clutch or drag applied.
Gamefish	A fish valued mainly for its fighting qualities when caught on a rod and reel.
Gimbal	A pivoted metal cup set on a fighting chair to take the butt socket of a rod.
Greyhounding	Fast, low, aerial travelling by a gamefish.
Harness	Leather or webbing waistcoat or belt clipped to rod and reel and worn by anglers to support the gear and free their hands to manipulate the line and reel.
Hook-up	Strike resulting in a fish being hooked.
Jag (or Paranaki)	A large three- or four-pronged hook on a handline, or a heavy casting rod and line, used for catching schooling baitfish, particularly trevally and mackerel.
Jig	A heavy rigid lure designed to be lowered to the bottom and retrieved in short upward jerks.
Knot	A speed measurement in terms of nautical miles per hour. A knot equals 1.152 statute miles per hour or 1.85 kilometres per hour.
Leader (or trace)	A short section usually of wire, monofilament or heavy line linking the hook to the main fishing line, either directly or via a double line. Leaders may be of any strength. Their permissible length, including hook etc, is 9.14 m for saltwater game fishing.
Line capacity	The length of specified strength line which a reel will hold.
Lure	An artificial bait usually designed to behave like natural food when trolled or drawn through the water at appropriate speeds.
Mile (sea or nautical)	Equivalent to 1.152 statute or land miles and 1.85 kilometres. All distances at sea in this book are given in sea or nautical miles.
Monofilament	Synthetic line consisting of a single strand or filament.
Outrigger	A device which spreads the trolled lines behind a big-game fishing boat. The lines are lightly clipped to halyards from the outriggers, from which they are pulled away by a strike.
Overrun	Occurs when reel spool revolutions exceed line travels, causing the turns of line in the spool to loosen, overlap and tangle.
Paranaki	See Jag
Pelagic	Applied to free-swimming fish which are largely independent of sea bottom.
Plankton	Free floating and free swimming small sea organisms.
Popper	In big gamefishing: a lure that regularly breaks surface. In fly fishing: one which relies on the disturbance it makes on the surface.
Pump	The action of lifting the rod tip, and winding in the line when lowering it again.
Reel	The device on which line is stored, from which it is run out and to which it is retrieved. Its ethical use is governed by strict rules which ban power drives, ratchet handles, and cranks for

Reel ctnd. the use of both hands at a time.

Reel seat — The metal fitting which locks the reel to the rod.

Retrieve — Winding back the line on to the reel.

Rod — A rod may be made of almost any material (usually fibreglass or carbon fibre) but unconventional rods may be disqualified if they give an angler an unfair advantage. The rod tip must be a minimum 101.6 cm in length and the rod butt cannot exceed 68.58 cm in length.

Roller guide — A guide mounted on the rod which uses a roller to reduce friction.

Run — The sprint of a hooked fish away from the angler.

Salinity — The percentage of salt in the (sea) water.

School — A community or large area of fish usually visible on or just under the surface when feeding.

Seine — A form of boat and launch-operated sea fishing net (Purse seine: a net which closes around and under a community of fish.)

Shoal — An area of shallow water.

Skipper — Runs the fishing boat and may advise but not participate in the fishing itself between the act of setting the bait, taking the trace and gaffing the catch.

Snotter — See Tailrope

Sound — Of a fish, to dive deep.

Sounder — An electronic depth indicator.

Spoon — A fishing lure usually of metal of a variety of spoon-like shapes.

Stern door (or tuna door) — An entry door in the tuck of modern boats; usually associated with self-draining cockpits and therefore well

Stern door ctnd. above waterline.

Star drag — Usually refers to the two-purpose friction clutch between the reel spool and the winding handle which acts also as the spool brake on line outrun.

Strip bait — Strips cut from fish large enough to provide fish-shaped pieces for use as trolling baits.

Strike — The actual taking of the bait by the fish sought.

Swivel — A free-turning connection between leader and line to overcome twisting up of line by bait or lure spin.

Tag — A metal or plastic marker attached to a fish so that it can be identified for scientific studies if and when re-caught.

Tailing or finning — Swimming (of a fish) with the upper lobe of the tail fin frequently showing above water.

Tailrope — A rope or cable used as a running noose to secure a gamefish when brought to the boat (Also: snotter).

Tailwalking — Describes a fast-moving marlin in near vertical attitude with only the tail immersed.

Teaser — A lure-like device used to attract fish, but without hooks.

Thermocline — A profile of sub-surface temperature change.

Tip — The top end of the rod.

Tippet — In fly fishing, a short length of line in the leader which determines the line class for the catch. A tippet (of minimum length 38.10 cm) must be of non-metallic material and be attached directly to the hook or (optionally) to a shock tippet of any material and strength with a maximum length of

Tippet ctnd.	30.38 cm. The breaking strain of tippets is graded at the time of writing in lbs, not kg.
Trace	See Leader
Troll	To trail baits or lures behind a moving boat.
Tuna door	See Stern door
Tuna tower	A high tower or ultra-flying bridge on a boat, designed originally for spotting tuna; useful with other fish and for photography.

BIBLIOGRAPHY

A Fisherman's Eldorado, by Zane Grey (Hodder and Stoughton), 1926.

Big Fish and Blue Water, by Peter Goadby (Angus and Robertson), 1970.

Fighting Fins, by Neil Illingworth (A. H. & A. W. Reed), 1961.

Fishing Methods and Devices of the Maori, by Elsdon Best (New Zealand Government publication).

Journals and Records of the New Zealand Big Game Fishing Council and the game fishing clubs of New Zealand.

Publications, Fisheries Research Division (Government publication).

New Zealand Sea Anglers Guide, by Raymond Dooge and John Moreland, Ills by John Heath (A. H. & A. W. Reed), 1960.

The Sport Fishery for Big Game Species at the Bay of Islands, by P. J. Saul, Ministry of Agriculture and Fisheries, 1981.

World Record Game Fishes – International Game Fish Association, annual.

A Rough Guide to New Zealand Big Game Fishing, by C. Alma Baker (Private publication), 1937.

LIST OF MAPS, DIAGRAMS

MAPS

DIAGRAMS

INDEX